Pro Functional PHP Programming

Application Development Strategies for
Performance Optimization, Concurrency,
Testability, and Code Brevity

Rob Aley

Apress®

Pro Functional PHP Programming: Application Development Strategies for Performance Optimization, Concurrency, Testability, and Code Brevity

Rob Aley
Oxford, United Kingdom

ISBN-13 (pbk): 978-1-4842-2957-6   ISBN-13 (electronic): 978-1-4842-2958-3
DOI 10.1007/978-1-4842-2958-3

Library of Congress Control Number: 2017954985

Copyright © 2017 by Rob Aley

This work is subject to copyright. All rights are reserved by the Publisher, whether the whole or part of the material is concerned, specifically the rights of translation, reprinting, reuse of illustrations, recitation, broadcasting, reproduction on microfilms or in any other physical way, and transmission or information storage and retrieval, electronic adaptation, computer software, or by similar or dissimilar methodology now known or hereafter developed.

Trademarked names, logos, and images may appear in this book. Rather than use a trademark symbol with every occurrence of a trademarked name, logo, or image we use the names, logos, and images only in an editorial fashion and to the benefit of the trademark owner, with no intention of infringement of the trademark.

The use in this publication of trade names, trademarks, service marks, and similar terms, even if they are not identified as such, is not to be taken as an expression of opinion as to whether or not they are subject to proprietary rights.

While the advice and information in this book are believed to be true and accurate at the date of publication, neither the authors nor the editors nor the publisher can accept any legal responsibility for any errors or omissions that may be made. The publisher makes no warranty, express or implied, with respect to the material contained herein.

Cover image by Freepik (www.freepik.com)

Managing Director: Welmoed Spahr
Editorial Director: Todd Green
Acquisitions Editor: Steve Anglin
Development Editor: Matthew Moodie
Technical Reviewer: Christopher Pitt
Coordinating Editor: Mark Powers
Copy Editor: Kim Wimpsett

Distributed to the book trade worldwide by Springer Science+Business Media New York, 233 Spring Street, 6th Floor, New York, NY 10013. Phone 1-800-SPRINGER, fax (201) 348-4505, e-mail orders-ny@springer-sbm.com, or visit www.springeronline.com. Apress Media, LLC is a California LLC and the sole member (owner) is Springer Science + Business Media Finance Inc (SSBM Finance Inc). SSBM Finance Inc is a **Delaware** corporation.

For information on translations, please e-mail rights@apress.com, or visit www.apress.com/rights-permissions.

Apress titles may be purchased in bulk for academic, corporate, or promotional use. eBook versions and licenses are also available for most titles. For more information, reference our Print and eBook Bulk Sales web page at www.apress.com/bulk-sales.

Any source code or other supplementary material referenced by the author in this book is available to readers on GitHub via the book's product page, located at www.apress.com/9781484229576. For more detailed information, please visit www.apress.com/source-code.

Printed on acid-free paper

Contents at a Glance

Contents

About the Author

Rob Aley I've been programming in PHP since late 2000. Initially it wasn't by choice because my preferred languages at the time were Perl and Delphi (also known as Object Pascal). Things began to change after I graduated from the University of Leeds with a degree in computer science in 1999 and started out in a career as a freelance web developer. After only a couple of months I was offered the opportunity to take over a (relatively speaking) substantial government web site contract from a friend who was exiting the freelance world for the safer and saner world of full-time employment. The only catch was that several thousand lines of code had already been written, and they were written in a relatively new language called PHP. Oh, and the only other catch was that I had about a week to learn it before taking over the site. So, as was the way at the time, I popped down to the local Waterstones bookshop. (For the younger among you that's where we used to get books. And we had to go out and get them. Or order online and wait many days for them to be delivered.) With my paper copies of *The Generic Beginner's Complete Guide to PHP* and *MySQL for Dummies Compendium* (I may not have recalled the titles completely correctly), I settled down with a pint of ale (I'm in Yorkshire at this point, remember) and set about reading them. A few days later I was coding like a pro (well, stuff was working), and 17 years later I haven't looked back. Over those 17 years PHP has changed vastly (the source code for the government web site I mentioned was littered with comments like "# Would have used a foreach here, if PHP had one...") and so have I. I like to think that both I and PHP have only improved and matured over the years.

After a varied career as a freelancer and starting up a couple of, er, startups (IT related and not) with varying (usually dismal) success, I spent the past ten years as a programmer at the University of Oxford. My day job involved performing medium-scale data acquisition and management, doing statistical analysis, and providing user interfaces for researchers and the public. The majority of my development work was done in PHP, either developing new projects or gluing together other people's software, systems, and databases. I've recently left the university to concentrate on writing books like this and providing consulting and training (in PHP, information governance, and related areas). But I'm still programming in PHP!

Throughout my career I've always used PHP for web development, but for desktop GUI work I initially used Delphi (and then Free-Pascal/Lazarus), complemented with Bash shell scripting for CLI-based tasks. This was mainly because I learned them while at university. However, as PHP has matured, I've increasingly used it beyond the Web, and now I rarely use anything else for any programming or scripting task I encounter. Having been immersed in other languages such as C++, JavaScript, Fortran, and Lisp (and probably others that my brain has chosen deliberately not to remember) by necessity during university and in some of my freelance jobs, I can honestly say that PHP is now my language of choice, rather than of necessity. At university (in the late 1990s) I took a couple of classes that involved functional programming, but at the time I really didn't "get the point." It's only in recent years that I've picked up functional-style programming again, partly because of the "buzz" that's developed around it and partly because as my programming styles have "matured," I've seen the advantages to functional coding.

When I'm not tied to a computer, I would like to say I have lots of varied and interesting hobbies. I used to have. I could write a whole book (which wouldn't sell well) about where I've been and what I've done, and I'd like to think it's made me a well-rounded person. But these days I don't have any. In large part, this is because of the demands of my three gorgeous young daughters, Ellie, Izzy, and Indy; my gorgeous wife, Parv; and my even more gorgeous cat, Mia. And I wouldn't have it any other way. That's what I tell myself, anyway....

—Rob Aley

About the Technical Reviewer

Christopher Pitt is a developer and writer, working at SilverStripe. He usually works on application architecture, though sometimes you'll find him building compilers or robots. He is also the author of several web development books and is a contributor on various open source projects like AdonisJs.

Acknowledgments

Isaac Newton said, "If I have seen further, it is by standing on the shoulders of giants." This book builds on, and I hope adds to, the work of many others, the most notable of whom I would like to acknowledge here.

- *The authors of, and contributors to, the official PHP Manual*: This is an invaluable reference for PHP functions and syntax, to which I referred frequently during writing this book, both for fact checking and as an aide-mémoir. Thanks!

- *The collective PHP and functional programming wisdom of the Internet*: For more than 17 years I've used you for learning, research, play, and profit. There are too many sites and too many people to list here; if you've written about PHP on the Web, then you may well be one of them. Thanks!

- *My family*: Thanks for allowing me a modicum of time to write this book and supporting me unconditionally in everything I do. Usually. If I ask first. And there's not something more important going on. And usually with conditions. Thanks!

PART I

■ ■ ■

Functional Programming in PHP 7

CHAPTER 1

■ ■ ■

Introduction

Functional programming isn't something that is often associated with PHP. Yet for quite a while PHP has had all the features necessary to create software using the functional paradigm. In this book, you'll take a look at what functional programming is, how to do it in PHP, and the different ways in which you can use it to improve your PHP software.

Who Is This Book For?

This book isn't an introduction to PHP itself; it assumes you have some basic (or, indeed, advanced) experience in PHP scripting. You don't need to be an expert to follow along; I'll cover all the key concepts in PHP you'll need to know to be able to implement functional designs in your code and point you in the direction of resources such as web sites and other books that you can use to learn or investigate any related concepts that I don't cover directly.

Absolute PHP beginners aside, this book is suitable for all programmers. Whether you have a pressing need to learn functional programming (perhaps you've taken over a functional PHP code base) or you are just interested in finding out what the "buzz" around functional programming is all about, there is something in this book for you. There's even likely to be something for those skeptical about creating software using the functional programming paradigm. I think that most programmers will find useful lessons and code patterns to take away from the functional programming style that will enhance their object-oriented or procedural programming work. If all else fails, knowledge of functional programming looks good on your résumé!

What Is Functional Programming?

Functional programming is a declarative programming paradigm that abstracts code into pure, immutable, side-effect-free functions, allowing the programmer to compose such functions together to make programs that are easy to reason about.

That is my definition of functional programming. Ask five other functional programmers to define functional programming and you'll get four more answers (two just copied the same answer from Wikipedia). There's no "standard" definition; different people and different programming languages implement functional programming elements differently. These differences are partly because of the practicalities of the language in question and sometimes because of the target platforms, data, and usage scenarios, but often they come down to what I call "programming religion": a fixed, sometimes irrational, but often deeply held belief of how a particular paradigm *should be*. Even within the small community of PHP functional programmers, you won't find an exact consensus. In PHP, functional programming is not a core concept, but even in languages where it is (e.g., Lisp, Scala, etc.), there are many "related" understandings of what constitutes true functional programming. While that may sound problematic, you'll still "know it when you see it," and when it gets woolly around the edges, you can choose to define it in any way you see fit!

© Rob Aley 2017
R. Aley, *Pro Functional PHP Programming*, DOI 10.1007/978-1-4842-2958-3_1

PHP isn't a pure functional programming language, but you can still use it for functional programming (which is good; otherwise this book wouldn't be very long). A few elements of what some purists consider to be essential functional programming concepts are harder to implement with PHP's standard syntax, so it's perhaps slightly more accurate to say that you can program in a functional programming "style" in PHP.

Let's now look a little more in depth at what functional programming actually is in practice. Functional programming is a "declarative" style of programming, which means you specify *what* you want it to do rather than *how* you want to do it. It's a higher level of abstraction than you may be used to with OO or procedural programming. However, you almost certainly use declarative programming on a day-to-day basis when using SQL, HTML, regular expressions, and similar languages. Consider the SQL snippet shown in Listing 1-1.

Listing 1-1. declarative.sql

```sql
SELECT forename,

       Surname

FROM   users

WHERE  username = 'rob'

       AND password = 'password1';
```

This is telling your database server what you want it to do (select the real name based on super-secret security credentials), but you don't tell it how to do it. You don't tell it the following:

- Where to look on disk for the data

- How to parse or search the data for matching records

- How to determine whether a record matches your criteria

- How to extract the relevant fields from the record

And so on. You simply tell it what you want it to achieve for you.

Now obviously, at some point, you need to tell the computer *how* to do something. With the SQL example in Listing 1-1, you do that by getting some rather clever people to write database management software (DBMS) for you. In functional programming, you'll tend to need to write the implementation code yourself, but to make it a manageable task, you break that down into the smallest possible chunks and then use a hierarchical chain of declarative function calls to tell the computer what to do with that code. If you use the Composer dependency management system, you will already be using a similar paradigm: there are many libraries of code available that abstract away the tasks that you need to do; you simply "compose" a list of libraries together to do what you want. In functional programming, you do exactly the same; you take functions that do something (like the libraries Composer provides) and compose them together into a program.

Having a program that is essentially a list of what you want to achieve sounds very good on paper, and indeed it makes it easy to understand and reason about your program. To make the idea a little more concrete, let's take a look at a small functional-style program (Listing 1-2).

Listing 1-2. example.php

```php
<?php

require_once('image_functions.php');

require_once('stats_functions.php');
```

```php
require_once('data_functions.php');

$csv_data = file_get_contents('my_data.csv');

$chart = make_chart_image (

                generate_stats (

                        data_to_array (

                                $csv_data

                        )

                )

        );

file_put_contents('my_chart.png', $chart);
```

This is clearly some code that has been abstracted into a set of functions that set out what it does (draw a chart based on some stats prepared from some data that is read in). You can also probably see that the *how* is hidden away in the required files at the top, but it is still clear as to what the program does. Should your requirements change and instead of drawing a chart you want to print a table, you can simply swap out draw_chart() for print_table() and it is clear what will happen. This is a (very loose) example of a functional program.

That all sounds great. But without even considering the code hidden away in the required files, your programmer instincts are probably telling you that chaining random functions together, and swapping out one for another, is a risky proposition particularly when you can't see how they're implemented. For instance, how do you know that read_data() will return data in the correct format for prepare_stats() to work on? And how can you be sure that you can swap out draw_chart() for prepare_stats() and it will all still work as you expect? Clearly, functional programming involves a little more than "chuck it all in a function with a descriptive name," and as you go through the book, you'll look at the various ways to structure functions so that you can use them as "little black boxes" of code that can be easily and reliably strung together.

Functional programming revolves around functions, as the name implies. However, functions in the functional programming sense aren't quite the same as functions in the PHP syntax sense, although you will use PHP's implementation of functions to implement FP functions. A functional programming function is often referred to as a *pure* function and has several important characteristics that can be mimicked with, but aren't enforced by, PHP's syntax. A pure function has the following traits:

- Is referentially transparent

- Is devoid of side effects

- Has no external dependencies

I'll talk more in detail about what these features mean in the next couple of chapters, but they boil down to a function being a small self-contained "black box" that takes well-defined inputs, produces well-defined outputs, and given the same inputs *always* produces the same outputs. In particular, the function only acts on the inputs it is given (it doesn't take into account any external state or data and relies only on the parameters it is called with), and the only effect it has is to return some output (which will be the same each time you give it the same input); thus, it doesn't alter the state of the program or system outside of itself.

In the example program in Listing 1-2, if you give exactly the same CSV file to read_data() each time, and assuming you have properly used functional programming, you can be sure that draw_chart() will produce exactly the same chart each time, regardless of anything else going on elsewhere in the program or on your system. This ability to be sure of, and reason about, the program flow leads to a number of benefits for the functional programming paradigm that you'll discover as you learn more about implementing functional programming programs.

Functional Programming Is SOLID

If you come from an object-oriented programming background, you are probably familiar with the SOLID principles for composing OO code. Although written for OOP, the SOLID principles actually embody the principles of functional programming very well; indeed, some are inherent in the way functional programming is defined. Understanding these principles will help you to understand some of the key traits of functional programming. If you're not familiar with SOLID, it is an acronym with each letter standing for one of the five basic principles of good OO design. I'll cover each in turn.

S: Single Responsibility Principle (SRP)

Each function is responsible for only one task. "Do one thing, and do it well." In functional programming, you break your program down into single-task functions. When any other function needs to do that task, they call that function. And when that task changes in specification, only that function has to be changed.

O: Open/Closed Principle (OCP)

Functions should be "open for extension but closed for modification." In functional programming, this means that when you need to extend the behavior of a function, you don't modify the existing function but compose it with (or call it from) other functions that create the new extended functionality.

L: Liskov Substitution Principle (LSP)

In OOP, this principle deals with the ability to substitute an object with an instance of a subtype of that object. In functional programming, that most precisely maps onto a concept called *contravariance* in functors, something that is more advanced (and also more theoretical and less practical) than you will learn in this book. However, there is a similar related principle that you will look at, that of referential transparency. This basically means that regardless of what else is happening in your program, a given function (with a given input) can be substituted with the value it returns in the program, and the program will continue to operate as expected.

I: Interface Segregation Principle (ISP)

This principle means that the parameters required for calling a function should only be those needed for the task you are carrying out. Interfaces to functions should be split down as specifically as possible, rather than providing general interfaces that contain parameters not relevant to the intent of the calling client code. Functional programming achieves this almost by default when chopped down into single responsibility functions because of the structured interface needed for efficient composition.

D: Dependency Inversion Principle (DIP)

This principle states the following:

- High-level modules should not depend on low-level modules. Both should depend on abstractions.

- Abstractions should not depend on details. Details should depend on abstractions.

This is more or less the definition of declarative programming. Your low-level functions that have the implementation details form an abstraction on which your higher-level "declarative" functions can operate.

Don't worry if all of these principles and terms don't make sense right now; just keep them in mind (or refer to them as needed) as you go through the book, and by the end you should be able to see how the SOLID principles apply naturally to the functional programming paradigm.

Further Reading

- The SOLID principles on Wikipedia

- https://en.wikipedia.org/wiki/SOLID_(object-oriented_design)

What Are the Benefits of Functional Programming?

I've touched on some of the benefits. But in case it isn't already clear, these are the key benefits that most programmers will gain from using functional programming techniques:

- You will create code that is easy to reason about. This means that it is less error prone, easier to update, and easier to understand the flow of the code.

- You will create code that is easier to test. This is a side effect of some of the properties of the functional programming paradigm, such as immutability, referential transparency, and lack of external dependencies.

- You can create higher-performance code, using techniques such as lazy evaluation, parallelization, and caching.

Who Uses Functional Programming, and Why?

I first learned functional programming some 20-odd years ago at university when I studied for my computer science degree. I really didn't see the point of it at the time and got quite a poor grade in that class because of my lack of interest in learning it, as I couldn't get my head around why anyone would want to use it "in real life." At the time, outside of academia and certain highly specialized domains such as engineering and finance, it wasn't in widespread use. However, over the years that has changed, and now many more people than you may think use functional programming, for many varied reasons.

It's prominent in many areas of mainstream IT these days, not just in specialized industries, academia, and startups run by "Silicon Valley hipsters"! Large companies such as Netflix, LinkedIn, and Twitter use functional programming to deliver robust services at scale. Some people use it because it is easy to reason about. Some use it because its lack of "side effects" makes it easy to parallelize and scale. Some use it because it maps neatly to mathematical constructs used in various fields of endeavor such as engineering, data science, and finance. It is being used in some industries because its declarative nature allows the creation of domain-specific languages (DSLs). DSLs can allow less skilled users to create or understand programs, allow easier mapping of business requirements and processes into software, and improve programmer productivity by providing task-specific abstractions.

Functional programming has been gaining more and more traction over the past few years. Modern functional languages like Racket, Clojure, and F# are building steam, and even PHP is getting in on the act with an ever-growing range of functional programming libraries becoming available on GitHub and through Composer.

But while it's currently a hot topic in modern computing, functional programming's history in computing stretches back to Lisp in the 1950s, while lambda calculus (the mathematical abstraction on which functional programming is based) and the more abstract field of combinatory logic began life in the 1920s and 1930s. Both directly in languages like Lisp and Scheme and indirectly in functional-style code written in most programming languages, functional programming has had an influence in many fields of computing over the years. Many companies write functional programming code and rely on functional programming software on a day-to-day basis (whether they realize it or not!).

Is Functional Programming "All or Nothing"?

When people start learning functional programming, they often start asking if they need to tear up their old OOP code and start from scratch. My answer is no (although the purists would say yes). Functional programming can happily live alongside OOP or procedural code, or indeed any other programming paradigm, as long as you understand where your functional programming code starts and stops. Because of the nature of functional programming, it is often easier to put functional programming structures *inside* objects or traditional functions/procedural code blocks, rather than the other way around.

Particular sections of code that can benefit from functional programming (such as business logic processes and high-performance algorithms) can often be good starting places for introducing functional programming into your code base. Because functional programming isn't a core feature of PHP, it actually makes it easier to mix and match paradigms as you see fit. In other traditional functional programming languages, things are more restrictive; for instance, Haskell doesn't have any OO capabilities, whereas F# is written around a specific FP-OO hybrid paradigm. Functional programming has many things in common with OOP; indeed, a closure (a function packaged with associated program state) is somewhat comparable to a streamlined object, and program flow control in many OO programming patterns somewhat mimics the functional programming style of flow. PHP is, as usual, flexible and says "do what you want," which can be both a blessing or (if you don't do it right) a curse. That's a common complaint about PHP in general, though, and is simply solved by always programming correctly!

If you're interested in learning the differences between the different programming paradigms that people have come up with over the years, then Wikipedia has got you covered with a fairly comprehensive comparison of the main features of each. Note that PHP is a "Turing complete" language, which basically means that if something can be computed, then PHP can compute it. This also means that any of the paradigms described can be implemented in PHP (whether you'd want to is another matter, although I think that most offer at least something that a good programmer can add to their mental toolbox for use at the appropriate time). If this book whets your appetite for doing things *a little differently*, then maybe check out the Wikipedia list for some more ways of mixing up your code.

Further Reading

- A comparison of programming paradigms on Wikipedia
  - https://en.wikipedia.org/wiki/Comparison_of_programming_paradigms

Why Use PHP for Functional Programming?

Just about everyone who has heard the title of this book has said to me, "You don't use PHP for functional programming" (besides my wife, who said, "That sounds super-boring"). Well, they're all wrong (including my wife). There's absolutely no reason not to use PHP (well, aside from the reasons listed in the "Why Not to Use PHP for Functional Programming" section). And it's not super-boring.

In all seriousness, PHP has just about everything you need to write good functional programming code. It has first-class support for functions, it has libraries that help abstract boilerplate code, and there is a growing body of documentation and help available (including the very book you're reading now). But most of all, *you already know PHP*. You're learning a new programming paradigm, so why burden yourself with getting to grips with a new language at the same time? Indeed, if you get to know the paradigm first in an environment you're already comfortable with, you will likely find it easier to pick up more specialized functional programming languages like Haskell later, where the language features implicitly rely on you being familiar with the functional programming paradigm.

Perhaps if you were not familiar with programming at all and wanted to learn functional programming, starting with something like Haskell may be fine. But you're coming with the baggage of familiarity of OO or procedural programming, and a pure functional programming language will feel alien to you until you're comfortable with functional programming as a concept. You'll waste a lot of time trying to work out how to implement features and constructs that just don't exist in the functional programming world, instead of getting on and writing code.

Why Not to Use PHP for Functional Programming

There are one or two cases where using PHP in this way might not be a good idea (just don't tell anyone I said so).

- You have a particular business case/requirement to *only* use functional programming. In PHP there is nothing to stop you from mixing your programming paradigms, and sometimes it is tempting (or pragmatic) to do so. So if you need to ensure you stick to functional programming code alone, then it's probably best not to use PHP.

- You need top-notch, first-rate commercial support. As noted earlier, there is growing, good-quality support for functional programming in the PHP community. But "traditional" functional programming languages have more, particularly in the area of paid commercial support.

- You think that PHP is dying, has serious issues, or isn't a real programming language. Some people still hold these views, even as PHP goes from strength to strength. Nevertheless, if the mention of PHP sends prickles up your spine, implementing your programs in functional programming within PHP won't magically make that feeling go away. As you're reading this book, it's more likely that you don't feel like that, but others around you (your boss or colleagues?) may, and as wonderful as this book is, it's unlikely to sway their opinion of PHP itself. You'll likely need to do what's pragmatic in that situation—quit and start your own company like I did.

- Your colleagues don't know functional programming, so your code may be harder for them to maintain. This is simple to solve: buy them a copy of this book!

PHP Versions

At the time of writing, the current stable release of PHP is 7.1.2, and it would be lovely if that was the version that everyone is running. However, it isn't; indeed, PHP versions all the way back to 5.2 can be found in mainstream use across hosting providers and inside companies. Tales of people using even older versions abound in the darker corners of the Internet, and with security updates available only for 5.6 and higher, such tales are the stuff nightmares are made of. So, which version should you choose (if indeed you have the choice) for functional programming?

All the code in this book was developed and tested on the current release of version 7.1 of PHP. However, most of the code will run with minor changes on any version from 5.4 onward. Versions older than 5.4 lack the language support for anonymous functions and closures, which means that functional programming isn't practical. I'll point out any differences between version support throughout the book, the most notable of which will be the lack of support for type declarations (also known as type hints) for scalar variables in the series 5 versions. Do note that "Active Support" for the last 5.x version, 5.6, has now ended, and "Security Fixes Only" support is due to be withdrawn in late 2018, so using a 7.x version is highly recommended if possible. As well as continued support from the PHP maintainers, you'll find that the lower resource requirements of PHP 7 will help in some areas of functional programming with PHP such as recursion. That said, you can do functional programming in PHP 5, and the inevitable upgrade lag in many workplaces may mean that you have no choice to use a 5.x version, so I'll do my best to cover the differences as I go along.

Conclusion

In this chapter, you started looking at what functional programming is and why it can be useful in your PHP development. Functional programming can be hard to grasp from such an abstract discussion, so don't worry if you don't "get it" yet. As you go through the next few chapters, you'll get a better feel for it as you see the programming concepts behind it and examples of functional code.

CHAPTER 2

■ ■ ■

Functional Programming: Key Concepts

In this chapter, you'll look at the key concepts, building blocks, and vocabulary that you'll need to understand before getting started on some actual functional programming. Although you are already likely to be using functions and closures in your everyday programming, it's worth taking the time to read the following sections that describe them from first principles as some of the details that you take for granted when using them in object-oriented or plain procedural programming can trip you up when applying them in the functional paradigm. As functional programming is rooted in math, you'll also take a look some language that you may be unfamiliar with and see it in terms that are easy to understand for a regular programmer.

The concepts presented in this chapter, taken individually, may paint a confusing picture about what functional programming is and what benefits it can bring. For instance, I'll talk about immutability, which is essentially the inability to change a value. That seems like a drawback at first rather than a benefit, but when you draw all of these concepts together over the next couple of chapters, you will see that immutability plays a key part in the flexible recipe-like nature of functional programming and is one of the factors that allows you to easily reason about your functional code.

So, for now, try to focus on understanding the individual concepts as presented and don't worry too much about how they all fit together. Learning functional programming is much like writing functional programming code—lots of small independent functions/ideas composed into an over-arching scheme that eventually does something!

Examining State

As you go through the book, particularly when you look at types, there may be times when you do not feel confident about the state of a variable, object, or function in your code. *State* includes the current contents of the thing you are examining and its current type. PHP provides a couple of handy functions, print_r and var_dump, to help you "look" at what's happening in your code. See Listing 2-1.

Listing 2-1. examine.php

```php
<?php

define('MY_CONSTANT', 'banana');

$my_function = function ($data) {
        return $data;
};
```

© Rob Aley 2017
R. Aley, *Pro Functional PHP Programming*, DOI 10.1007/978-1-4842-2958-3_2

```
$my_array = [1,2,'apple',MY_CONSTANT,$my_function];

echo "print_r output :\n\n";

print_r($my_array);

echo "\n\n var_dump output :\n\n";

var_dump($my_array);
```

Running the script in Listing 2-1 gives the output shown in Listing 2-2.

Listing 2-2. examine-output.txt

```
print_r output :

Array
(
    [0] => 1
    [1] => 2
    [2] => apple
    [3] => banana
    [4] => Closure Object
        (
            [parameter] => Array
                (
                    [$data] => <required>
                )

        )

)

 var_dump output :

array(5) {
  [0]=>
  int(1)
  [1]=>
  int(2)
  [2]=>
  string(5) "apple"
  [3]=>
  string(6) "banana"
  [4]=>
  object(Closure)#1 (1) {
    ["parameter"]=>
    array(1) {
      ["$data"]=>
      string(10) "<required>"
    }
  }
}
```

12

As you can see, the functions produce similar output. print_r is formatted for easier reading by humans, and var_dump provides slightly more information about basic types. I usually use var_dump, reverting to print_r when I have a particularly dense data structure to look through as the formatting can make it easier.

Another function that's particularly useful in functional programming is debug_print_backtrace(). Functional programming usually involves composing many single-purpose functions together into stacks of functions that represent your program. When an error does occur, it can be hard to track down exactly which of the many functions you have used in your stack is causing the error. A backtrace shows where you are in the function call stack at that moment and is commonly displayed by debuggers and code profilers. The debug_print_backtrace() function can allow you to print the call stack from within your code, as the contrived example in Listing 2-3 demonstrates (Listing 2-4 shows the output).

Listing 2-3. backtrace.php

```php
<?php

function prepare_text($text) {

    return make_headline($text);

}

function make_headline($text) {

    return add_h_tags( upper_case($text) );

}

function upper_case($text) {

    return strtoupper($text);

}

function add_h_tags($text) {

    debug_print_backtrace();

    return '<h1>'.$text.'</h1>';

}

$title = prepare_text('testing');

echo $title;
```

Listing 2-4. backtrace-output.txt

```
#0  add_h_tags(TESTING) called at [backtrace.php:12]
#1  make_headline(testing) called at [backtrace.php:6]
#2  prepare_text(testing) called at [backtrace.php:30]
<h1>TESTING</h1>
```

The top of the list has the most recent function called (in this case, add_h_tags()), all the way down to the initiating function (prepare_text()). Note that although the make_headline() function calls the upper_case() function, it is not in the backtrace. This is because it has completed its execution and is not waiting for the output of the next function in the chain before it returns its own output (as is the case for the other three functions, which are still in the stack).

The three functions mentioned are most useful when you're learning and experimenting with code, particularly if you use a read-eval-print-loop (REPL; see Appendix B for more information) to test and hack on code. In proper development and production code, you should use debuggers, profilers, and secure logging to keep track of what your code is doing; using print_r and var_dump can accidentally spill internal data to the outside world and cause various security issues.

Mutability and Immutability

If something is *mutable*, it means you can change it. Variables are mutable. Consider the code in Listing 2-5 and Listing 2-6.

Listing 2-5. mutable.php

```php
<?php
$a = 1;

var_dump($a);

$a = 2;

var_dump($a);

$a = "Banana";

var_dump($a);
```

Listing 2-6. mutable-output.txt

```
int(1)
int(2)
string(6) "Banana"
```

First, $a is set to 1. Then, because it is mutable, you can "mutate" (change) it to be equal to 2. Finally, you mutate it again to Banana. Note that in the last change, you not only mutate the variable but also the type, from int to string.

In functional programming, you want values (represented by functions) to be immutable. This is important in helping you to reason about your program and to allow you to loosely couple functions together. You'll look at this more in detail later.

PHP has limited support for immutability, mainly in the form of "constants" defined using either the define() function or the const keyword. There are a few differences between how and what you can declare constant when using define() versus const, but once declared, the constants created by either method are the same. One thing they both have in common is that only scalars or arrays can be constants. Listing 2-7 tries to create a constant from a variable holding an anonymous function. Listing 2-8 shows the output.

Listing 2-7. constant-func.php

```php
<?php

$double = function ($input) {
    return $input * 2;
};

define('DOUBLE',$double);

echo "Double 2 is " . $double(2) . "\n";

echo "Double 2 is " . DOUBLE(2) . "\n";
```

Listing 2-8. constant-func-output.txt

```
PHP Warning:  Constants may only evaluate to scalar values or arrays in constant-func.php on
line 8
Double 2 is 4
PHP Fatal error:  Uncaught Error: Call to undefined function DOUBLE() in constant-func.
php:12
Stack trace:
#0 {main}
  thrown in constant-func.php on line 12
```

Here you can see that you get a warning when trying to use the variable holding the function in define(), and when you try to use the DOUBLE constant, you get confirmation (via a fatal error) that it did indeed fail to be defined.

So, without much help from PHP, you will need to ensure immutability yourself through discipline when coding. One of the key ways to help achieve this is to avoid using assignment, and you'll look at ways to do this as you go through the book. The lack of support for immutability in PHP (compared to other languages) is one of the main things people will point out when you tell them you are using PHP for functional programming. However, it does not in any way stop you from writing functional programs in PHP; you simply need to keep it in mind as you code.

As well as watching what you do yourself, you need to keep half an eye on what PHP is doing. A key thing to think about is how PHP's own functions operate on your variables. For instance, the function sort() mutates (i.e., sorts) the array it is passed, rather than returning a new array that is a sorted version of the old array (and leaving the old array unmutated). However, you can make your own immutable version of sort() quite easily (see Listing 2-9 and Listing 2-10).

Listing 2-9. sort.php

```php
<?php

function immutable_sort($array) {

    sort($array);

    return $array;

}
```

```
$vegetables = ['Carrot', 'Beetroot', 'Asparagus'];

# Sort using our immutable function

$ordered = immutable_sort( $vegetables );

print_r( $ordered );

# Check that $vegetables remains unmutated

print_r( $vegetables );

# Do it the mutable way

sort( $vegetables );

# And see that the original array is mutated

print_r( $vegetables );
```

Listing 2-10. sort-output.txt

```
Array
(
    [0] => Asparagus
    [1] => Beetroot
    [2] => Carrot
)
Array
(
    [0] => Carrot
    [1] => Beetroot
    [2] => Asparagus
)
Array
(
    [0] => Asparagus
    [1] => Beetroot
    [2] => Carrot
)
```

This works because by default PHP function parameters are passed *by value* and not *by reference*. This means that when you call a function, it gets a *copy* of any variables that you give as parameters, rather than a reference to the variable itself. Anything the function does to that copy does not affect the original variable. PHP does allow you to pass in a parameter by reference (which is what sort() uses to mutate the original array), but this is not the default. When you pass in an object or resource, you are passing in an object or resource *variable*, which is a pointer to that object or resource. The variable is still passed by value; however, the new copy of the variable is still pointing to the original object or resource, so it acts in a similar manner to passing by value. You'll look at that issue in depth in Chapter 7.

In most cases, it is obvious which functions will mutate their parameters; they usually don't supply their output as a return value, but some take a mixture of *by value* and *by reference* parameters, so always check the PHP Manual if you're not sure.

Further Reading

- Constants in the PHP Manual
  - http://php.net/manual/en/language.constants.php
- A comprehensive synopsis of the differences between define() and const
  - http://stackoverflow.com/a/3193704

What Is a Function?

You probably have a reasonable idea about what a function is, and you probably use them regularly in your PHP code. However, I'll cover functions from scratch because a good understanding of the fundamentals of how PHP implements functions, and the different ways of handling them, is necessary to understand how to implement functional programming in PHP.

You'll develop a better feeling for exactly what a function is, in terms of functional programming, over the course of this chapter. But here's a good starting definition:

A *function* is a set of instructions, encapsulated into a self-contained, reusable block of code.

PHP lets you work with several different invocations of functions, which you'll look at in turn next.

Named Functions

A standard named function is the basic way to use functions in PHP. A named function looks something like the my_function() function in Listing 2-11 (the output is shown in Listing 2-12).

Listing 2-11. named_function.php

```php
<?php

function my_function ( $parameter_1, $parameter_2) {

        $sum = $parameter_1 + $parameter_2;

        return $sum;

}

$value1 = my_function(10,20);

var_dump( $value1 );

$value2 = my_function(6,9)

var_dump( $value2 );
```

Listing 2-12. named_function-output.txt

```
int(30)
int(15)
```

The function is created using the "function" language construct. It has a name (`my_function`), which is used to call it later. It has parameters (in this case two), which allow you to pass values to the code inside the function. It carries out some useful work (in this case adding the parameters together and returning them). It has a `return` statement that sets the *value* of the function. As you can see from this example, the function's value is often dependent on external values, in this case by changing the parameters given as input. The return value, however, can depend on external sources of state not directly passed in by parameters, as demonstrated by Listing 2-13 and Listing 2-14.

Listing 2-13. returns.php

```php
<?php

$oranges = 3;

function count_fruit($apples, $bananas) {

    global $oranges;

    $num_fruit = $apples + $bananas + $oranges;

    return $num_fruit;

}

function get_date() {

    return trim ( shell_exec('date') );

}

var_dump( count_fruit(6,7) );

var_dump( get_date() );
```

Listing 2-14. returns-output.txt

```
int(16)
string(28) "Tue 21 Feb 13:12:37 GMT 2017"
```

`count_fruit()` uses the global variable $orange, the value of which is set outside of the function, in its calculation of the return value. `get_date()` doesn't ask for any parameters at all and calculates its return value based on an external shell command. In both cases, these are potential causes of "side effects," which you will look at later, and show that functions in PHP aren't restricted to operating on only the parameters supplied.

This is a key difference with mathematical functions. The *functional* in functional programming refers to the mathematical concept of a function and not the programming concept of a function. Mathematical functions are *pure* functions, which you'll look at shortly.

The following are the primary limitations with named functions:

- They cannot be destroyed.

- Their functionality (the code in the function) cannot be changed once defined.

- They are harder to "pass around" because they cannot be assigned to a variable.

- Only the name of the function can be assigned to a variable, rather than the function itself.

There are limited options for "dynamically" handling named functions, although the call_user_func() function does offer one way to work in such a manner, as shown in Listing 2-15 and Listing 2-16.

Listing 2-15. userfunc.php

```php
<?php

function list_fruit($item) {

    return ['apple','orange','mango'][$item];

}

function list_meat($item) {

    return ['pork','beef','human'][$item];

}

$the_list - 'list_fruit';

var_dump( call_user_func($the_list, 2) );

$the_list = 'list_meat';

var_dump( call_user_func($the_list, 1) );
```

Listing 2-16. userfunc-output.txt

```
string(5) "mango"
string(4) "beef"
```

As you can see, you can pass call_user_func() the name (as a string) of a function (plus any parameters you want to supply the function), and call_user_func() will return the return value from the function you called as its own return value. And as you can see, you can change the name of the function in $the_list (as it is a string *variable*) and run call_user_func() again, this time running a different function. This allows you a little dynamism but is quite limited. A similar method is called a *variable function*, which you'll look at in the next section. Since PHP 7.0, you can also use the fromCallable static method of PHP's closure object to wrap a named function into something called a closure, which you'll look at later.

The *scope* of named functions is also unintuitive. As you'll see in the section "Scope" later in this chapter, when you create a variable within a function, by default it isn't available to code outside of that function. However, when a named function is instantiated within another function, it is created in the global scope, such that it can be called from anywhere, and thus it also needs to have a globally unique name. Consider the demonstration in Listing 2-17 of nested functions, which return a string to illustrate their nesting (Listing 2-18 shows the output).

Listing 2-17. name-scope.php

```php
<?php

function a() {

    function b() {

        return "a -> b";

    }

    return "a";

}

function c() {

    function d() {

        function e() {

            return "c -> d -> e";

        }

        return "c -> d";

    }

    return "c";

}

var_dump( a() );

var_dump( b() );

var_dump( c() );

var_dump( d() );

var_dump( e() );
```

Listing 2-18. name-scope-output.txt

```
string(1) "a"
string(6) "a -> b"
string(1) "c"
string(6) "c -> d"
string(11) "c -> d -> e"
```

Note that you are defining the functions b(), d(), and e() within the scope of other functions, but when you call them with var_dump, you are calling them from outside their "parent" functions. You can alter this script to show another property of named functions; they are not created until the scope within which they are defined is created. In Listing 2-19, you swap the order in which you call c() and d() in the var_dump() section (with the output shown in Listing 2-20).

Listing 2-19. name-scope2.php

```php
<?php

function a() {

    function b() {

        return "a -> b";

    }

    return "a";

}

function c() {

    function d() {

        function e() {

            return "c -> d -> e";

        }

        return "c -> d";

    }

    return "c";

}

var_dump( a() );

var_dump( b() );

var_dump( d() );

var_dump( c() );

var_dump( e() );
```

Listing 2-20. name-scope2-output.txt

```
string(1) "a"
string(6) "a -> b"
PHP Fatal error:  Uncaught Error: Call to undefined function d() in name-scope2.php:38
Stack trace:
#0 {main}
  thrown in name-scope2.php on line 38
```

Because you haven't yet called c(), d() doesn't exist, and so you get a fatal error. b() could be accessed fine, as you had already called a(), even though you were in the main program scope when you called it. As a final demonstration of the problems of named functions, let's look at the need for a globally unique name. With a normal variable, you can use the same variable name for different variables, as long as they are in a different scope (e.g., in different functions). With a named function, that won't work, as you can see from Listing 2-21 and Listing 2-22.

Listing 2-21. name-scope3.php

```php
<?php

function f() {

    function g() {

        return "1st g()";

    };

    return "f()";

}

function h() {

    function g() {

        return "2nd g()";

    };

    return "h()";

}

var_dump( f() );

var_dump( g() );

var_dump( h() );
```

Listing 2-22. name-scope3-output.txt

```
string(3) "f()"
string(7) "1st g()"
PHP Fatal error:  Cannot redeclare g() (previously declared in name-scope3.php:7) in name-
scope3.php on line 17
```

As you can see, you've defined g() twice, once inside f() and once inside h(). Despite this, things run smoothly at first when you call f() and g(), but as soon as you try to call h(), the second instance of g() tries to declare itself, leading to a fatal error.

Using unique names for functions doesn't seem like too much of a terrible restriction, until you consider that if you start including external code libraries with include() or require() or via an autoloader, those become part of the scope in which your function name must be unique, and it's harder to ensure that other people won't tread on your functional toes! PHP does allow you to "namespace" functions, which mitigates this issue somewhat; however, that can be considered a somewhat inelegant solution (depending on who you talk to).

Variable Functions

PHP supports the concept of "variable" functions. This is a dynamic way of calling named functions with a slightly more succinct syntax than the call_user_func() example you looked at in the previous section. In essence, if you put parentheses (round brackets) at the end of a variable, PHP will call the named function stored in the *value* of that variable (with any parameters you put in the parentheses). See Listing 2-23 and Listing 2-24.

Listing 2-23. variable.php

```php
<?php

function vehicles( $index ) {

    $types = ["car", "motorbike", "tractor"];

    return $types[$index];

}

function animals( $index ) {

    $types = ["cow", "pig", "chicken", "horse"];

    return $types[$index];

}

$get_thing = 'animals'; # string with the name of a function

var_dump( $get_thing(2) ); # add ($index) to call it

$get_thing = 'vehicles'; # change the function

var_dump( $get_thing(2) ); #same "code", different function
```

```
# Just to show that $get_thing is just a
# standard string, and nothing special...

$get_thing = strrev('selcihev'); # do string things

var_dump( $get_thing ); # it's a string

var_dump( $get_thing(2) ); # call it

var_dump( $get_thing ); # afterwards, still just a string

unset( $get_thing ); # we can destroy it, because it's a string

var_dump( $get_thing );

var_dump( vehicles(2) ); # But the function still exists

# However, it needs to be set to a function that exists

$get_thing = 'people';

var_dump( $get_thing(2) );
```

Listing 2-24. variable-output.txt

```
string(7) "chicken"
string(7) "tractor"
string(8) "vehicles"
string(7) "tractor"
string(8) "vehicles"
PHP Notice:  Undefined variable: get_thing in variable.php on line 41
NULL
string(7) "tractor"
PHP Fatal error:  Uncaught Error: Call to undefined function people() in variable.php:49
Stack trace:
#0 {main}
  thrown in variable.php on line 49
```

As you can see, the variable $get_thing is just a string holding the name of the function you want to call, and you can change that name whenever you want. However, the actual functions operate just like named functions (because that is what they are).

Language Constructs

strtoupper()—that's a function, right? Yup. How about echo()? It's got the parentheses like strtoupper(), and it takes parameters, so it must be a function, right? Sorry, nope! Some PHP "functions" are not actually functions at all but "language constructs," built-in parts of the language syntax. You can usually spot these because even though they accept parameters in parentheses, you don't *have* to use parentheses. You can also read the relevant page in the PHP Manual to discover which they are. Examples of function-like constructs include echo(), print(), unset(), isset(), empty(), include(), and require(). The distinction between language constructs and functions matters sometimes. Variable functions, described in the previous section, will not work with language constructs. See Listing 2-25 and Listing 2-26.

Listing 2-25. constructs.php

```php
<?php

$var_func = 'echo';

$var_func('hello world!');
```

Listing 2-26. constructs-output.php

```
PHP Fatal error:  Uncaught Error: Call to undefined function echo() in constructs.php:5
Stack trace:
#0 {main}
  thrown in constructs.php on line 5
```

However, if you do need to treat a construct like a function, then all you need to do is to wrap it up in your own function, as shown in Listing 2-27 and Listing 2-28.

Listing 2-27. constructs2.php

```php
<?php

function my_echo($string) {

    echo $string;

}

$var_func = 'my_echo';

$var_func('hello world!');
```

Listing 2-28. constructs2-output.php

```
hello world!
```

Return Values

As you saw in the "Named Functions" section, you can use a `return` statement to assign a value (or *return value*) to your functions. There are several properties of return values that you need to understand to get a good handle on functions.

If you don't put a `return` statement in your function or if the execution path on a particular run doesn't hit a `return` statement, then your function will return NULL. See Listing 2-29 and Listing 2-30.

Listing 2-29. null-return.php

```php
<?php

function reverse($string) {

 $string = strrev($string);

}
```

```php
function capitals($string) {

    if ($string != 'banana') {

        $string = strtoupper($string);

        return $string;

    }

}

# no return statement
var_dump( reverse('hello') );

# returns a value
var_dump( capitals('peaches') );

# execution flow misses return statement
var_dump( capitals('banana') );
```

Listing 2-30. null-return-output.txt

```
NULL
string(7) "PEACHES"
NULL
```

In the reverse() function, you forgot to return any value at all, so the reversed string didn't make it back outside the function. Captials() capitalized the peaches fine, but the bananas didn't pass through a code path with a return statement, so you just got a NULL back for your troubles.

In a similar manner, the return statement without a parameter also returns NULL, as shown in Listing 2-31 and Listing 2-32.

Listing 2-31. null-return2.php

```php
<?php

function fruits($type) {

    if ($type == 'mango') {

        return 'Yummy!';

    } else {

        return;

    }

}
```

```php
var_dump( fruits('kiwi') );

var_dump( fruits('pomegranate') );

var_dump( fruits('mango') );
```

Listing 2-32. null-return2-output.txt

```
NULL
NULL
string(6) "Yummy!"
```

Calling fruits() on kiwi and pomegranate hits the second return statement without a parameter, so NULL is returned for them. Mango, possibly the greatest fruit of all time, causes the fruits() function code path to hit the first return statement, which has the Yummy! string as a parameter, so fruit() returns that string in this case.

The other point to note about the return statement is that it can occur at any point in the function and immediately terminates the function execution at that point. See Listing 2-33 and Listing 2-34.

Listing 2-33. return.php

```php
<?php

function my_funct() {

    $a = 23;

    return $a;

    $a = 45;

    return $a;

}

var_dump( my_funct() );
```

Listing 2-34. return-output.txt

```
int(23)
```

As you can see, the function returns after the first return statement, and the code that sets $a equal to 45 (and the subsequent second return call) is never executed.

To sum up, you need to ensure you've done all the processing you need to do before you call return and make sure all of your code paths hit a return statement before the function finishes.

Lambda/Anonymous Functions

You've looked at "traditional" named functions and seen some of their drawbacks. Luckily, from PHP 5.4 onward, you can use anonymous functions in PHP. These are also known as *anonymous function literals* or *lambda functions* in other languages. They are called *anonymous* functions because, unlike named functions, they don't have a function name. Your first question is probably, "Well, how do you call them then?" There are a number of different ways to do that, but it's helpful first to take a look at how PHP implements anonymous functions "under the hood." See Listing 2-35 and Listing 2-36.

Listing 2-35. anon.php

```php
<?php

var_dump(

  # An anonymous function

    function ($a) { return $a; }

);
```

Listing 2-36. anon-output.txt

```
object(Closure)#1 (1) {
  ["parameter"]=>
  array(1) {
    ["$a"]=>
    string(10) "<required>"
  }
}
```

You can see that the function definition is the same as for a named function, but *sans* the name. Looking at the var_dump output, you can see that the function is in fact an object (of class Closure, something you'll look at later in this chapter).

So, what does that mean? It means you can treat it like any other object in PHP. You can assign it to a variable, and you can pass it around, destroy it, copy it, and more. But how do you actually *call* it to get it to something useful? The straightforward way is to assign it to a variable and then use the methods you learned about earlier (variable functions and call_user_func) to execute it. PHP can tell from the type of the variable (a closure object rather than a string) that it is an anonymous function rather than a named function and knows what to do with it. Let's look at some examples. See Listing 2-37 and Listing 2-38.

Listing 2-37. call_anon.php

```php
<?php

# create an anonymous function and assign it to a variable
$double = function ($a) { return $a * 2; };

var_dump( $double );

# call the anonymous function
var_dump( $double(4) );

var_dump( call_user_func($double, 8) );

# Copy it to another variable;

$two_times = $double;
```

```
var_dump( $two_times(4) + $double(6) );

# pass it as a parameter to another function

$numbers = [1,2,3,4];

var_dump( array_map( $two_times, $numbers ) );

# redefine it

$double = function ($a) { return $a * 4; };

var_dump( $double(10) );

# but the earlier copy is definitely a copy not a reference

var_dump( $two_times(10) );

# destroy it

unset($double);

var_dump( $double(9) );
```

Listing 2-38. call_anon-output.txt

```
object(Closure)#1 (1) {
  ["parameter"]=>
  array(1) {
    ["$a"]=>
    string(10) "<required>"
  }
}
int(8)
int(16)
int(20)
array(4) {
  [0]=>
  int(2)
  [1]=>
  int(4)
  [2]=>
  int(6)
  [3]=>
  int(8)
}
int(40)
int(20)
PHP Notice:  Undefined variable: double in call_anon.php on line 39
PHP Fatal error:  Uncaught Error: Function name must be a string in call_anon.php:39
Stack trace:
#0 {main}
  thrown in call_anon.php on line 39
```

You don't always need to assign anonymous functions to a variable to be useful. You can define them as parameters to other functions, for instance. See Listing 2-39 and Listing 2-40.

Listing 2-39. call_anon2.php

```php
<?php

# Define a function that is assigned to a variable,
# that takes a function as its first parameter
# and a parameter to call that function with as its
# second

$function_caller = function ($function, $parameter) {

    $function($parameter);

};

# Define a named function

function double($a) {

    echo ($a * 2)."\n";

}

# use the anonymous function to call the named function
# using the Variable Function technique

$function_caller('double', 4);

# this time, define a new anonymous function right in the
# calling parameter code

$function_caller( function($a) { echo 'Function says ' . $a . "\n"; },
    'Hello There');

# Do it again, but with a different anonymous function. Note that
# the anonymous function no longer finishes once the function
# has finished executing.

$function_caller( function($a) { echo $a . ' backwards is '. strrev($a) . "\n"; },
    'Banana');

# It's not only our own functions that can accept inline definitions
# of anonymous functions ...

var_dump(
    array_map( function($a) { return $a * 2; }, [1,2,3,4])
);
```

Listing 2-40. call_anon2-output.txt

```
8
Function says Hello There
Banana backwards is ananaB
array(4) {
  [0]=>
  int(2)
  [1]=>
  int(4)
  [2]=>
  int(6)
  [3]=>
  int(8)
}
```

Higher-Order Functions

A *higher-order* function is a function that can take one or more functions as input and/or return one or more functions as output, and I touched on them in at the end of the previous section. Higher-order functions are functions that work on other functions. In functional programming, you'll look at using higher-order functions for program control (rather than imperative control statements like for and while).

I've covered the building blocks you need for higher-order functions in the previous sections of this chapter, but if it hasn't quite clicked with you yet, then consider that you've already discovered that anonymous functions are in fact objects internally in PHP. You're probably familiar with passing around traditional objects in PHP, and you can do the same with function objects. They can be used as parameters to a function and returned as the result of a function. Let's look at an example; see Listing 2-41 and Listing 2-42.

Listing 2-41. higher-order.php

```php
<?php

# Define some data. I should stop writing code
# when I'm hungry...

$fruits = ['apple', 'banana', 'blueberry', 'cherry'];
$meats = ['antelope','bacon','beef','chicken'];
$cheeses = ['ambert','brie','cheddar','daralagjazsky'];

# Create a function that filters an array and picks out the

# elements beginning with a specified letter

$letter_filter = function($list, $letter) {

  # Rather than a foreach loop or similar, we'll use PHP's
    # higher-order array_filter function. Note it takes two
    # paramters, an array ($list in our case) and a
    # function (which we've defined inline)

    return array_filter($list, function($item) use ($letter)  {
```

```
        return $item[0] == $letter;

    });

};

# We can call the function on our data as normal.

print_r( $letter_filter($fruits,'a') );
print_r( $letter_filter($meats,'b') );
print_r( $letter_filter($cheeses,'c') );

# But let's use a single call to the higher-level array_map function
# to demonstrate a simple "loop" over three arrays & parameters.
# It should give the same output as the three functions above,
# wrapped up into a single array.

print_r(
    array_map( $letter_filter, [$fruits, $meats, $cheeses], ['a', 'b', 'c'])
);
```

Listing 2-42. higher-order-output.txt

```
Array
(
    [0] => apple
)
Array
(
    [1] => bacon
    [2] => beef
)
Array
(
    [2] => cheddar
)
Array
(
    [0] => Array
        (
            [0] => apple
        )

    [1] => Array
        (
            [1] => bacon
            [2] => beef
        )
```

```
    [2] => Array
        (
            [2] => cheddar
        )

)
```

The last array_map clause may give you some hints as to how you can replace loops and other imperative program control structures using functions.

You may also have spotted that in the anonymous function you used as the last parameter to array_filter, there was a use ($letter) clause. array_filter doesn't provide any way for you to pass additional variables to the filtering function, and $letter is out of the scope of the function when it is executed. use allows you to bind data to your functions, so you can take advantage of variables that wouldn't normally be available to it. I'll discuss scope in the next section and talk more about the use clause when you look at closures.

It's not all about consuming functions as input, though; higher-order functions often return them as output as well. Let's take a look at an example of that. See Listing 2-43 and Listing 2-44.

Listing 2-43. higher-order2.php

```php
<?php

# Create a higher order function to return a
# function to "add" two variables using a user selectable
# method

function add($method) {

    if ($method == 'sum') {

        # our return value is actually an anonymous function

        return function($a, $b) { return $a+$b;};

    } else {

        # this is returning a different function object

        return function($a, $b) { return $a.$b; };

    }

}

# Let's call the function. Note, that as the function
# returns a function, we can simply stick an extra
# set of parentheses on the end with some parameters
# to call that newly returned function.

print_r( add('sum')(2,3) ."\n" );
print_r( add('concatenate')('hello ', 'world!') ."\n" );
```

```php
# We can also pass the function to returned to other
# higher order functions like array_map

$a = [1, 2, 'cat', 3, 'orange', 5.4];
$b = [6, 3, 'ch', 9.5, 'ish', 6.5];

print_r( array_map(add('sum'), $a, $b) );
print_r( array_map(add('concatenate'), $a, $b) );

# and we can assign the returned function to a
# variable as with any anonymous function

$conc = add('concatenate');

print_r( array_map($conc, $a, $b) );

print_r( $conc("That's all, ", "folks!\n") );
```

Listing 2-44. higher-order2-output.txt

```
5
hello world!
Array
(
    [0] => 7
    [1] => 5
    [2] => 0
    [3] => 12.5
    [4] => 0
    [5] => 11.9
)
Array
(
    [0] => 16
    [1] => 23
    [2] => catch
    [3] => 39.5
    [4] => "orange" and "ish"
    [5] => 5.46.5
)
Array
(
    [0] => 16
    [1] => 23
    [2] => catch
    [3] => 39.5
    [4] => "orange" and "ish"
    [5] => 5.46.5
)
That's all, folks!
```

As you saw in a previous section, language constructs such as echo() aren't real functions, so you can't use them directly as input to or output from a higher-order function, but you can always wrap them in your own custom function if you need to use them in this way.

Scope

The *scope* of a variable determines which parts of your code can access it. In PHP, a variable exists in the *global* scope, unless it is declared in a user-defined function (including as one of the parameters to the function). If the variable is in the global scope, you can access it from everywhere in your program *except* from within user-defined functions (by default). If you want to manipulate it in your function, you need to either pass it in as a parameter *by reference* or use the global keyword to pull it into the function's scope. If you pass it in as a parameter *by value*, your function gets a copy of the value of the variable, but even if you give it the same name, your function's copy is independent of the global variable. Assigning a new value to the function's copy will not alter the global one. Likewise, if you simply declare a variable in a function with the same name as one in the global scope (or indeed one within another function), they are separate variables and will not interact.

Variable scope is an important concept to keep in mind when you are writing functional programs. One of the advantages of using PHP when programming functionally is that you have to go out of your way to bring variables from the global scope into your function or to change the values within your function from the outside. In functional programming you want your functions to have no *side effects*, which means you don't want the external state of your programs (e.g., global variables) to affect the operation of our function, as it makes it harder to reason about exactly what the function will do at any given time. Be aware that "external state" when I'm talking about functions isn't just anything external to your program (databases, system state, etc.) but any state outside of your function (e.g., other state within your program) that was not passed in through the parameters to the function.

The slight caveat to the scope rules are so-called superglobals, which are variables that exist literally *everywhere* in your program. $_SESSION, $_GET, $_POST, etc., are examples that you may be aware of from typical web-based PHP applications. The best advice here is to simply avoid accessing these from your functions!

Listing 2-45 demonstrates the general rules of scope (with the output shown in Listing 2-46).

Listing 2-45. scope.php

```php
<?php

# Define some variables in the "Global" scope
$a = 2;
$b = 6;

function double($a) {

  # In this function's scope, we'll double $a
  $a = $a * 2;

  return $a;

}

# This is like the function above, except
# we've passed in the variable by reference
# (note the & before $a in the parameters)
function double_ref(&$a) {
```

```
  $a = $a * 2;

  return $a;

}

function double_add($a) {

  # We'll pull in $b from the global scope
  global $b;

  # and double it
  $b = $b * 2;

  # and double $a from the local function scope
  $a = $a * 2;

  return $a + $b;

}
# a in the global scope = 2
echo("a = $a \n");

# a in the function scope, doubled, = 4
echo("double a = ". double($a). " \n");

# but a in the global scope still = 2
echo("a = $a \n");

# now we pass it in by reference
echo("double_ref a = ". double_ref($a). " \n");

# and now $a = 4;
echo("a = $a \n");

# b in the global scope = 6
echo("b = $b \n");

# doubled and added = 8 + 12 = 20
echo("double_add a+b = ". double_add($a). " \n");

# a is still = 4 in the global scope
echo("a = $a \n");

# but b in the global scope is now doubled = 12
echo("b = $b \n");
```

Listing 2-46. scope-output.txt

```
a = 2
double a = 4
a = 2
double_ref a = 4
a = 4
b = 6
double_add a+b = 20
a = 4
b = 12
```

Further Reading

- Scope, in the PHP Manual

    - http://php.net/manual/en/language.variables.scope.php

State

Have you ever spent a long time trying to re-create an error that a user is experiencing, without luck? That's likely because of you being unable to re-create the user's state. *State* is the condition of the environment the program is running in at any given time. This includes internal and external conditions. External conditions include the following:

- The content of files

- Memory contents

- Network conditions

- Environmental variables

- The state of other running processes

Examples of internal conditions include the following:

- The values (and existence) of variables and other data structures

- The amount of resource (memory, disk space, etc.) used by the process

In functional programming, you try to avoid relying on state. State is bad because it is hard to re-create (as with the example of re-creating a user's problem earlier) and because it makes it hard to reason about a piece of code. For instance, let's say I give you a function written in PHP and a known input variable. Can you tell me what the return value of that function will be? If the only information that the function requires is the input variable, then yes, you can. However, if the function references the content of an external file, references the value of a global variable, or calls a remote API, then it's going to be a lot harder for you to determine what the function will actually return without also knowing the exact state of those external resources.

Of course, your programs aren't going to be very useful if you can't read from files or talk to remote systems, so you need to manage state. As you'll see in this book, you usually do this by passing any necessary state information into your chains of functions as parameters directly so that given the inputs to the function you can fully determine the output of it.

Parameters/Arguments/Operands, Arity, and Variadic Functions

Parameters, arguments, and operands. They're different words for the same thing, at least for our purposes. They are the things that you use to explicitly pass values to a function. You'll see the terms used interchangeably in various literature (particularly if you start exploring the mathematical background to function programming). In the PHP Manual, the term *argument* is usually (but not always) used. For the avoidance of doubt, the things I am talking about are $arg1, $stringB, and so on, in Listing 2-47.

Listing 2-47. arguments.php

```php
<?php

function func_one($arg1, $arg2, $arg3) {

    return $arg1 + $arg2 + $arg3;

};

function func_two($stringA, $stringB) {

    return $stringA.$stringB;

};
```

Arity is a term borrowed from mathematics and logic and is used in programming to describe the number of parameters a function accepts. The func_one function in Listing 2-47 accepts three parameters and so has an arity of three (sometimes termed a *3-ary function*), and func_two has an arity of two as it accepts two parameters.

Now if you have lots of arguments to pass into a function, the function definition is going to quickly get unwieldy. And what happens if you don't know how many arguments your calling code will need to use? These are both situations that you try to avoid in functional programming, but PHP being ever the pragmatist, does have you covered when you find the exception to that rule. It's called the *variadic function*, and it's implemented using the "splat" operator ... (that's three full stops in a row, called the *splat operator*, and not me trailing off at the end of that sentence). Be careful to use three full stops and not the Unicode ellipsis symbol, which looks similar. The splat operator allows you to say "put all the remaining arguments into this array," as demonstrated by Listing 2-48 and Listing 2-49.

Listing 2-48. splat.php

```php
<?php

function my_func($a, ...$b) {

  var_dump($a);

  var_dump($b);

}
```

```
# Call it with 4 arguments, $a will be a string
# and $b will be an array of 3 strings

my_func('apples', 'bacon', 'carrots', 'doughnut');

# Define some colorful arrays

$array1 = ['red', 'yellow', 'pink', 'green'];
$array2 = ['purple', 'orange', 'blue'];

# $a will be an array with 4 elements,
# $b will be an array with 1 element, which itself is an
# array of 3 elements

my_func($array1, $array2);

# We can also use the splat operator in reverse when
# calling an array. In this case, the splat
# unpacks $array2 into 3 separate arguments, so
# $b will be an array with 3 elements.

my_func($array1, ...$array2);
```

Listing 2-49. splat-output.txt

```
string(6) "apples"
array(3) {
  [0]=>
  string(5) "bacon"
  [1]=>
  string(7) "carrots"
  [2]=>
  string(8) "doughnut"
}
array(4) {
  [0]=>
  string(3) "red"
  [1]=>
  string(6) "yellow"
  [2]=>
  string(4) "pink"
  [3]=>
  string(5) "green"
}
array(1) {
  [0]=>
  array(3) {
    [0]=>
    string(6) "purple"
    [1]=>
    string(6) "orange"
```

```
    [2]=>
    string(4) "blue"
  }
}
array(4) {
  [0]=>
  string(3) "red"
  [1]=>
  string(6) "yellow"
  [2]=>
  string(4) "pink"
  [3]=>
  string(5) "green"
}
array(3) {
  [0]=>
  string(6) "purple"
  [1]=>
  string(6) "orange"
  [2]=>
  string(4) "blue"
}
```

As you can see from Listing 2-48 and Listing 2-49, you can use the splat in reverse when calling a function to split an array into separate arguments. If you're using type hinting (see Chapter 4), you can add a single type hint to variadic parameters to ensure all values passed are of the right type (assuming you want them all to be the same type).

Further Reading

- Variadic functions in the PHP Manual

  - `http://php.net/manual/en/functions.arguments.php#functions.variable-arg-list`

Closures

I briefly mentioned closures in a previous section, but now I'll explain them in more detail. A *closure* is a function, together with an *environment* that is "enclosed" with it. It's a bit like a streamlined object: the function is the (one and only) method, and the environment consists the properties of the object. In PHP, the environment that is enclosed in a closure is a set of one or more variables.

As you've seen, one of the great properties of anonymous functions is that you can pass them around as if they were a variable or object (and, as I noted, they are indeed implemented as an object of the closure class). The key downside to this is that while they are being passed around, they are typically going from scope to scope (often up and down a chain of functions). This means that when you create the function in one scope, you can't be sure it will still be in that scope to have access to variables from it as arguments when it is called.

By turning an anonymous function into a closure, you can "close the function over" one or more variables from the current scope. You do that with a use clause in the function definition.

Let's say that you want to create a function called get_multiplier that returns an anonymous function to multiply any number by a fixed amount. A first stab at such a function might look like Listing 2-50.

Listing 2-50. closure.php

```php
<?php

function get_multiplier($count) {

  return function ($number)  {

    return $number * $count;

  };

}

$times_six = get_multiplier(6);

print_r( $times_six(3) );
```

So when you call get_multiplier(6), it returns (into $times_six) an anonymous function that multiplies $number by $count (which you specified as 6). Then when you call the anonymous function on 3 (using $times_six(3)), you should get 18 returned (3×6), right? Well, Listing 2-51 shows what actually happens.

Listing 2-51. closure-output.txt

```
PHP Notice:  Undefined variable: count in closure.php on line 7
0
```

Hmm. It says that $count is undefined. But it's passed in as a parameter to get_multiplier, and you're in get_multiplier when you define the anonymous function, aren't you? Well, yes and no. A function, no matter where it's defined, has its own scope. And at the point where you call your anonymous function on the last line of the script, you're definitely out of the scope of get_multiplier in any case. So, you need to use a use clause to enclose $count into your function (see Listing 2-52 and Listing 2-53).

Listing 2-52. closure2.php

```php
<?php

function get_multiplier($count) {

  return function ($number) use ($count) {

    return $number * $count;

  };

}

$times_six = get_multiplier(6);

print_r( $times_six(3) );
```

41

Listing 2-53. closure2-output.txt

18

Perfect. You can use the use clause to enclose just about anything into the closure, including variables, objects, and of course (because they're implemented as objects) other closures and anonymous functions! Simply add a comma-separated list of parameters to the use clause, just like adding extra parameters to the function clause.

Side Effects

In functional programming, you don't want your functions to create or experience "side effects." Side effects occur when a function changes the state of something outside of its scope or when something outside of its scope affects the internal operation of a function. The only thing you want to affect a function's operation is the parameters it's given, and the only effect you want your function to have is to set an appropriate return value.

Here are examples of side effects:

- The function changing a variable that exists outside of its scope (e.g., a global variable)

- The function using the value of a variable that exists outside of its scope (e.g., $_SESSION)

- A parameter passed by reference instead of value

- Reading in user input (e.g., through readline())

- Getting data from a file (e.g., via file_get_contents())

- Writing to a file (e.g., via file_put_contents())

- Throwing an exception (apart from where it is caught and handled within the function itself)

- Printing to screen or returning data to the web user (e.g., via echo())

- Accessing databases, remote APIs, and any other external resources

You get the idea. Basically, anything that means the function isn't fully self-contained.

Referential Transparency

Referential transparency in functional programming means that given a function, you can always replace that function with its return value as long as its parameter input is the same. Listing 2-54 shows an example (with the output shown in Listing 2-55).

Listing 2-54. referential.txt

```
<?php

# This function is Referentially Transparent. It has no
# side effects, and its output is fully determined
# by its parameters.
```

```
function is_RT($arg1, $arg2) {

    return $arg1 * $arg2;

}

# This function is not RT, it uses the rand() function
# which introduces a value (a side effect) that
# isn't passed in through the parameters

function is_not_RT($arg1, $arg2) {

    return $arg1 * $arg2 * rand(1,1000);

}

# So let's call our RT function with the values 3 and 6
$val = is_RT(3,6);

# if it really is RT, then in an expression like the
# following, we can replace the function call...
$a = is_RT(3,6) + 10; # with itself
$b = $val + 10; # with the value it returned earlier
$c = 18 + 10; # with the hard coded value

# and all output should be the same
var_dump( $a == $b ); # true
var_dump( $a == $c ); # true

# The following demonstrates that this is not the case
# for non-RT functions
$val = is_not_RT(3,6);

$a = is_not_RT(3,6) + 10;
$b = $val + 10;
$c = 2372 + 10;
#(2372 was the value from my first run of this script)

var_dump( $a == $b ); # false
var_dump( $a == $c ); # false
```

Listing 2-55. referential-output.txt

```
bool(true)
bool(true)
bool(false)
bool(false)
```

Referential transparency is only reliably possible when you have no side effects.

Pure Functions

A *pure function*, in functional programming terms, is one that has no side effects and is referentially transparent. Pure functions are what you will be aiming to write in your functional programming,

Lists and Collections

When reading about the topic of functional programming, you will come across references to data structures such as lists and collections. There are different pros and cons to such data structures in various languages, but in PHP you have the Swiss Army knife of data structure types (misleadingly) called an *array*.

An array in PHP is actually implemented in the background as an "ordered map," but its implementation is flexible enough that as well as a normal array, it can be treated as a list, a hash table, a dictionary, a collection, a stack, a queue, and other less common data structures. So, it is what you will use in this book, and if you're trying to implement in PHP an algorithm that you've found in a different language and come across a list, say, you can usually just think to yourself "that'll be an array then." Lists and collections are perhaps the most commonly found data structures in functional programming (beyond simple types such as integers and strings), and you'll simply implement them as standard arrays. The Standard PHP Library (SPL) does offer some more efficient data structures, but they can be harder to work with and aren't strictly necessary for functional programming, so I won't cover them in this book. You can take a look at the PHP Manual for more information if you are interested in them.

Further Reading

- The Standard PHP Library (SPL)
    - http://php.net/manual/en/book.spl.php

Conclusion

Phew, that was a lot to cover, but you should now be familiar with the key concepts and terminology you'll need to understand to start getting to grips with functional programming. There were tantalizing glimpses of some of the features that you'll explore over the next few chapters as you start piecing these concepts together to make some functional programs. Don't worry if you still don't have a concrete idea of what functional programming is yet; you're only just getting started!

■ ■ ■

## CHAPTER 3

Getting Started with Functional Patterns

In the previous chapter, you looked at some of the key concepts and vocabulary that you'll use as you develop functional-style code. You'll now turn your attention to looking at some of the core programming patterns that differentiate functional code from imperative and that you'll use to structure the flow of your functional code. You'll first look at some ways to use map, filter, and reduce functions to perform common operations on sets of data. They're useful in most scenarios where, as an imperative programmer, you would have used loops based on foreach or for to iterate through a collection of data. You'll then look at recursive functions and explore the benefits they have for certain problems. Finally, you'll look at partial functions and functional composition, which are different ways to mix up your functions for different uses.

Map, Filter, and Reduce

Some of the key functional patterns that replace typical loops in functional programs are the map, filter, and reduce functions, which simplify iterating over collections of data. In PHP, these are already implemented for you with three native functions (array_map, array_filter, and array_reduce) ready for use on your favorite data type. The purpose of each function is as follows:

- Array_map: Maps (applies) a function to all elements of an array, returning a new array with the output of each mapping as an element. The output array will have the same number of elements as the input array.

- Array_filter: Filters the elements of an array to a smaller array by applying a function to each element to decide whether it appears in the output array. The output array will be the same size or smaller than the input array.

- Array_reduce: Reduces an array to a single value by applying a function to each element in turn. The output of each call of the function is fed back into the function as a parameter when it is called on the next element. The output value of the last function call is the value that array_reduce returns.

These are easier to understand in action, so let's look at an example script using all three (see Listing 3-1 and Listing 3-2). Put on your chef's hat and imagine you're opening a new restaurant. You need to get inspiration for a new dish to cook for your guests. Your function will take a range of ingredients and dish types, come up with some exciting recipes, and finally pick the best recipe for you to cook for your guests. What could possibly go wrong…?

© Rob Aley 2017
R. Aley, *Pro Functional PHP Programming*, DOI 10.1007/978-1-4842-2958-3_3

Listing 3-1. map_filter_reduce.php

```php
<?php

# Set up some arrays of data

$ingredients = [
  "cod", "beef", "kiwi", "egg", "vinegar"
];

$dish_types = [
  "pie", "smoothie", "tart", "ice cream", "crumble"
];

$baked = [
  "pie", "tart", "crumble", "cake"
];

# A function which creates a "recipe" by combining
# an ingredient with a type of dish

$make_recipe = function ($ingredient, $dish) {

  return $ingredient.' '.$dish;

};

# A function to check if a recipe involves baked
# goods by seeing if it has any of the words in
# the $baked array in it

$is_baked = function ($recipe) use ($baked) {

    # We need to return a value that evaluates to
    # true or false. We could use a foreach to loop
    # through each $baked item and set a flag to true
    # but instead we'll do it the functional way and
    # filter the $baked array using a function that calls
    # strpos on each element. At the end, if no match is
    # made, array_filter returns an empty array which
    # evaluates to false, otherwise it returns an array of
    # the matches which evaluate to true

  return array_filter($baked,
                            function($item) use ($recipe) {

                                return strpos($recipe, $item) !== false;

                            }
                        );

};
```

```
# A function which returns the longest of $current_longest or $recipe

$get_longest = function ($current_longest, $recipe) {

  return strlen($recipe) > strlen($current_longest) ?
                          $recipe : $current_longest;

};

# the PHP function shuffle is not immutable, it changes the array it is
# given. So we create our own function $reshuffle which is immutable.
# Note that shuffle also has a side effect (it uses an external source
# of entropy to randomise the array), and so is not referentially
# transparent. But it will do for now.

$reshuffle = function ($array) { shuffle($array); return $array;};};

# Now we actually do some work.

# We'll take a shuffled version of $ingredients and $dish_types (to add
# a little variety) and map the $make_recipe function over them, producing
# a new array $all_recipes with some delicious new dishes

$all_recipes = array_map($make_recipe,
                                $reshuffle($ingredients),
                                $reshuffle($dish_types)
                    );

print_r($all_recipes);

# Everyone knows that only baked foods are nice, so we'll filter
# $all_recipes using the $is_baked function. If $is_baked returns
# false for a recipe, it won't appear in the $baking_recipes output array.

$baking_recipes = array_filter($all_recipes, $is_baked);

print_r($baking_recipes);

# Finally we need to pick our favorite dish, and everyone knows that food
# with the longest name tastes the best. $get_longest compares two strings
# and returns the longest. Array_reduce applies the $get_longest
# function to each element of $baking_recipes in turn, supplying the result
# of the last call to $get_longest and the current array element. After all
# elements have been processed, the result of the last $get_longest call
# must be the longest of all of the elements. It is returned as the output

$best_recipe = array_reduce($baking_recipes, $get_longest, '');

print_r($best_recipe);
```

Listing 3-2. map_filter_reduce-output.txt

```
Array
(
    [0] => kiwi smoothie
    [1] => vinegar crumble
    [2] => egg ice cream
    [3] => cod tart
    [4] => beef pie
)
Array
(
    [1] => vinegar crumble
    [3] => cod tart
    [4] => beef pie
)
vinegar crumble
```

So, there you go—vinegar crumble. It sounds delicious (this may be why I'm a programmer and not a chef). But why would you want to use functions such as map, filter, and reduce instead of foreach loops, for instance? Reusability is the main advantage. On their own, loops such as foreach, while, for, and so on, need to be rewritten each time they need to be used. You can, of course, wrap them into their own bespoke functions, and of course if you need something not exactly implemented by the built-in array_* functions, then you'll need to do that anyway, but if the built-in ones do match your use case, then using them will often a) save you the time of creating your own, and b) typically be more performant than your own implementations. Having common control structures like this wrapped into functions (either as the native PHP functions or as your own custom functions) also allows you to use the full power of functional programming on them, for instance, by creating partial functions from them or composing them into combined functions, topics that you'll look at later in this chapter.

Recursive Functions

A *recursive* function is simply a function that calls itself, and any type of function (named, anonymous, or closure) can be recursive. You'll first take a look at a couple of examples of recursive functions and see why they are useful. You'll then take a look at how you can implement program control functions using recursion.

Basic Recursion

Let's jump right into an example. You have a shopping list, stored as a PHP array (see Listing 3-3).

Listing 3-3. shopping_list1.php

```php
<?php

$shopping = [
    "fruits" => [ "apples" => 7, "pears" => 4, "bananas" => 6 ],
    "bakery" => [ "bread" => 1, "apple pie" => 2],
    "meat" => [ "sausages" => 10, "steaks" => 3, "chorizo" => 1 ]
];
```

This is a multidimensional array; at the top-level you have "groups" of food (fruits, bakery, meat), each of which is an array of items (apples, pears, bananas, etc.) with the number of each that you want to purchase. Let's say you want to know how many items in total are in your list. Listing 3-4 is a typical procedural way to count up the items (with the output shown in Listing 3-5).

Listing 3-4. foreach.php

```php
<?php

require('shopping_list1.php');

$total = 0;

foreach ($shopping as $group) {

    foreach ($group as $food => $count) {

        $total += $count;

    }

}

echo "Total items to purchase : $total\n";
```

Listing 3-5. foreach-output.txt

```
Total items to purchase : 34
```

You use two foreach loops, the first to loop through the groups of food and then a second to loop through each food in the group and add the count to the total. That's a perfectly good way to complete the task. However, with fussy children, simply buying seven apples is not good enough. Four must be red apples, and three must be green, or war will ensue. So, let's alter the list and break the apples entry down into a further nested array (see Listing 3-6).

Listing 3-6. shopping_list2.php

```php
<?php

$shopping = [
    "fruits" => [ "apples" => [ "red" => 3, "green" => 4], "pears" => 4, "bananas" => 6 ],
    "bakery" => [ "bread" => 1, "apple pie" => 2],
    "meat" => [ "sausages" => 10, "steaks" => 3, "chorizo" => 1 ]
];
```

Now run the foreach.php script against the new list (see Listing 3-7).

Listing 3-7. foreach2-output.txt

```
PHP Fatal error:  Uncaught Error: Unsupported operand types in foreach.php:11
Stack trace:
#0 {main}
  thrown in foreach.php on line 11
```

The new apples subarray is causing a problem. When the script reaches this new array, it assumes it will be a numeric value and tries to add it to $total, causing PHP to throw an error. The situation could be remedied by adding a third foreach loop, but then you would need to convert all the other foods (pears, bananas, etc.) to arrays as well. And what happens when someone insists that red apples needs breaking down further into Gala and Braeburn varieties? This way of structuring your code is clearly fragile and hard to maintain as the task at hand evolves. What you need instead is a bit of code that can walk through an array of arbitrary depth and add up all the "leaf nodes" (elements like bread that contain a single value rather than an array of further values) wherever it finds them. This is where recursion can help us. See Listing 3-8 and Listing 3-9.

Listing 3-8. recursive.php

```php
<?php

function count_total ($list) {

    # we start like before, with a variable to hold our total

    $total = 0;

    # and then we loop through each value in our array

    foreach ($list as $food => $value) {

        # for each value in the array, which check if it
        # is infact another array ...

        if (is_array ($value)) {

            # ... in which case we call *this* function
            # on the new (sub)array, and add the result
            # to the $total. This is the recursive part.

        $total += count_total ($value);

        } else {

            # ... or if it's just a plain old value
            # we add that straight to the total

        $total += $value;

        }

    }

    # once we've finished the foreach loop, we will have
    # added ALL of the values of the array together, and
    # also called count_total() on all of the sub-arrays
    # and added that to our total (and each of those
    # calls to count_total() will have done the same on
    # any sub-arrays within those sub-arrays, and so on)
    # so we can return the total.
```

```
        return $total;

};

# Let's call it on our original shopping list

require('shopping_list1.php');

echo "List 1 : ".count_total($shopping)."\n";

# and then on the list with the apples sub-array

require('shopping_list2.php');

echo "List 2 : ".count_total($shopping)."\n";

# and finally on a new list which has sausages broken
# into pork and beef, with pork broken down to a third
# level between chipolatas and cumberland sausages.

require('shopping_list3.php');

echo "List 3 : ".count_total($shopping)."\n";
```

Listing 3-9. recursive-output.txt

```
List 1 : 34
List 2 : 34
List 3 : 34
```

As you can see, no matter how you split your list into arrays and subarrays, the same function will always get to every part of the array. It may take a while to get your head around how a function can call itself. The key to understanding this is that each time you call a function (whether from within itself or not), a new "copy" of the function state is created in memory. This means each invocation of the function is effectively separate from others of the same function. As they are called, the state of each function call is placed into a *call stack* in memory, and looking at the call stack can help you visualize recursion. To demonstrate, Listing 3-10 (its output is in Listing 3-11) is a simple recursive function that sums all the numbers up to the given number (e.g., for sum(3) it does 3+2+1). The debug_print_backtrace() line prints out the call stack each time the function is (recursively) called.

Listing 3-10. recursive_stack.php

```php
<?php
function sum($start) {

echo "---\n";
debug_print_backtrace();

    if ($start < 2) {

        return 1;

    } else {
```

```
        return $start + sum($start-1);
    }
}

echo "The result is : ".sum(4);
```

Listing 3-11. recursive_stack-output.txt

```
---
#0  sum(4) called at [recursive_stack.php:17]
---
#0  sum(3) called at [recursive_stack.php:13]
#1  sum(4) called at [recursive_stack.php:17]
---
#0  sum(2) called at [recursive_stack.php:13]
#1  sum(3) called at [recursive_stack.php:13]
#2  sum(4) called at [recursive_stack.php:17]
---
#0  sum(1) called at [recursive_stack.php:13]
#1  sum(2) called at [recursive_stack.php:13]
#2  sum(3) called at [recursive_stack.php:13]
#3  sum(4) called at [recursive_stack.php:17]
The result is : 10
```

In the stack traces in Listing 3-11, #0 is the most recently called function, and you can see how each time through the function calls the same function again with the next number to add to the total.

Recursion is good, but you have to be careful to ensure your recursive loop will definitely terminate at some point. Consider Listing 3-12 and Listing 3-13.

Listing 3-12. forever.php

```php
<?php

ini_set('memory_limit','1G');

function forever() {
  forever();
}

forever();
```

Listing 3-13. forever-output.txt

```
PHP Fatal error:  Allowed memory size of 1073741824 bytes exhausted (tried to allocate
262144 bytes) in forever.php on line 6
```

The function forever() recursively calls itself each time it is called; there is no bounds check or other mechanism to cause it to return. As I noted earlier, each time a function is called, a copy is created in memory, and in this case, with no way to exit the function, more and more memory is consumed with each call, and it is never released by exiting a function. Note that I explicitly set a memory limit for the script with ini_set. Unlike web scripts, PHP CLI scripts do not have a memory limit by default. Without a limit, this script would likely bring your machine to its knees by consuming all available memory.

Every variable you use in your function, every debug statement, and every other resource allocated all take up valuable memory when a function is called. Called once, it may not add up to much, but called recursively many hundreds or thousands of times, it can quickly become an issue. Thus, you should always try to keep every form of state within a recursive function to the absolute minimum.

Tail recursion is a form of recursion where the recursive call is made as the very last part of function. In many languages, the compiler can optimize tail recursion because it doesn't require a "stack frame" for the compiler to store state in to come back to. Unfortunately, the PHP virtual machine doesn't offer such an optimization, so I won't go into detail about tail recursion. In the next chapter, you will instead look at "trampolines," which are a way that you can get a similar optimization by automatically flattening a recursive function into a loop.

Implementing a Recursive Function

In the "Map, Filter, and Reduce" section, you created a script to generate tasty new recipes. You generated your candidate recipes by using `array_map` to combine elements of two arrays of size n, giving you n combined recipes as output. But what if you wanted to expand your culinary horizons and get a candidate list based on every possible combination of $ingredients and $dish_types (i.e., n × n combinations)? You can do that with two embedded foreach loops, as shown in Listing 3-14 and Listing 3-15.

Listing 3-14. all_recipes.php

```php
<?php

$ingredients = [
    "cod", "beef", "kiwi", "egg", "vinegar"
];

$dish_types = [
    "pie", "smoothie", "tart", "ice cream", "crumble"
];

$all_recipes = [];

foreach ($ingredients as $ingredient) {

    foreach ($dish_types as $dish) {

        $all_recipes[] = $ingredient.' '.$dish;

    }

}

print_r($all_recipes);
```

Listing 3-15. all_recipes-output.txt

```
Array
(
    [0] => cod pie
    [1] => cod smoothie
    [2] => cod tart
    [3] => cod ice cream
    [4] => cod crumble
    [5] => beef pie
    [6] => beef smoothie
    [7] => beef tart
    [8] => beef ice cream
    [9] => beef crumble
    [10] => kiwi pie
    [11] => kiwi smoothie
    [12] => kiwi tart
    [13] => kiwi ice cream
    [14] => kiwi crumble
    [15] => egg pie
    [16] => egg smoothie
    [17] => egg tart
    [18] => egg ice cream
    [19] => egg crumble
    [20] => vinegar pie
    [21] => vinegar smoothie
    [22] => vinegar tart
    [23] => vinegar ice cream
    [24] => vinegar crumble
)
```

These foreach loops are very specific; they take particular variables as input, and as they aren't part of a function, they can't be reused elsewhere. And print_r is a bit all-or-nothing; perhaps you only want to print the first n items from the list. So, let's look at how you can make this more *functional*.

You'll create two functions. The first will be a recursive version of the foreach loops shown in Listing 3-14. The second will be a more flexible version of the print_r call. You'll save these in a separate reusable PHP file, and then you'll call them from your main script. See Listing 3-16, Listing 3-17, and Listing 3-18.

Listing 3-16. recipe_functions.php

```php
<?php

function combine($a,$b) {

    $combinations = [];

    if (is_array($a)) {
        foreach ($a as $i) {
            $combinations = array_merge( $combinations, combine($i, $b) );
        }
    } else {
            foreach ($b as $i) {
                $combinations[] = $a.' '.$i;
```

```php
        }
    }

    return $combinations;

}

function print_first($items, $count) {
        for ($counter=0; $counter<$count; $counter++) {
            echo "$counter. ${items[$counter]} \n";
        }
}
```

Listing 3-17. all_recipes_recursive.php

```php
<?php

require_once('recipe_functions.php');

$ingredients = [
  "cod", "beef", "kiwi", "egg", "vinegar"
];

$dish_types = [
  "pie", "smoothie", "tart", "ice cream", "crumble"
];

$all_recipes = combine($ingredients, $dish_types);

print_first($all_recipes, 5);
```

Listing 3-18. all_recipes_recursive_output.txt

```
Showing 5 of 25 items:
1. cod pie
2. cod smoothie
3. cod tart
4. cod ice cream
5. cod crumble
```

So, why is this better than the original imperative foreach version? Consider what happens if you have a need for a different structure for the $ingredients list. For instance, if you change your ingredients supplier and their data feed is structured differently, you have Listing 3-19 and Listing 3-20.

Listing 3-19. new_ingredients.php

```php
<?php

require_once('recipe_functions.php');

$ingredients = [
  ["ham", "beef"],
    ["apple", "kumquat"],
    "vinegar"
];
```

```
$dish_types = [
  "pie", "smoothie", "tart", "ice cream", "crumble"
];

$all_recipes = combine($ingredients, $dish_types);

print_first($all_recipes, 11);
```

Listing 3-20. new_ingredients-output.txt

```
Showing 11 of 25 items:
1. ham pie
2. ham smoothie
3. ham tart
4. ham ice cream
5. ham crumble
6. beef pie
7. beef smoothie
8. beef tart
9. beef ice cream
10. beef crumble
11. apple pie
```

As you can see, the recursive `combine` function didn't need any alterations to cope with the new structure of the `$ingredients` array and recursively went down into each subarray.

As well as the benefits discussed earlier, recursive functions help to ensure program correctness. By often eliminating the need to explicitly keep the state of the "loop" via counters or similar, the opportunities to introduce off-by-one errors and the like are substantially reduced.

Partial Functions

In Chapter 1, you looked at how functional programming embodies the SOLID principles from OOP. One of those principles, Interface Segregation Principle (ISP), means that only the parameters necessary for completing the current task should be those that you are required to pass to your function.

Consider the `print_first` function in `recipe_functions.php` in the previous section. It requires two parameters, the array of items to be printed and the number of items to print. Normally it would be reasonable to require both parameters as typically they will both vary for a given task. But what if you are writing a new web site, theTopFiveBestEverListsOfStuff.com, where you are only ever going to ever want to print out the first five items of any list you are given. You can of course repeatedly type `print_first($list, 5)` throughout your scripts. But when the market for top-five-best-ever lists becomes saturated and you need to move on to the top-ten-best-ever market, you'll need to find and replace all of those 5s with 10s. And if you accidentally mistype 4 instead of 5 or 1 instead of 10, you'll lose half your market share in an afternoon.

You could, of course, replace 5 with a variable, say $count, and later set $count = 10 when needed. But doing that in the global scope means extra work to ensure it is available to calls within other function scopes, and when another programmer accidentally uses $count as a loop counter somewhere, weird errors will abound.

Partial functions give you a solution to these woes. Partial functions are new functions that take an existing function and reduce its arity by binding a value to one (or more) of the parameters. Put another way, a partial function makes a more specific version of an existing function by fixing one or more of its parameters to a particular value, thus reducing the number of parameters needed to call it. Let's create a partial function for printing lists on the top-five site. See Listing 3-21 and Listing 3-22.

Listing 3-21. top_five.php

```php
<?php

require_once('print_first.php');

# Some data ...
$best_names = ["Rob", "Robert", "Robbie", "Izzy", "Ellie", "Indy",
    "Parv", "Mia", "Joe", "Surinder", "Lesley"];

# Calling the function in full

print_first($best_names, 5);

# Now let's define a partial function, print_top_list, which
# binds the value 5 to the second parameter of print_first

function print_top_list($list) {
    print_first($list, 5);
};

# Calling the new partial function will give the same
# output as the full function call above.

print_top_list($best_names);
```

Listing 3-22. top_five-output.txt

```
Showing 5 of 11 items:
1. Rob
2. Robert
3. Robbie
4. Izzy
5. Ellie
Showing 5 of 11 items:
1. Rob
2. Robert
3. Robbie
4. Izzy
5. Ellie
```

You can happily use the print_top_list partial function throughout the web site now, safe in the knowledge that a) you can change the number 5 to 10 in one single central place at any time, b) you can still benefit from any updates or changes to the underlying print_first function, and c) you can still call the print_first function directly with any number for a second parameter in any other scripts that happens to use the same function but needs a different number.

While this demonstrates the benefits of a partial function, the manual way you created it is a little clunky and isn't reusable. So, let's be real functional programmers and create a function to create your partial functions! I talked about higher-order functions in Chapter 2; as a reminder, these are functions that can take other functions as input and/or return them as output. You'll define a function called partial that takes a function and one or more parameters to bind to it and spits out a ready-made partial function for you to use. See Listing 3-23, Listing 3-24, and Listing 3-25.

Listing 3-23. partial_generator.php

```php
<?php

# Our function to create a partial function. $func is
# a "callable", i.e. a closure or the name of a function, and
# $args is one or more arguments to bind to the function.

function partial($func, ...$args) {

        # We return our partial function as a closure

    return function() use ($func, $args) {

                # The partial function we return consists of
                # a call to the full function using "call_user_func_array"
                # with a list of arguments made up of our bound
                # argument(s) in $args plus any others supplied at
                # calltime (via func_get_args)

        return call_user_func_array($func, array_merge($args, func_get_args() ) );

    };
}


# The partial function generator above binds the given
# n arguments to the *first* n arguments. In our case
# we want to bind the *last* argument, so we'll create
# another function that returns a function with the
# arguments reversed.

function reverse($func) {

    return function() use ($func) {

                return call_user_func_array($func,
                                array_reverse(func_get_args()));

    };

}
```

Listing 3-24. partial.php

```php
<?php

require_once('print_first.php');

require_once('partial_generator.php');

$foods = ["mango", "apple pie", "cheese", "steak", "yoghurt", "chips"];
```

```php
$print_top_five  = partial(reverse('print_first'), 5);

$print_top_five($foods);

$print_best = partial(reverse('print_first'), 1);

$print_best($foods);
```

Listing 3-25. partial-output.txt

```
Showing 5 of 6 items:
1. mango
2. apple pie
3. cheese
4. steak
5. yoghurt
Showing 1 of 6 items:
1. mango
```

This example uses a named function rather than as a closure, despite what I said about named functions earlier. This is deliberate for the scope of this book; you will be using it again later, and in the simple programs that you are writing, using it as a named function means you don't need it in each and every function you want to call it from. In your programs, you may want to change it to be a closure if that offers you benefit.

As you can see, the partial function generator allows you a reusable way to create multiple partial functions as you need them, and you made two different partials ($print_top_five and $print_best). You can use this function to reduce the arity of any function, by any amount. Consider the function in Listing 3-26, which has an arity of four, which you'll reduce by two. Listing 3-27 shows the output.

Listing 3-26. concatenate.php

```php
<?php

require_once("partial_generator.php");

$concatenate = function ($a, $b, $c, $d) {

    return $a.$b.$c.$d;

};

echo $concatenate("what ", "is ", "your ", "name\n");

$whatis = partial($concatenate, "what ", "is ");

echo $whatis("happening ", "here\n");
```

Listing 3-27. concatenate-output.txt

```
what is your name
what is happening here
```

Partial functions help you to break your functions down into single-purpose, reusable, and maintainable functions. They allow you to share core functionality of broader "monolithic" functions among several different tasks, while still benefiting from the centralization of functionality in the full function. They also allow you (if you so want) to approach parity with pure mathematical functions, which accept only a single argument. In the next chapter, you will look at *currying*, which despite my focus on food isn't a way to functionalize Indian cuisine but instead a method for automatically decomposing multi-arity functions into a chain of single-argument functions.

Functional Expressions

Functional programming tends to use "functional expressions" for program control, rather than the traditional imperative control structures, and you've indirectly looked at some examples of these already. You can use the techniques you've already explored to put together some more useful expressions.

Some of the easiest examples to convert and understand tend to be numeric functions. After all, functional programming is derived from mathematics. In many languages, the functions inc and dec exist for incrementing and decrementing an integer. In PHP you are accustomed to using the ++ and -- operators instead, but there's no reason why you can't write your own functional expressions using functions called inc and dec. You might be tempted to create these functions as shown in Listing 3-28 to achieve this (with the output shown in Listing 3-29).

Listing 3-28. inc_dec.php

```php
<?php

function inc($number) {
    $number++;
    return $number;
}

function dec($number) {
    $number--;
    return $number;
}

var_dump( inc(3) );
var_dump( dec(3) );
```

Listing 3-29. inc_dec-output.txt

```
int(4)
int(2)
```

That's perfectly valid, but let's consider a different approach, using the technique of partial functions that you looked at earlier. See Listing 3-30 and Listing 3-31.

Listing 3-30. inc_dec_partial.php

```php
<?php

require_once('partial_generator.php');

# First define a generic adding function

function add($a,$b) {

    return $a + $b;

}

# Then create our inc and dec as partial functions
# of the add() function.

$inc = partial('add', 1);

$dec = partial('add', -1);

var_dump( $inc(3) );
var_dump( $dec(3) );

# Creating variations is then a simple one-liner

$inc_ten = partial('add', 10);

var_dump( $inc_ten(20) );

# and we still have our add function. We can start
# to build more complex functional expressions

$answer = add( $inc(3), $inc_ten(20) );

var_dump ( $answer );
```

Listing 3-31. inc_dec_partial-output.txt

```
int(4)
int(2)
int(30)
int(34)
```

Note that you can mix and match named and anonymous functions as you please using these techniques. For a little extra effort initially, you get more flexibility and the easier creation of other derived functions. Another example might be the ability to create versions of a function depending on the use case. For instance, you and I might think a dozen is 12, but to a baker it's 13. See Listing 3-32 and Listing 3-33.

Listing 3-32. dsl.php

```php
<?php

require_once('partial_generator.php');

# Define a multiply function

function multiply($a,$b) {    return $a * $b;}

# And then create two ways to count in
# dozens, depending on your industry

$programmers_dozens = partial('multiply', 12);
$bakers_dozens = partial('multiply', 13);

var_dump( $programmers_dozens(2) );
var_dump( $bakers_dozens(2) );
```

Listing 3-33. dsl-output.txt

```
int(24)
int(26)
```

This ability to create functions that *describe* what they're going to do, rather than spell out how to do it, is one of the properties that makes functional programming ideal for creating domain-specific languages (DSLs). DSLs are languages, or adaptions of existing languages, that are tailored for specific application "domains" (e.g., specific industries or types of software).

Functional Composition

You've dealt with one way of creating new functions by reducing the arity of existing ones, but what if you want to make new ones by combining multiple existing functions? You could call one function after the other with intermediate variables to pass the output from one into the next. Alternatively, you could chain them together by directly using one function as the parameter to the next. This is a form of functional composition, and as always, there is a better "functional" way to do it.

Let's say you have a secret formula to work out the optimum temperature for making the world's best mango ice cream. The formula takes the number of mangoes you are using (say 6), doubles it (12), negates it (-12), and adds 2 (-10°C). You need to embed this formula as a function in the PHP software running your ice-cream-making machine. However, you do make other flavors of ice cream, each of which has its own unique formula. So, you need to start from a set of reusable basic math functions and compose them into a formula specifically for mango, while still allowing yourself room to easily implement the formula for strawberry ice cream later. One way would be to compose several functions together into a mango_temp function, as shown in Listing 3-34 and Listing 3-35.

Listing 3-34. sums1.php

```php
<?php

function double($number) { return $number * 2; };

function negate($number) { return -$number; };

function add_two($number) { return $number + 2; };
```

```php
function mango_temp ($num_mangos) {

        return    add_two(

                        negate (

                            double (

                                $num_mangos

                            )

                        )

                    );
};

echo mango_temp(6)."°C\n";
```

Listing 3-35. sums1-output.txt

-10°C

That works, but it's not quite intuitive to read. Because each function is nested inside the previous one, you effectively have to read it backward and from the right to get an understanding of the order of execution. Pure functional languages usually have a syntax or function for composing functions together like this but in a way that is easier to read. PHP doesn't, but fear not, because it's easy to create your own (see Listing 3-36).

Listing 3-36. compose.php

```php
<?php

# This is a special function which simply returns it's input,
# and is called the "identity function" in functional programming.

function identity ($value) { return $value; };

# This function takes a list of "callables" (function names, closures etc.)
# and returns a function composed of all of them, using array_reduce to
# reduce them into a single chain of nested functions.

function compose(...$functions)
{
    return array_reduce(

            # This is the array of functions, that we are reducing to one.
        $functions,

            # This is the function that operates on each item in $functions and
            # returns a function with the chain of functions thus far wrapped in
            # the current one.
```

```
        function ($chain, $function) {

            return function ($input) use ($chain, $function) {

                return $function( $chain($input) );

            };

        },

            # And this is the starting point for the reduction, which is where
            # we use our $identity function as it effectively does nothing

        'identity'
    );
}
```

To see how you can use this, examine the new version of your mango ice cream script, shown in Listing 3-37.

Listing 3-37. sums2.php

```php
<?php

include('compose.php');

function double($number) { return $number * 2; };

function negate($number) { return -$number; };

function add_two($number) { return $number + 2; };

$mango_temp = compose(

    'double',
    'negate',
    'add_two'

);

echo $mango_temp(6)."°C\n\n    ";

print_r ($mango_temp);
```

I hope you agree that this is much easier to read and follow the chain of execution. Because the mango_temp function is a closure, you can use print_r to see the structure that the compose function created (see Listing 3-38).

Listing 3-38. sums2-output.txt

-10°C

```
    Closure Object
(
    [static] => Array
        (
            [chain] => Closure Object
                (
                    [static] => Array
                        (
                            [chain] => Closure Object
                                (
                                    [static] => Array
                                        (
                                            [chain] => identity
                                            [function] => double
                                        )

                                    [parameter] => Array
                                        (
                                            [$input] => <required>
                                        )

                                )

                            [function] => negate
                        )

                    [parameter] => Array
                        (
                            [$input] => <required>
                        )

                )

            [function] => add_two
        )

    [parameter] => Array
        (
            [$input] => <required>
        )

)
```

You can see the identity function right at the start of the chain (the middle of this output), with each successive function following on as the property of each "chain" closure in turn.

In Chapter 1, you looked a sample of functional-type code. I didn't want to introduce composition functions at that stage so as not to muddy the waters early on. However, now that you know about composition, you could rewrite that example as shown in Listing 3-39.

Listing 3-39. example2.php

```php
<?php

require_once('image_functions.php');

require_once('stats_functions.php');

require_once('data_functions.php');

require_once('compose.php');

$csv_data = file_get_contents('my_data.csv');

$make_chart = compose(

'data_to_array',

'generate_stats',

'make_chart_image'

);

file_put_contents('my_chart.png', $make_chart( $csv_data ) );
```

One thing to note from these examples is that your `compose` function works only with functions that take one single parameter. This is deliberate, as a function can return only a single return value. If a function accepted two parameters, how would the `compose` function know where to use the single return value from the previous function call?

You can use the techniques like partial functions that I've already covered to create functions of single arity to use with `compose`. And of course that single parameter can be an array or similar data structure, if you need to move sets of data between functions. Enforcing single parameters also helps to ensure that your functions are kept as simple and as limited in scope as possible. However, it's often pragmatic (or sometimes necessary if you're using other people's functions or code) to be able to compose a function using other functions that take more than one parameter. Functional programming has you covered here too; you simply wrap the function in another function that returns a function! Listing 3-40 and Listing 3-41 show using PHP's native `str_repeat` function (which takes two parameters: a string and the number of times to repeat it) should make that a little clearer.

Listing 3-40. strrepeat.php

```php
<?php

include('compose.php');

# A function to format a string for display

function display($string) {
  echo "The string is : ".$string."\n";
};
```

```
# Our function to wrap str_repeat.
# Note it takes one parameter, the $count

function repeat_str($count) {

  # This function returns another (closure) function,
  # which binds $count, and accepts a single parameter
  # $string. Note that *this* returned closure is the
  # actual function that gets used in compose().

  return function ($string) use ($count) {

    return str_repeat($string, $count);

  };

};

# Now let's compose those two functions together.

$ten_chars = compose(

    repeat_str(10),
    'display'

  );

# and run our composed function

echo $ten_chars('*');
```

Listing 3-41. strrepeat-output.txt

```
The string is : **********
```

The key to understanding what you did in this script is to realize that when you use repeat_str(10) in the compose statement, that *isn't* the function that you are passing in. Putting parentheses after a function name executes it there and then and replaces itself with the return value. So, you are calling repeat_str(10) in the compose statement definition, and the function that repeat_str(10) returns is what is actually being received by compose as the parameter. repeat_str(10) returns a closure that accepts one parameter (which is what you need for your compose function) as $string but sneakily has a second parameter (the 10) bound into it by use ($count).

You don't have to do it this way, of course; you can start creating partial functions for example (e.g., a repeat_ten_times($string) function), but this is a more pragmatic way to compose multi-arity functions in many circumstances.

Conclusion

You're starting to write functional code now. In this chapter, you looked at various ways to structure your functions in a "functional" way and looked at how techniques such as recursion and partial functions let you write more flexible functions. You can use the techniques you've looked at thus far to make other common program control structures, and you'll look at those as you go through the rest of the book. In the next chapter, you'll start looking at some more advanced functional programming topics.

CHAPTER 4

■ ■ ■

Advanced Functional Techniques

By now you have gained some understanding of the functional style of programming and the advantages it can bring. You can take those techniques away to start using today, with no need to read further. Ideally, though, I've whetted your appetite to take it further and learn more functional techniques to add to your programmer's toolbox.

In this chapter, you'll look at some more advanced aspects of functional programming that will let you structure your PHP code in ever more functional ways. This chapter is the last section of "theory" before you start moving onto practical examples in the next part of the book. You'll start by looking at currying, which extends the concept of partial function application into an automatable way of decomposing them into lower-arity versions. Next, you'll look at the fabled monads, which help you with program flow control and allow you to deal with the pesky side effects you will come across when working in the real world. After that, you'll take a look at trampolines, which are a method for keeping recursion under control. Finally, I'll talk a little about strict versus dynamic typing with type declarations, which while not strictly a functional concept can be useful in some ways (and not in others).

Currying Functions

You looked at the advantages of partial functions in the previous chapter, and I alluded to a method for automating this decomposition of functions. *Decomposition* is the act of breaking down multi-arity functions into functions with smaller signatures by fixing the value of one or more of the parameters. The method of automatic decomposition you're going to look at is called *currying* and is named after Haskell Curry, a man whose name is (literally) all over functional programming!

Currying is indeed closely related to partial function application, and a currying function at first glance can look a lot like the partial function generator you created. However, there are some subtle but important differences. That said, partial function application is just a type of currying (or the other way around, depending on who you talk to), so the benefits of each are similar. Which you choose to use depends on what works for you in your situation.

In the partial function generator, you took a function, plus a value to bind to the first parameter, and returned a function whose signature was one parameter shorter. In currying, you make this more flexible by taking a function and a list of one or more parameters and binding all of them given to the new function returned. So far, currying is similar (if more general). To get the actual result of your function, you need to get to a point where you have bound and/or passed in all of the function's parameters, and the function will then execute and return a value.

The partial functions returned by the generator and the currying function (which in both cases are closures) hold the key to the difference between the two. With the simple partial generator you looked at, the function returned was a function with a reduced signature (i.e., a reduced number of parameters required to call it). If you wanted to reduce it even further to create another partial function, you would call the partial function generator again on the returned closure. In contrast, the closure returned by a currying routine is a stand-alone function that can automatically curry itself further. For instance, if you have a function

© Rob Aley 2017

R. Aley, *Pro Functional PHP Programming*, DOI 10.1007/978-1-4842-2958-3_4

with five parameters and you curry it by fixing two parameters, you will get a closure that accepts three parameters. If you then call that closure with one more parameter, then rather than executing without a full set of parameters (as the partial function shown earlier would), it will automatically curry itself and return a further closure that accepts two parameters (and again has the ability to curry itself further if called with another single parameter). Contrast this with the partial functions from your generator; if you supply one parameter to a partial function that accepts three, it will attempt to execute with the reduced parameter set, often leading to an error.

As always, this is likely to be clearer with an example. As writing a properly formed currying function is nontrivial, you'll use a library called php-curry written by Matteo Giachino to help you. This is available on GitHub at https://github.com/matteosister/php-curry and can be installed either via Composer or directly by including it as shown in Listing 4-1 and in Listing 4-2.

Listing 4-1. currying.php

```php
<?php

include('Curry/Placeholder.php');
include('Curry/functions.php');

use Cypress\Curry as C;

# Let's make a function place an order with our chef
# for some delicious curry (the food, not the function)

$make_a_curry = function($meat, $chili, $amount, $extras, $where) {

    return [
                "Meat type"=>$meat,
                "Chili hotness"=>$chili,
            "Quantity to make"=>$amount,
                "Extras"=>$extras,
            "Eat in or take out"=>$where
                ];
};

# We think that everyone will want a mild Rogan Josh, so
# let's curry the function with the first two parameters

$rogan_josh = C\curry($make_a_curry, 'Lamb','mild');

# $rogan_josh is now a closure that will continue to
# curry with the arguments we give it

$dishes = $rogan_josh("2 portions");

# likewise $dishes is now a closure that will continue
# to curry

$meal = $dishes('Naan bread');

# and so on for meal. However, we only have 1 parameter
# which we've not used, $where, and so when we add
# that, rather than returning another closure, $meal
# will execute and return the result of $make_a_curry
```

```
$order  = $meal('Eat in');

print_r( $order );

# To show that our original function remains unmutated, when
# we realize that actually people only want 1 portion of curry
# at a time, with popadoms, and they want to eat it at home, we
# can curry it again. This time, the parameters we want to bind
# are at the end, so we use curry_right.

$meal_type = C\curry_right($make_a_curry, 'Take out', 'Poppadoms', '1 portion');

$madrass = $meal_type('hot', 'Chicken');

print_r( $madrass );

# We could curry the function with all of the parameters
# provided, this creates a parameter-less closure but doesn't
# execute it until we explicitly do so.

$korma = C\curry($make_a_curry,
                    'Chicken', 'Extra mild', 'Bucket full', 'Diet cola', 'Eat in');

print_r($korma());
```

Listing 4-2. currying-output.txt

```
Array
(
    [Meat type] => Lamb
    [Chili hotness] => mild
    [Quantity to make] => 2 portions
    [Extras] => Naan bread
    [Eat in or take out] => Eat in
)
Array
(
    [Meat type] => Chicken
    [Chili hotness] => hot
    [Quantity to make] => 1 portion
    [Extras] => Poppadoms
    [Eat in or take out] => Take out
)
Array
(
    [Meat type] => Chicken
    [Chili hotness] => Extra mild
    [Quantity to make] => Bucket full
    [Extras] => Diet cola
    [Eat in or take out] => Eat in
)
```

Currying offers a cleaner way to manage partial functions, particularly if you frequently need many different versions of a given function or set of partial functions. The trade-off is a bigger overhead in your closures because of the extra currying code, but that is usually a marginal consideration. You also lose the ability (at least with currying as implemented here) to allow optional parameters; the function won't execute until all parameters have been given a value.

As well as currying, there exists the reverse process, usually called *decurrying* or *uncurrying*, which takes a set of *n* single-parameter functions and composes them up into a single *n*-arity function. This usually has limited application, so I won't cover it in this book.

The Mysterious Monad

Monads are a versatile form of program control, a solution to the problem of real-world side effects (like reading from files and printing to the screen), and arguably one of the hardest concepts to understand in functional programming (or life in general). If you look up introductory articles or videos on monads, they'll invariably start by telling you that experts say you need to understand the mathematical topics of category theorem, endofunctors, and possibly other related esoteric concepts. They'll then say that, actually, you don't need to understand these, as they have found a simple-to-understand way of explaining monads. They'll then launch into a discussion of functors (the math functor, not the programming one), applicative functors, monoids, and such, finally ending up defining monads in terms of those concepts and losing 90 percent of their readers along the way. They'll then claim that they gave a brief nontechnical overview and here's a link to the full mathematical explanation to help clear it all up, at which point everyone gives up on monads, functional programming, and sometimes their whole way of life to date. So I'm not going to do that.

Renowned JavaScript educator Douglas Crockford, in his Google Tech Talk "Monads and Gonads," famously said this:

"The monadic curse is that once someone learns what monads are and how to use them, they lose the ability to explain [them] to other people."

A less flippant way of saying this is, perhaps, that your understanding of what a monad is and can do typically develops over time. By the time you've got a full grasp of their power and the concept has fully "clicked," it's hard to remember all of the smaller "eureka" moments that led to that understanding of how they work.

So, I'll start at the other end of the problem. Rather than trying to derive monads from first principles, I'll tell you what they are, what you use monads for, and show you some examples. Once you get used to using them, you'll ideally have your own "oh yeah, I get it now" moment, even if you don't understand the math behind it. I'll of course provide the obligatory links to the math-heavy explanations at the end as well.

What Is a Monad?

A *monad* is a type of function that encapsulates values and applies functions to those values within the context of the monad. You can think of them as a container for working on state, with different types of monads undertaking different kinds of work on the state. What can you use monads for?

- Controlling program flow (as a form of function composition)

- Encapsulating side effects (taking them out from your pure functions and making them merely an effect of the program itself)

- Reducing code complexity (well, once you've got your head around monads themselves)

While monads are "just" functions and you *could* implement them with PHP functions, it is usually more convenient to create them using objects because this gives you more flexibility (and allows you to cheat at times with extra helper methods). This is the approach that most PHP libraries that implement monads take. Remember that a method is essentially just a function called within the context of the object (and, indeed, a closure is essentially an object with a single method that operates over a set of data encapsulated in its context).

So, what does a monad in the wild look like? It will have two key methods.

- A constructor method that takes a value and creates a monad object that "wraps" that value

- A "bind" method that

  - Takes a function (or other callable) as input

  - Calls it on the value wrapped by the constructor mentioned earlier

  - Returns a *new* monad created by calling the constructor method on the result of the called function

As you can see, the bind method is key here. It takes a function, applies it to the value (i.e., the state) stored in the monad, and returns a new monad object with the result (the "new" state) as the value of that new monad. It also has three key mathematical properties, which distinguish it from other structures that happen to protect a value and bind a function. You'll look at those in detail later and see how you can use them to test whether something is actually a monad.

It's time to look at an example. Rather than writing your own monad class, you'll use a library written Anthony Ferrara called MonadPHP (available on GitHub at https://github.com/ircmaxell/monad-php). This is a simplistic "toy" implementation of monads, which is great for learning from. I strongly suggest taking a look at the source code as it is well written and easy to follow. You can install it with Composer or simply require the files, as I'll show. You'll first look at the Identity monad in Listing 4-3 (with the output shown in Listing 4-4), whose only job is to call the passed function on the wrapped value. It isn't very useful but demonstrates the structure and properties of a basic monad.

Listing 4-3. monad.php

```php
<?php

require('MonadPHP/Monad.php');
require('MonadPHP/Identity.php');

# Use the namespace

use MonadPHP\Identity;

# Define a couple of pure functions

$double = function ($n) { return $n*2; };

$add_ten = function ($n) { return $n+10; };

# Create a monad by calling the static unit method,
# with a value (33). The unit method is a constructor
# which checks if what we are passing in is already
# an instance of this monad, or create a new one if
# not by calling the _construct method to bind
# our value (33) and return a monad object
```

```
$monad_a = Identity::unit(33);

# Let's check it is an object of class MonadPHP\Identity
# encapsulating the value 33

var_dump( $monad_a );

# Now we bind one of our functions to the monad

$monad_b = $monad_a->bind($double);

# $monad_b should be a new monad object.
# Let's check that it is and that we haven't
# just mutated monad1

var_dump( $monad_a ); # should be the same as above

var_dump( $monad_b ); # should be a new monad encapsulating 66

# This library includes a helper method "extract" to
# get the encapsulated value back out of the monad

var_dump( $monad_b->extract() ); #66

# Let's bind that function again to the new monad...

$monad_c = $monad_b->bind($double);

var_dump( $monad_c->extract() ); #132

# ... and check that monad_b is unchanged

var_dump( $monad_b->extract() ); #66

# finally, bind the function again to monad_b,
# to demonstrate again that its encapsulated value
# isn't mutated.

$monad_d = $monad_b->bind($double);

var_dump( $monad_d->extract() ); #132

# Let's now repeatedly bind methods
# in a chain

$monad_e = $monad_d->bind($double)   # *2
                        ->bind($add_ten)  # +10
                        ->bind($add_ten); # +10

var_dump( $monad_e->extract() ); # 284
```

```
# and take a look at the returned monad_e,
# take note of the object identifier (#7)

var_dump( $monad_e );
```

Listing 4-4. monad-output.txt

```
object(MonadPHP\Identity)#3 (1) {
  ["value":protected]=>
  int(33)
}
object(MonadPHP\Identity)#3 (1) {
  ["value":protected]=>
  int(33)
}
object(MonadPHP\Identity)#4 (1) {
  ["value":protected]=>
  int(66)
}
int(66)
int(132)
int(66)
int(132)
int(284)
object(MonadPHP\Identity)#7 (1) {
  ["value":protected]=>
  int(284)
}
```

In the last part of that example, you chained together a set of bind calls, which looks suspiciously like the kind of functional composition you looked at in the previous chapter. And while you can indeed use the identity function in this manner for composing functions, monads do more than just passing the output from the previous function into the input of the next. Take a look at the hash numbers (#3, #4, etc.) in the var_dump output in Listing 4-4. These are PHP's internal identifiers (in numeric form) for objects created in the current context. (It starts at #3 because #1 and #2 are your pure functions $double and $add_ten, which are objects of the closure type.) Specifically, #3 corresponds to $monad_a, and #4 is $monad_b. You don't use var_dump on them, but $monad_c would be #5, and $monad_d would be #6. #7 is monad_e. Why is this important? It demonstrates that each time you call bind on a monad, you get another object completely. You are changing the context (state) around your bound value each time, not just passing it along as you do with simple composition. This allows you to create some fancy monads that do interesting (and useful) things, which you'll look at in a moment.

But what about that "chain" of bind calls you do on $monad_d to create $monad_e? You've applied three functions, but you got only one new monad out at the end. You are, in fact, creating three new monads and using PHP's object dereferencing to bind the next function to the monad from the previous one. The monads are created and then destroyed "behind the scenes" in the blink of an eye, which is why you don't explicitly see them. If you're not convinced, you can add an impure echo('creating') call to the Identity constructor method and you'll see it output creating for each bind call.

So, those are the basics of a monad. Let's do something useful now. While you can invent monads to do just about anything you can think of, there are some common monads that you'll come across that solve common functional programming problems and implement typical functional patterns. In pure functional languages like Haskell, monads were popularized because they are pretty much the only way to get real work done. You're going to look at a couple of the most common monads to demonstrate the possibilities and power of this kind of structure.

The Maybe Monad

In the previous example, the Identity monad just called the bound function with the value encapsulated in the monad. The Maybe monad takes this one step further and adds a test on the value before calling the bound function with it.

"I call it my billion-dollar mistake." No, that's not me talking about writing this book. Those are the words of Sir Charles Antony Richard Hoare, inventor of the NULL reference. Null, while being a great tool for conveying information such as failure or lack of a value, has its problems. Functions often return null to indicate that there was no actual value to return, usually because of an error or such in the function or a problem with the parameters passed into the function. This allows the caller to be able to tell whether this is the case, for instance, if the return value is legitimately a 0, false, empty array, or similar that may otherwise be used as an error code if null didn't exist. The caller can then test for null and deal with it as appropriate.

To see why this can be problematic, consider the chains of functions that you have been looking at in the examples of functional composition. What happens if one of the functions returns null as its return value? The null value gets fed into the next function in the chain as input, which means you now need to alter all of your functions to test for and handle null values, or you'll start having problems. Step forward the Maybe monad, which allows you to deal with functions that "maybe" will fail or "maybe" work correctly, without having to write extra code in every function to check. The Maybe monad achieves this by checking for a null return value after each call of a function and not calling the next function if it finds a null. Let's take a look at an example (see Listing 4-5 and Listing 4-6), and then I'll discuss how and why it works. You'll use the MonadPHP library again.

Listing 4-5. maybe_monad.php

```php
<?php

require('MonadPHP/Monad.php');
require('MonadPHP/Maybe.php');

use MonadPHP\Maybe;

# We'll use the shopping list array from the previous chapter.
# It's a nested array, and not all elements have the
# same level of nesting.

$shopping_list = [
    "fruits" => [ "apples" => [ "red" => 3, "green" => 4], "pears" => 4, "bananas" => 6 ],
    "bakery" => [ "bread" => 1, "apple pie" => 2],
    "meat" => [ "sausages" =>
                        ["pork" => ["chipolata" => 5, "cumberland" => 2], "beef" => 3],
                        "steaks" => 3, "chorizo" => 1 ]];

# Let's create some functions.

# This function takes a category (e.g. fruits) and returns either
# a) a closure that returns that category from the supplied list
# or
# b) null if the category doesn't exist.

$get_foods = function ($category) {

    return function ($list) use ($category) {
```

```
        echo("get_foods return closure called\n");

        return isset($list[$category]) ? $list[$category] : null;

    };

};

# This function does the same, except it returns a closure that returns
# the  foods (e.g. apples, pears...) from the category (fruit), or null

$get_types = function ($food) {

    return function ($category) use ($food) {

        echo("get_types return closure called\n");

        return isset($category[$food]) ? $category[$food] : null;

    };

};

# and lastly another function of the same type to get the types of food
# (e.g. red, green) from the food, or null

$get_count = function ($type) {

    return function ($types) use ($type) {

        echo("get_count return closure called\n");

        return isset($types[$type]) ? $types[$type] : null;

    };

};

# Now let's create a Maybe monad, encapsulating our
# shopping list as its value.

$monad = Maybe::unit($shopping_list);

# We'll repeatedly bind our functions against it as
# we did in the previous example.

var_dump( $monad  ->bind($get_foods('fruits'))
                            ->bind($get_types('apples'))
                            ->bind($get_count('red'))
                            ->extract() # returns 3
            );
```

```
# None of our closures test for null parameters, so what
# happens if we try to look for something that doesn't exist?

var_dump( $monad  ->bind($get_foods('fruits'))
                            ->bind($get_types('apples'))
                            ->bind($get_count('purple')) # doesn't exist
                            ->extract() # returns null
            );

var_dump( $monad  ->bind($get_foods('cheeses')) # doesn't exist
                            ->bind($get_types('cheddar')) # doesn't exist
                            ->bind($get_count('mature')) # doesn't exist
                            ->extract() # returns null
            );

var_dump( $monad  ->bind($get_foods('bakery'))
                            ->bind($get_types('pastries')) # doesn't exist
                            ->bind($get_count('danish')) # doesn't exist
                            ->extract() # returns null
            );
```

Listing 4-6. maybe_monad-output.txt

```
get_foods return closure called
get_types return closure called
get_count return closure called
int(3)
get_foods return closure called
get_types return closure called
get_count return closure called
NULL
get_foods return closure called
NULL
get_foods return closure called
get_types return closure called
NULL
```

(Note that if you run this on PHP 7, you'll get a warning thrown because the library hasn't been updated since PHP 5; you can either alter the bind declaration in the library or safely ignore the warning.)

I've peppered some impure echo statements in there so that you can see when the closures get called. As you can see, where you try to get items from your array that don't exist (and hence your closures return null), the subsequent function calls in the chain *don't* get executed, even though you bind them to the monad. So, how and why does this work? The Identity monad, in this situation, would function as follows:

1. First you create a monad with the shopping list as its value.

2. Then you bind your first function to it, which it calls with the shopping list value.

3.   This returns a value (either the requested part of the array or null), which is put into a new monad object and returned.

4.   Then you bind your next function to the new monad as earlier, and so on, until all the functions have been bound.

The key difference to the Identity monad is that at the stage where you bind the function, a conditional statement checks the value of the monad, and if it is null, instead of calling the function, it just returns null into the new monad. Thus, as soon as one function in the chain returns a null execution, all of the subsequent functions are skipped because the value encapsulated in every monad is null (and won't change because none of the functions can ever be called on it because it's null...!). The monad is still created each time in your chain, but the encapsulated value (null) just propagates along the chain.

So, you as the programmer will still need to write a null check but only once at the end of the chain and not for each individual function. This allows you to write simpler functions that can assume that they will get valid (or, at least, not null) values as input to operate on. If your functions have other common requirements for their input values (e.g., they always require an integer as input), you can easily construct similar conditional monads that check their encapsulated value in any way you want.

This ability to execute code on each function call is one of the advantages monads have over the simple functional composition technique you looked at in the previous chapter. It has been likened to "programmable semicolons" in that PHP (like many programming languages) executes statements one after the other with a semicolon in between. Imagine if you could make that semicolon do something; that should give you an idea of the power of monads in this type of situation.

Monad Axioms

As I alluded to in the monad introduction, there are three axioms (or laws) that monads must obey to be classed as a monad. It can be useful to understand these to be able to tell whether something you are using is indeed a monad. To be clear, some monad-like structures that have only one or two of these mathematical properties can still be very useful, but you will need to take extra care to ensure that they are behaving in the *functional* ways that you intend to ensure your code carries the properties you expect of fully functional code.

Again, I'm not going to try to derive or explain the *hows* and *whys* of these axioms, but I will present the *what* in a useful way. I'll present them as pseudocode using PHP, rather than in their math notation.

Monad Axiom 1

```
bind( unit($i), $func ) == $func( $i )
```

This says if you bind a function $func to a monad created with the value $i, it is equivalent to calling $func on $i directly. unit is the commonly used name for monad constructor functions.

Monad Axiom 2

```
bind($monad, unit) == $monad
```

This says that if you bind the constructor unit function to a monad, the result is equivalent to that monad.

Monad Axiom 3

```
bind ( bind($monad, $f1), $f2) == bind ($monad, function($i) {return bind($f1($i), $f2($i)})
```

Now this one is the hard one!

The left side says, "Bind a function $f1 to a monad, and bind another function $f2 to the resulting monad."

The right side says that this is equivalent to taking a monad $monad and binding a function that returns a monad that is the result of the binding function $f2($i) applied to $function $f1($i), where $f1 is a function that returns a monad.

Don't worry if you didn't follow that or understand any of the axioms (particularly the last one). In practice, if you need to use them at all, it will invariably be as a test, and you can apply them as is. If you really want to understand them better, see the "Further Reading" section later in this chapter.

Testing the Monad Axioms

So, let's see whether the Identity monad is really a monad after all (see Listing 4-7 and Listing 4-8). An easy litmus test is to create a test value and function, create a monad, and then take the previous axioms and write them in proper PHP, testing whether each evaluates to true.

Listing 4-7. monad_test.php

```php
<?php

require('MonadPHP/Monad.php');
require('MonadPHP/Identity.php');

use MonadPHP\Identity;

# 1. bind( unit($i), $func ) == $func( $i )

// define some test variables and functions

$i = 10;
$func = function ($i) {    return $i*2; };

// create a new monad to test

$monad = Identity::unit($i);

// see if the 1st Axiom holds (should output true)

var_dump ( $monad->bind($func)->extract() == $func($i) );

# 2. bind($monad, unit) == $monad

// and see if the 2nd Axiom also holds

var_dump ( $monad->bind(Identity::unit) == $monad );
```

```
# 3. bind ( bind($monad, $f1), $f2) ==
#          bind ($monad, function($i) { return bind( $f1($i), $f2($i) } )

// create some more test functions

$f1 = function ($i)  { return Identity::unit($i); }; // returns a monad
$f2 = function ($i) { return $i*6; };

// and see if Axiom 3 holds

var_dump (

    $monad->bind($f1)->bind($f2) ==
        $monad->bind(function ($i) use ($f1, $f2)
                    { return $f1($i)->bind($f2); }
                )

);
```

Listing 4-8. monad_test-output.txt

```
bool(true)
bool(true)
bool(true)
```

Well, that all looks good. How about the slightly more functional Maybe monad? You'll approach this in exactly the same way (see Listing 4-9 and Listing 4-10).

Listing 4-9. maybe_test.php

```php
<?php

require('MonadPHP/Monad.php');
require('MonadPHP/Maybe.php');

use MonadPHP\Maybe;

# 1. bind( unit($i), $func ) == $func( $i )

// define some test variables and functions

$i = 10;
$func = function ($i) {    return $i*2; };

// create a new monad to test

$monad = Maybe::unit($i);

// see if the 1st Axiom holds (should output true)

var_dump ( $monad->bind($func)->extract() == $func($i) );

# 2. bind($monad, unit) == $monad
```

```
// and see if the 2nd Axiom also holds

var_dump ( $monad->bind(Maybe::unit) == $monad );

# 3. bind ( bind($monad, $f1), $f2) ==
#           bind ($monad, function($i) { return bind( $f1($i), $f2($i) } )

// create some more test functions

$f1 = function ($i)  { return Maybe::unit($i); }; // returns a monad
$f2 = function ($i) { return $i*6; };

// and see if Axiom 3 holds

var_dump (

    $monad->bind($f1)->bind($f2) ==
        $monad->bind(function ($i) use ($f1, $f2)
                        { return $f1($i)->bind($f2); }
                    )

);
```

Listing 4-10. maybe_test-output.txt

```
bool(true)
bool(true)
bool(true)
```

That passes all three axiom trials as well. Of course, this isn't a comprehensive test; the axioms must hold for any and all (well-constructed) inputs/functions passed to the monad, but it should give you some clues as to how to proceed if you want to more thoroughly test the behavior of a monad you have created.

Other Useful Monads

You've looked at what a monad is and how it can be a versatile way to compose functions together. In the introduction to this chapter, I said that I would explain how to use monads to solve some of the issues with functional programming, such as dealing with operations that would otherwise be classified as side effects. That is what I will do in this section.

First you will look at a common monad call the Writer monad. A common task when writing software is to log information to disk as your program progresses. This can be anything from debug information or audit logs to tracking information and transaction records. Typically, messages bound for the log are written to disk as and when they are recorded, either directly or by calling a logging function. In a functional program, you could create a logging function, but if it wrote anything to disk, it wouldn't be a pure function. And if it didn't, it wouldn't be of much use as a logging function!

One of the techniques (or, as it might be better called, *compromises*) used to deal with side effects is to push all "impure" actions to the end of the program run. In this way, the bulk of the program is "properly" functional and able to be fully tested and is easy to reason about, and at least if there's a problem with the messy impure bit, it's all in one place, and you know where it happened.

So, how could you push all of your log writing to the end of the program? One way would be to create a global variable to gather the information to be logged, finally writing it to disk all in one go at the end. However, as I've already discussed, global state is generally considered a bad idea in functional programming, as you're introducing state outside the flow of your functions that you can't (easily) reason about or be confident about at any one time. Another alternative is to pass the logging information along your function chain as you go; each function can take the "log" in its input from the previous function, add its own log records, and pass the log out as part of its return value to the next function in the chain, writing to disk only once you have your final values out of your chain of functions. This would be a perfectly good functional way to do it, except that it would mean you would need to alter the signature of each and every function to accept passing this additional data, possibly using arrays or similar to keep the log information and actual function output separate and organized. As you may have guessed, the answer to the problem is the Writer monad.

The Writer monad provides a way to write and compose your functions together as you would expect, without having to alter the parameters they accept. In the background, the Writer monad builds up a separate data structure with the "written" information (e.g., in this case, strings to be logged), and at the end of the chain of monad functions, two values (the normal return value and the log data) are returned. To demonstrate this in practice, you will use a different monad library this time called php-fp-writer, written by Tom Harding, which you can download from https://github.com/php-fp/php-fp-writer. You can install it with Composer or simply include the files as I show here.

Before you implement the Writer example, though, you need to create a structure called a *monoid*. As you run your chain of functions, you need a structure in the monad to "gather" and hold the log messages (or whatever data the Writer monad is going to handle for you), with the monad itself dealing with the actual function return value as in the previous examples.

What is a monoid? Well, its two key properties are that it has a single "associative binary operation" and that it has an "identity element." In some ways, a monoid feels a bit like a monad; it wraps a value (which remains static), applies a function, and returns a new monoid as output rather than mutating itself. Saunders Mac Lane, a mathematician, says the following in *Categories for the Working Mathematician*:

"All told, a monad in X is just a monoid in the category of endofunctors of X, with product X replaced by composition of endofunctors and unit set by the identity endofunctor."

Interpreting that quote for the layperson who doesn't know what an endofunctor is, a monad is, in fact, just a special case of the more general monoid. Like monads, you're going to create monoids as objects. As they are much simpler, you'll write your own monoid class (see Listing 4-11). The "associative binary operation" your object is going to carry out is concatenation, and in this case you're going to concatenate strings (of log entries) together into an array. An identity element is an element (or value) that leaves other values the same when the operation is carried out on them. For concatenation (into an array), the identity element is an empty array. In this case, you're not going to use the identity element, so you'll leave it out for clarity, but you could add an empty() method that returns a monoid with an empty array as its encapsulated value if you wanted.

Listing 4-11. monoid.php

```php
<?php

class Monoid {

    public function __construct($value) {

        $this->value = $value;

    }
}
```

```php
        public function concat($to) {

        return new Monoid(array_merge($to->value, $this->value));

    }

};
```

You're going to use the monoid as a structure to add and hold your log data. You're then going to write your "useful" pure functions so the following happens:

- The return value is a Writer monad.

- The monad is created by calling the `Writer::tell` static method that does the following:

    - Creates a Writer monad object with the monoid attached

    - Binds your actual "useful" function, ready to be called on the main function value

This allows you to chain functions together using the monad's chain method.

To make this clearer, look at Listing 4-12 (and Listing 4-13). You're going to use the ice cream temperature example from the previous chapter, which will give you the temperature as an integer as the return value of your chain of functions. You'll also receive a second return value that is a set of statements ready to be logged to disk or screen. As you'll notice, this library has a slightly different method of creating and chaining monads than the first library you looked at, which demonstrates that there's more than one way to skin the monad cat, but it should look familiar enough to understand what is happening. If you want, you can always test the monads created in this way with the axioms you looked at earlier to make sure you are happy that that is what you are using.

Listing 4-12. writer_monad.php

```php
<?php

include('src/Writer.php');
include('monoid.php');

use PhpFp\Writer\Writer;

function double($number) {

    $log = new Monoid(["Doubling $number"]);

    return Writer::tell($log)->map(

            function () use ($number)
            {
                    return $number * 2;
            }
    );
};
```

```php
function negate($number) {

    $log = new Monoid(["Negating $number"]);

    return Writer::tell($log)->map(

            function () use ($number)
            {
                    return -$number;
            }
    );
};

function add_two($number) {

    $log = new Monoid(["Adding 2 to $number"]);

    return Writer::tell($log)->map(

            function () use ($number)
            {
                    return $number + 2;
            }
    );

};

list ($mango_temp, $log) = double(6)->chain('negate')->chain('add_two')->run();

echo $mango_temp."°C\nLog :\n";

print_r($log->value);
```

Listing 4-13. writer_monad-output.txt

```
-10°C
Log :
Array
(
    [0] => Doubling 6
    [1] => Negating 12
    [2] => Adding 2 to -12
)
```

Looking at the previous output, you can see that you get the correct -10°C. You also get a second array out, containing three "log" strings as a result of the three functions you called, which you can now use in your "impure" code (e.g., by writing to disk, etc.). These two outputs are wrapped into an array, so you use the list language construct to separate the array into two variables ($mango_temp and $log).

Another interesting point to note about the previous code is the use of the run() method at the end of the chain of functions. If you omit that and run the script, you'll find that none of the functions in your chain is actually called. This type of monad builds up the function chain and then "runs" it only once it is built. This can be useful for testing purposes and is typical of monads that help you deal with potential side effects, as you'll see in the next type of monad you look at, the IO monad.

The IO Monad

In the previous example, the Writer monad, you push all of your impure actions to the end of the script by gathering the information you want to act on up into an array, carrying it along until all of the pure functions have completed, and then returning it alongside your main return value for your script to deal with the nasty side effect of writing to disk or similar. This is a great way to deal with side effects, but in many cases it's not practical to wait until the end of your code to start talking to outside systems. For instance, you may need to gather input from external sources (APIs, files, databases) that vary depending on calculations made partway through one of your pure functions and on which further functions will rely for their calculations. You need another tool to utilize impure actions as you go, and that tool is the IO monad. You'll use the php-fp-io library by Tom Harding, available on GitHub at https://github.com/php-fp/php-fp-io, which is a sister library to the earlier php-fp-writer and so follows the same structure and style.

Take a look through the code that follows. The pattern should be familiar from the Writer monad example, but as you'll see, you have calls to three functions/language constructs that are considered to be impure (they have side effects) that you need to call as you go along.

- random_bytes: This introduces values from an external source of state (usually /dev/urandom on Linux) and when used in creating the function's return value obviously means that from a given set input parameters you won't be able to determine the return value.

- file_put_contents: This (like most file system functions in general) function cannot be guaranteed not to have side effects, even though you're not reading unknown values from it. For instance, errors and exceptions can be generated if the files or file systems are not in the state that you may expect, and so you can't reliably reason that your function perform the action intended.

- echo: As it's only outputting to the screen (or web server), perhaps you think that nothing could go wrong with echo to cause problems/side effects for your function? Consider that if your script has somewhere called fclose(STDOUT), or the STDOUT stream has been closed from outside your program without your knowledge; then calling echo would cause your program to terminate without warning.

And of course there are many other functions with different types of side effects related to I/O that you could use instead to demonstrate the principles here.

So, let's look at your script. You get 100 random bytes and convert them to a hex string (to make it easier to print in a book!), write them to a file called random.txt, and finally output a message to the screen to confirm that you've finished your task. But you're actually going to break this down into two scripts. The first, io_monad.php, sets up all the functions needed to complete your task and creates a chain of them. It then "returns" the chain on the last line. If you haven't seen return used like this (i.e., outside of a function), fear not. You are writing it this way so that in the second script you can "include" the first script as the body of a function. Note the parentheses around the include call in run_io.php; these forms an immediately invoked functional expression (IIFE), which does what it says on the tin: it invokes the code within the parentheses immediately as if it were a function being called. This is part of the PHP RFC on uniform variable syntax that was introduced as part of PHP 7. Because the code in the first file is being called as a function, the return statement should make more sense now! See Listing 4-14, Listing 4-15, Listing 4-16, and Listing 4-17.

Listing 4-14. io_monad.php

```php
<?php

include('src/IO.php');

use PhpFp\IO\IO;
```

```php
# Some functions that define how to create
# some other, impure functions

# Make a random string of hex characters from $length random bytes

$string_maker = function($length) {

    return new IO( function () use ($length) {

                            return bin2hex(random_bytes($length));

                        }

                    );
};

# Write a string to $filename on disk

$file_writer = function($filename) {

    return function ($string) use ($filename)  {

        return new IO( function () use ($filename,$string) {

                            file_put_contents($filename,$string);

                        }
                    );
        };
};

# Send ($string) to STDOUT

$printer = function($string) {

    return function () use ($string)  {

        return new IO( function () use ($string) {

                            echo($string."\n");

                        }

                    );
        };
};

# Chain those functions together, and return the resulting
# monad

return  $string_maker(100)
                                ->chain($file_writer('random.txt'))
                                ->chain($printer('All done'));
```

Listing 4-15. run_io.php

```php
<?php

# Start an IIFE

(

    # Execute the io_monad.php file to get the monad

    require('io_monad.php')

    # At this stage, we have a monad full of functions
    # that have not been called (and so haven't done)
    # any "impure" work

# Finally call the unsafePerform() method on the monad to
# call the "impure" functions

)->unsafePerform();
```

Listing 4-16. run_io-output.txt

```
All done
```

Listing 4-17. random.txt

```
935998b29780e9f8f56435120208f7196854f677a666abcc510fee8a7162d12f6d923e470b4373f232dfbb0bf1
a9da28e9b8a3f84af15273fc516ccf74c493ebce3931922a59d83ba80d77cfc41e8c76ffd90d79d91e32bcf2
fbdf15a85ec38b1c5186cc
```

So, what happens here is that in io_monad.php you set up your chain of functions using the IO monad in a similar manner to the Writer monad. In the second file, run_io.php, you actually call that chain of functions using the aptly named unsafePerform() method. Why structure it this way? All of the functions in the first file remain "pure" up until you actually run them. The functions in the first file merely construct the impure functions (often termed as *deferring* the functions); they don't actually run them or do any I/O, so they remain as pure as the driven snow. This means that io_monad.php, on its own, is a pure functional program and can be fully tested, reasoned about, and so on. If this seems a little like cheating, it's because it is. The testing may be of limited value as it may not test the "meat" of your program where much of the functionality depends on impure actions. Of course, you're not restricted to using impure functions in this manner; you can ably mix them with pure calls and other monads, so where more of your program is pure rather than impure, the testability of structuring it like this increases.

Learn More About Monads

If the previous sections have got you excited about monads, then the following "Further Reading" section will help you get up to speed on the mathematical details and theory behind them. Warning: it can make heavy reading at times, so make yourself a coffee first. If you're not so taken with monads, then you'll be interested in Chapter 7 that looks at structuring applications (spoiler: I'll be suggesting it's perfectly OK to ignore monads and their ilk).

Further Reading

- Wikipedia entry for monads, which gives a general background

    - https://en.wikipedia.org/wiki/Monad_(functional_programming)

- Wikipedia entry for monoids, again giving a general background

    - https://en.wikipedia.org/wiki/Monoid

- *Monads and Gonads* video of a Google Tech Talk by Douglas Crockford, where he explains monads in JavaScript, in a reasonably understandable way

    - https://www.youtube.com/watch?v=b0EF0VTs9Dc

- *Don't Fear the Monad*, MSDN video of Brian Beckman explaining monads, this time with more math

    - https://www.youtube.com/watch?v=ZhuHCtR3xq8

- The Haskell Manuals section on monads (Haskell was responsible for popularizing monads in programming, and this is a fairly succinct treatment of them.)

    - https://wiki.haskell.org/Monad

- A (Haskell-oriented) explanation of the three Monad axioms

    - https://wiki.haskell.org/Monad_laws

- A physical analogy for monads, from the Haskell wiki via The Wayback Machine

    - https://web.archive.org/web/20100910074354/http://www.haskell.org/all_about_monads/html/analogy.html

- A fairly comprehensive timeline of monad tutorials and related articles; although it's on the Haskell wiki, it isn't Haskell specific

    - https://wiki.haskell.org/Monad_tutorials_timeline

Recursion with Trampolines

If you thought trampolines were only fun for kids, you're clearly not a functional programmer! In the previous chapter, you looked at recursion and saw how it is a useful form of program control that can be used in many cases to replace traditional imperative loops. I also mentioned one of the key downsides, that of (potentially) unlimited resource usage resulting in stack overflows and the like.

In recursion, you create a function that, in turn, calls itself. The way PHP (and most programming languages operate) is that for each function that is still active, information about that function is held in the call stack. Each time your function calls itself, a new function becomes active; therefore, another frame of information is added to the stack, using more memory to hold the current state of the program. The original function is still active, waiting for the result of the copy of itself it just called, so it can't be removed from the stack until the copy completes, and so on. The stack is unwound only when the innermost call of the recursive function is complete, and all previous functions can then also complete. If you run out of allocated memory before this happens, you get a stack overflow error (or a crashed machine, depending on any enforced limits to the stack size). Compare this to a simple while or for loop, where the only state held is the current state of any variables involved. Each loop may alter them but (usually) doesn't add to the *amount* of state information held.

So, one way to avoid the problem of recursion is to not use it and rewrite any recursive functions that may potentially blow the stack as imperative loops. However, that's not very *functional* and means that you miss out on the benefits of writing recursive code. You can, of course, put some hard-limit checks into your code to ensure that your recursion will be called only on values for which you can guarantee it will complete within the available stack/memory limits, but those can be hard to determine beforehand and means that some computations cannot be completed at all.

A number of languages provide a solution with what is called *tail call optimizations* (TCO). This is a trick employed by the compiler that lets it flatten out certain recursive functions into imperative-like loop structures. This can happen when the recursive call (the actual call to itself) is the last call in the function (the *tail* call), calling only itself. At this point, the compiler can reuse the frame containing the state of the function instead of creating an additional frame, as it knows there are no other operations to conduct for the calling function. This dramatically reduces the information stored, in effect flattening out the recursion into a kind of loop.

The PHP virtual machine, unfortunately for you, doesn't use TCO. If it did, you could just ensure that your recursive functions are written with the recursive call at the tail end of the function. Instead, you can use a trampoline function to do essentially the same task. In computing, a *trampoline* is a function that automatically creates another function to assist in calling to yet another function, "bouncing" your function around in this case to avoid recursion!

Before you look at the trampoline function, it is necessary to fully understand what a tail call is. A tail call has the following traits:

- Is recursive (i.e., it must be the function calling itself)

- Must be a return statement (i.e., `return this_function()`)

- Must only return itself

- Must be the last executed function, which it will be if it is a "return" value

- Must have no other operation occur in the call (i.e., not return `$something+this_function()`)

If your function does not satisfy these criteria, then it can't be TCO'd and your trampoline won't work. There are ways to rewrite most recursive functions to be tail call recursive (TCR), which you can google for if you need them.

For this example, you'll use the classic example that most TCO articles use, the factorial function. If you're not familiar, the factorial of a number x (often written as x!) is x * (x-1) * (x-2) * ... * (1). In other words, $5! = 5 \times 4 \times 3 \times 2 \times 1 = 120$. This can be implemented in a standard recursive function and invariably has a recursive tail call. You'll use a trampoline implementation from the Functional PHP library written by Gilles Crettenand and available on GitHub at `https://github.com/functional-php/trampoline`; you can install it via Composer or directly include it. See Listing 4-18 and Listing 4-19.

Listing 4-18. bounce.php

```php
<?php

# Include and use the trampoline library

include('trampoline/src/Trampoline.php');
include('trampoline/src/functions.php');

use FunctionalPHP\Trampoline as T;

# First define our standard recursive function

$factorial = function ($i, $total = 1) use (&$factorial) {
```

```
        # if $i is 1, return the total, otherwise
        # recursively call the function on $i-1,
        # multiplying the accumulating total by $i

    return $i == 1 ? $total : $factorial($i - 1, $i * $total);

        # note that $factorial is the tail call here
        # when it is returned

};

# Now the same function again, but this time using the
# trampoline function. The only difference (other than
# the name!) is that we wrap the tail call in T\bounce()

$bounced_factorial = function ($i, $total = 1) use (&$bounced_factorial) {

    return $i == 1 ? $total : T\bounce($bounced_factorial, $i - 1, $i * $total);

};

# We use T\trampoline() to call the "bounced" function.
# We'll wrap it in a helper function called $trampolined
# for ease of use

$trampolined = function ($i) use ($bounced_factorial) {

    return T\trampoline($bounced_factorial, $i);

};

# We'll create a function to time how long our
# function runs take, in seconds

$timer = function($func, $params) {

    $start_time = microtime(true);

    call_user_func_array($func,$params);

    return round(microtime(true) - $start_time,5);

};

# So let's run our normal recursive function
# and the trampolined version, both to
# calculate the factorial of one hundred thousand.
# The result will be the same, we're only
# interested in the time they take here.

var_dump ( $timer($factorial, [100000]) );
```

```
var_dump ( $timer($trampolined, [100000]) );

# Now let's limit the memory we're working with
# and run them again, this time to calculate
# the factorial of one million. We'll run the
# trampolined first, for reasons that you will
# see.

ini_set('memory_limit','100M');

var_dump ( $timer($trampolined, [1000000]) );

var_dump ( $timer($factorial, [1000000]) );
```

Listing 4-19. bounce-output.txt

```
float(0.0254)
float(0.07143)
float(0.63219)
PHP Fatal error:  Allowed memory size of 104857600 bytes exhausted (tried to allocate 262144
bytes) in bounce.php on line 18
```

If you look at the output, you'll see that the standard recursive function (first line) runs much faster than the trampolined version (second line). However, when you start crunching the big numbers, while the trampolined version takes longer still to run (third line), the recursive version (fourth line) runs out of memory and takes down the script.

So, the trade-off for using a trampoline is lower performance (in terms of time to execute). In some cases, this may mean you stick with the normal recursive version. Always keep in mind, though, that a slower function that completes is usually better than a quicker one that doesn't! Consider what resources the users of your script will have available, and what inputs you can expect your scripts to handle, and play it safe with a trampolined version where appropriate.

Recursive Lambdas

As an interesting aside, notice the way I wrote the factorial functions earlier. I used closures rather than named functions, which in a toy program like this is purely by choice, but you may have good reasons to do so in a real program to allow you the advantages that closures bring that I talked about earlier in the book. Now, a recursive function (be it a named function or a closure) needs to be able to call itself. That's easy in the case of a named function; it has a name in the global space, so you can call it from within itself easily. In a closure, however, it is less straightforward. Because it is technically an object and here you are declaring it in the global scope by assigning it to a global variable, it doesn't exist in the scope of, well, itself. You may think that you just need to "use" the variable you've assigned it to, as you would with any variable you want to use in a closure. If you try that, you'll get an error, because you can only "use" a variable that exists (and thus has a value because by default you pass by value in PHP). The variable doesn't exist until the closure is created, during which the error will have occurred as the variable didn't exist! As you'll see from my code, the way around that is to pass it by reference to the use clause (placing an ampersand before the variable), which side-steps the fact there is no value yet to pass in.

This kind of recursive closure is more commonly called a *recursive lambda* (lambda being another word for anonymous functions) or *anonymous recursion*. Conventional programming wisdom (whatever that may be) declares this to be undesirable, with recursion to be implemented on named functions to keep code clear and understandable. However, many languages embrace anonymous recursion, like JavaScript, which provides reflection capabilities to make it easier, and as you can tell, I like it! As ever, be pragmatic, and see what suits your code the best.

The PHP Type System

As you probably know, PHP is a dynamically typed language, as opposed to a statically typed one. It is also weakly typed rather than strongly typed. This means you do not have to specify the type (integer, string, Boolean, etc.) of a variable when you declare it (at compile time). The type is implicit and determined by the value the variable is assigned at runtime. Weak typing means you can change the type by assigning a different value to it. And when it comes time to work with the variables, PHP helps you out by automatically casting the type of the variable to the type needed, for instance, when you try to add an integer and a string. It's incredibly useful to have weak dynamic typing in PHP, but it's also something that trips up a lot of newcomers (in particular those coming from statically or strongly typed languages) and leads to some of PHP's negative attention. Why is PHP dynamically/weakly typed? Well, back in the mists of time, when Rasmus Lerdorf created PHP, it was intended as a simple, straightforward way to create interactive web sites and not a fully fledged, general-purpose programming language. It seemed obvious at the time to use weak dynamic typing; after all, it was designed to handle web sites, and with HTTP there isn't a concept of integers and Booleans—everything is a string! So, to get any useful values as input and send anything back as output, your script would need to do a lot of type wrangling if everything in it was strongly statically typed. So, why not take all the hassle out and make it weak and dynamic?

In most functional programming languages, by contrast, strong static typing is all the rage. Take Haskell, for example; it has a strong static type system, although even this language, which is held up as the paragon of functional programming, does make a nod toward the utility of dynamic languages with its aptly named dynamic type. The key reason that static typing is big in functional programming goes back to one of the key advantages that programming in a functional style brings: the ability to easily read and reason about your code. The thinking goes that if you are forced to explicitly declare the types of your variables in your code (including the types of parameters to your functions), then given the definition of a particular function, you can easily reason about what will happen to any given input as you read through your function implementation. There are of course other good reasons for static typing beyond those specific to functional programming, such as the ability for compilers/interpreters to pick up certain classes of errors before the program has even begun to run.

Of course, there are downsides too, and not everyone (including me) thinks that static typing is a totally positive thing in functional programming, particularly in PHP. As you'll see in a moment, although it is essentially dynamic, PHP does have a system for *type declarations*, previously known as *type hints*, which can be used to suggest or enforce particular types for function parameters and return types. Using this syntactical facility only brings limited benefits, though. It is not strong typing, so while you (and the compiler) can reason about the type of a variable when it is passed in as a parameter, any explicit type guarantees go out of the window as soon as you do anything with the variable inside your function. And that assumes you are calling the function from within a file that turns on strict type checking; otherwise, it is nothing more than "guidance" and doesn't give any guarantees at any stage at all, only an attempt to wrangle one type into another. For the little benefit it brings, the extra syntax to declare each type reduces the brevity and readability of your code. But without typing information, how can you reason about your code? I suggest that you reason about it in the same way that you would have to even if you used type declarations. As mentioned, the internals of your function (so, a large part of your code base) will have no respect for the type declaration you made. Take Listing 4-20 (and Listing 4-21), for example.

Listing 4-20. types1.php

```php
<?php

declare(strict_types=1);

function my_function(bool $a) {

var_dump($a);
```

```
$a = $a * 22;

var_dump($a);

};

my_function(true);
```

Listing 4-21. types1-output.txt

```
bool(true)
int(22)
```

As you can see, you've turned on strict typing with the declare statement, and you've used a type declaration to declare that $a is a Boolean. All is good in the first var_dump, but hang on, the second var_dump tells you that $a is an integer. "Of course," you say, "when you multiply a Boolean by a number, PHP cast the Boolean to an int, and true becomes 1, so 1 * 22 is 22, which is an int, so this is expected." Good. I've just shown how you reason about your code when using type declarations, which is by understanding the dynamic type system that PHP uses. And you can use this knowledge to reason in the same way about untyped functions. The fact that you don't necessarily know the type that you start with doesn't leave you far behind the case where you do. In fact, if your functions may be used by others who do not employ strict typing, it may be dangerous to assume that your type declarations will be respected rather than coding defensively. PHP only enforces strict type checking for functions that are *called* from files with the declare(strict_types=1) statement, regardless of whether the file that *defines* the function has that declaration. So if your function assumes it will receive an integer because you've specified int as a type declaration and turned on strict types in your file, but someone else includes that file who doesn't use strict typing, your function may well get called with a float instead. And when that happens, in many cases where PHP can coerce one type into another, there won't be a type error thrown. The float will be quietly coerced into an integer value (truncation, anyone?). That coercion happens under the normal PHP rules that happen when it needs to wrangle types, but your code has no knowledge that it has happened, and even if you anticipate it, you can't test for it. Without a type declaration, your function will get the float, so you can test for it and choose how to deal with it when what you wanted was an integer.

As an aside, pure functional programming languages (and/or programmers) often eschew assignment in their code, in part to ensure immutability. For instance, in this case, not assigning new values to a variable would guarantee that the type stayed the same. However, the lack of assignment leads to madness, so you won't practice that dark art here.

An additional problem (although more theoretical) when using type declarations for functional programming is that PHP only allows you to catch and handle type errors outside of the function (for instance, by wrapping your function calls in a try/catch block), which means that such errors are effectively side effects. If you look back at the discussion of side effects in Chapter 2, you will see that if you catch and deal with an error within the function itself, then there is no side effect. The best way to do this is to handle the parameters and any necessary testing/conversion within your function, which means not using type declarations.

As you can guess, many developers and experts think that the pros of even PHP's limited type enforcement outweigh the cons, and at the end of the day it's often a matter of either personal choice or pragmatic considerations that will determine whether you use type declarations in a particular program or function. You won't use them in the rest of the book to keep the code clean and focused on the other topics, but here I'll outline how to use the PHP type system if you want or need.

Type Declarations

Type declarations were known as type hints in PHP 5. The key differences (aside from the name change) between 5 and 7 are as follows:

- In 5, violating a type hint results in a recoverable fatal error; in 7, not conforming to the type declaration results in a type error.

- In 5, the only types supported by hinting are class/interface, self, array, and callable. Declarations in 7 add the scalar (bool, float, int, string) types.

- Strict typing is only supported in 7.

- Return types are only supported in 7.

Note that type aliases are not supported at all, so for instance you cannot use boolean to specify to the bool type. PHP treats aliases as class names, so it would assume that a parameter of type boolean was expecting an object from the boolean class, rather than a bool (true/false) scalar variable.

You can also set the parameter to be "nullable." That is, it will accept null values as well as values of the specified type. To do this, set the default value for the parameter to be null by adding =null after the parameter name.

As well as specifying a type for each parameter, you can also specify a type for the return value. Parameter types go before each parameter, and the return type is specified with a colon and type after the parameter list.

With strict typing (available in PHP 7) turned on, parameters or return values that do not match the specified type will result in a type error. With strict typing turned off (which is the default), parameters and return values will be coerced into the specified type where possible under PHP's normal rules, without an error being thrown. Where coercion isn't possible (e.g., from the string "hello" to an integer), a type error is thrown.

You can mix and match parameters with and without declared types in the same function. Likewise, specifying a return type is optional and doesn't depend on having parameter types specified.

Let's look at these points in some example code (see Listing 4-22, Listing 4-23, Listing 4-24, and Listing 4-25).

Listing 4-22. types2.php

```php
<?php

# Examples of non-strict typing

# Our function accepts two nullable ints, and returns an int

$add = function (int $a = null, int $b = null) : int {

    return $a + $b;

};

var_dump( $add(7, 3) ); #10

var_dump( $add(2.5, 4.9) ); #6, not 7.4

var_dump( $add("5Three", "6Four") ); #11, plus Notices thrown

var_dump( $add(true, false) ); #1 (true == 1, false == 0)
```

```php
var_dump( $add(null, null) ); # 0 (null is coerced to 0)

var_dump( $add("Three", "Four") ); # Type Error
```

Listing 4-23. types2-output.txt

```
int(10)
int(6)
PHP Notice:  A non well formed numeric value encountered in types2.php on line 7
PHP Notice:  A non well formed numeric value encountered in types2.php on line 7
int(11)
int(1)
int(0)
PHP Fatal error:  Uncaught TypeError: Argument 1 passed to {closure}() must be of the type
integer, string given, called in types2.php on line 23 and defined in types2.php:7
Stack trace:
#0 types2.php(23): {closure}('Three', 'Four')
#1 {main}
  thrown in types2.php on line 7
```

Listing 4-24. types3.php

```php
<?php

# Turn on strict typing

declare(strict_types=1);

# A function which accepts $a of any type,
# and a nullable int $b, and return a
# value of type int

$divide = function ($a, int $b = null) : int {

    if ( ($a / $b) == intdiv($a, $b) )  {

        return intdiv($a, $b); # returns an integer

    } else {

        return $a / $b; # returns a float (not good!)

    }

};

# As we'll be experiencing a lot of errors, lets create
# a function to catch and deal with the errors so the
# script can complete all of our calls without dying

function run($func, $args) {
```

```php
    try {

        # run the function and var_dump the return result

        var_dump( call_user_func_array($func, $args) );

    } catch ( Error $e ) {

        # print the error message if one occurs

        echo "Caught : ".$e->getMessage()."\n";

    }

};

run( $divide, [10, 2] ); # int(5)

run( $divide, ["10","2"]); # Type Error, as no type coercion

run( $divide, [10, 2.5] ); # Type Error, as no type coercion

run( $divide, [true, false] ); # Type Error, as no type coercion

run( $divide, [23, null] ); # Division by zero warning & intdiv type error.
# Note that our input parameter is declared an int, and intdiv requires
# an int. But we still get an error, because ints are nullable in
# user function parameters, but not in all PHP function parameters

run( $divide, [10,3]); # Return Type Error (float 3.3333333...)

run( $divide, [6.4444 % 4.333, 9.6666 % 2.0003]); # int(2)
# all that matters is the type of the value of an expression passed
# as a parameter, not the types of the operands of that expression.
```

Listing 4-25. types3-output.txt

```
int(5)
Caught : Argument 2 passed to {closure}() must be of the type integer, string given, called
in types3.php on line 36
Caught : Argument 2 passed to {closure}() must be of the type integer, float given, called
in types3.php on line 36
Caught : Argument 2 passed to {closure}() must be of the type integer, boolean given, called
in types3.php on line 36
PHP Warning:  Division by zero in types3.php on line 13
Caught : intdiv() expects parameter 2 to be integer, null given
Caught : Return value of {closure}() must be of the type integer, float returned
int(2)
```

So, as you can see, if you're using type declarations, it's good to make sure that you know all the caveats as to how they operate and don't lull yourself into a false sense of security. For instance, what do you think happens if you have strict typing turned on, you declare the return type for your function to be a float, and you try to return an int? Remember I said that PHP won't try to coerce types? So, you should get a return type error, right? Let's try (see Listing 4-26 and Listing 4-27).

Listing 4-26. types4.php

```php
<?php

# Turn on strict typing

declare(strict_types=1);

# Declare two functions that are EXACTLY
# the same apart from the return type (and name).
# intdiv returns an integer. (int) casting
# ensures that even if we've somehow messed
# up, intdiv returns an int into $a, and
# the return value is forced to int.

$the_func_int = function () : int {

    $a = (int)intdiv(10,2);
    return (int)$a;

};

$the_func_float = function () : float {

    $a = (int)intdiv(10,2);
    return (int)$a;

};

var_dump( $the_func_int() ); # int(5). As expected.
var_dump( $the_func_float() ); # float(5). Errr?!
```

Listing 4-27. types4-output.txt

```
int(5)
float(5)
```

There's no error, and returning something that is definitely, positively an int when it leaves your hands comes out the other end as a float! It makes sense when you think about it because any valid int in PHP can be represented as a valid float. But assuming that strict typing insists on *exactly* the same type name reported by, for example, var_dump, can lead to trouble. You can learn more about the ins and outs of type declarations in the PHP Manual.

Further Reading

- Type declarations in the PHP Manual

  - `http://php.net/manual/en/functions.arguments.php#functions.arguments.type-declaration`

- Return type declarations in the PHP Manual

  - `http://php.net/manual/en/functions.returning-values.php#functions.returning-values.type-declaration`

As a somewhat flippant afterthought, consider that there is nothing new in this world. Strong static typing was the predominant form of type management all those years ago, before the new upstarts like Perl, PHP, and Python came along with their fancy modern weak dynamic systems, which were the way of the future. Read a recent PHP "best practices" web site or listen to the great PHP reformers speak about how they want to advance the language, and you'll soon find out that for PHP to truly complete its transformation into a modern paradigm, it needs to have proper strong static typing...and so the wheel turns again.

Summary

In this chapter, you looked at several more advanced functional programming topics. You won't be surprised to learn that many programmers in purely functional languages will consider these to be run-of-the-mill topics, and indeed you may well find that they can be useful in solving many functional "issues." Given the lack of imperative and "impure" functionality in some functional languages, they are a necessity to get any real work done. However, with the flexibility afforded by PHP to mix and match functional with imperative code and assuming you aren't hell-bent on writing *only* functional code, you can often get away with writing function-*style* code without using any of these techniques. Use your judgement and experience as a programmer to determine when they will enhance your programs and when you are just writing such code for the sake of "being functional."

PART II

Application Development Strategies

■ ■ ■

## CHAPTER 5

Strategies for High-Performance Applications

In the first part of this book, I covered the theory behind functional programming, outlining how to write code in a functional style. I touched on some of the benefits of functional programming, but in this second part I'm going to double down on the benefits by creating some programs that demonstrate some of the real-life tasks that functional programming can make easier.

This chapter looks at using functional programming to improve the performance of your scripts. In the past, PHP has gotten a bad rap in the performance department, which is not entirely unsurprising given it is essentially a high-level interpreted language. However, performance has vastly improved in the past few major versions, with version 7 in particular pushing performance way beyond anything PHP has had before. So, before you even start looking at the techniques in this chapter, make sure you're running the latest version of PHP, as that is likely to be the easiest way to improve performance. With that said, even when you've upgraded to the latest and greatest version, there'll often be times when you can do with an extra boost in performance for problematic scripts. You'll look at functional programming techniques such as memoization and lazy evaluation, which can help speed up your scripts, as well as how functional programming can help you to utilize parallel programming to improve performance. But before you get started, it's important to understand exactly what I mean by performance and how you can measure it.

Understanding and Measuring Performance

When your script runs, it will use a certain amount of memory and CPU and/or wall time. A reduction in any of those is usually considered to be a performance increase. Sometimes other resources, such as disk space, network bandwidth, or API calls, are considered to be performance issues. Your particular performance requirements will determine in what circumstances you consider performance to have improved. For instance, on a NAS box with lots of disk space but a limited processor, you may consider that optimizing for lower memory and CPU usage at the expense of increased disk space usage for caching is ideal. However, if you're targeting high-performance laptops with small SSDs, you may consider using memory because cache storage is a better trade-off. In this chapter, you'll mainly be looking at memory usage and wall time, which are often the two biggest performance problems that PHP scripts encounter.

Measuring Performance: Profiling

You've probably come across slow-running scripts (often your own!), and usually the first response is to start looking up ways to increase PHP's speed. Compiling, caching, refactoring code, accelerators—these are all topics that will readily turn up when googling for *PHP performance* or *speed issues*. You may have already read about them and wanted to dive right in to try them out.

© Rob Aley 2017
R. Aley, *Pro Functional PHP Programming*, DOI 10.1007/978-1-4842-2958-3_5

My advice (derived from bitter personal experience) is to *stop right now*. Throwing performance trick after performance trick against your code (often that you find online or in good books like this)—even when they appear sensible and you can see the logic—can end up complicating your code or adding dependencies for no good reason. Why? Because when you don't know the root cause of the problem, you don't know whether a particular solution, no matter how good on paper, will address the issue you are having in your particular case. Even if it does appear to work, you don't know if it is the simplest way to fix it and thus whether you're saddling yourself with extra "technical debt" when you don't have to.

The step you often miss is to ask your script directly, "Why are you running so slowly?" If your script tells you, you can then attempt to fix the issue without the use of external tools such as compilers and caching systems. So, how do you ask your script the *why* question? By profiling it.

A profiler watches a piece of software (usually from the "inside") as it runs and breaks down the time (and sometimes resources) that each part of the program uses. The profile information is often reported down to the level of an individual line of code or function call. This helps you spot exactly where your scripts are slowing down. Is it that complex database query? A badly written loop? A function that's called more times than expected? Disk or network access pausing execution? Whatever the problem, the profiler will tell you. Once you know the exact cause of the slowdown, the solution is usually apparent (or at the very least, you can rule out potential solutions that won't actually fix it). It may just mean rewriting a few lines of code or caching some data instead of repeatedly generating it. The profiler may point out problems external to PHP, such as a slow database server or a laggy network connection or resource. Of course, in some cases you may end up having an intractable problem from a PHP programming point of view that does indeed require the help of an accelerator or external caching system. In any case, you will likely save time and prevent making unnecessary changes to your code or deployment environment by using a profiler to ask the *why* before you start trying the *what*.

With PHP, you have several choices when it comes to profiling. You can manually profile your code by adding profiling/measuring statements directly to your code base, or you can use a tool to automatically profile your code for you. The former is quick and easy to do, with no changes to your development environment, if you know roughly where in your code the problem lies. The latter, while requiring the setup and configuration of the tool and learning how to use it the first time, provides more comprehensive profiling. It also doesn't rely on you knowing where your problems may be located and usually requires minimal or no changes to your code base. You'll look at both options in the following sections.

Manual Profiling

Manual profiling entails adding code to your source to measure time or resources directly from within the scripts. Listing 5-1 shows an example of measuring execution time of different lines of code, with the output shown in Listing 5-2.

Listing 5-1. manual.php

```php
<?php

# A script to do some "busywork", filling
# some strings with some characters.

# Let's create a "checkpoint" by recording the current time and memory
# usage

$time1 = microtime(true);

$memory1 = memory_get_usage();
```

```php
# Now let's do a loop 10 times, having a quick usleep and
# adding just a little data to our variable each time

$a_string = (function () {

  $output = '';

  for ($counter = 0; $counter < 10; $counter++) {

    usleep(10);

    $output .= 'a';

  };

  return $output;

})(); //we execute the function straight away

# Now create a second checkpoint

$memory2 = memory_get_usage();

$time2 = microtime(true);

# Let's do this second loop 1000 times, having a longer
# sleep and adding lots of data to our variable each time

$b_string = (function () {

  $output = '';

  for ($counter = 0; $counter < 10; $counter++) {

    usleep(100);

    $output .= str_repeat('abc',1000);

  };

  return $output;

})(); //again we execute straightaway

# and create a final checkpoint

$memory3 = memory_get_usage();

$time3 = microtime(true);
```

```
# Now let's output the time and memory used after each function.

echo "1st function : ".($time2-$time1)." secs, ".
    ($memory2-$memory1)." bytes\n";

echo "2nd function : ".($time3-$time2)." secs, ".
    ($memory3-$memory2)." bytes\n";

echo ("Peak memory usage : ". memory_get_peak_usage()." bytes\n");
```

Listing 5-2. manual-output.txt

```
1st function : 0.0007178783416748 secs, 40 bytes
2nd function : 0.0016269683837891 secs, 32768 bytes
Peak memory usage : 392504 bytes
```

As you can see, the second function takes a lot longer than the first. You now know that the problem making your script slow is the second loop, and you can fix it by removing the usleep statement and maybe removing the loop altogether and using str_repeat('abc',1000000) to fill your string.

You need to be slightly more cautious when looking at the amount of memory used before and after each function call. As you can see, the difference in memory usage after the second function is much greater than the first, which is to be expected because you've returned a large string. However, the peak memory usage of the script is higher than both individual measurements added together. Functions use memory while they are running, but once they return, that memory is usually freed (static variables and generators not withstanding), leaving only the memory footprint of whatever value was returned (assuming you chose to capture it). Even if you add a memory_get_usage() call right before your return statement, it may not capture all the memory used by your function if you destroy or replace variable values as the function executes. You'll need to carefully consider what your script is doing and where the best places to put manual profiling statements are, as you go along.

This is obviously a simple, contrived example, but the principles apply to real-world code as well. As you can see, manual profiling is quick and simple for a few lines of code or a function here or there. However, profiling larger code bases can quickly become cumbersome, massively increasing the size of the code base if you're not careful. When hunting down a particular problem, you can profile larger sections of code, and when the larger section at fault is found, you can profile that into smaller chunks, and so on, until the problem code is found (effectively doing a binary search). If you're spending a lot of time doing it this way, the time necessary to implement and learn a profiling tool like those detailed next would probably be time well spent instead.

One other thing to remember is that manual profiling code adds a performance penalty to your scripts—which, although usually small, can add up, especially if you are repeatedly logging profiling information to disk as you go. So, it may be worth considering stripping out or disabling profiling code before the code hits production (perhaps as part of your build/deployment process). In some cases, of course, consciously adding profiling code to the production code base can be helpful (for example, when it is necessary/useful to collect profiling information from your end users who aren't likely to have dedicated profiling software installed). Automatic profiling tools also usually add some overhead, although it is often smaller (they are typically written in lower-level languages and often integrate directly with the PHP interpreter) and is usually easier to switch on and off. These automatic tools are often used only in the development environment and not on live production machines, so any overhead is restricted to development work.

Profiling Tools

Several profiling tools are available for PHP. While the popular Xdebug debugger provides some profiling options (and is worth looking at if you already have it installed for debugging), the most common and comprehensive tool is XHProf. Originally developed by Facebook, it is available as a PECL extension and so can be simply and easily installed. The data collection side is written in C, and a graphical PHP interface is provided for viewing the collected profile data, including call graphs (visual graphs of which functions call which) if you have Graphviz installed. Two related projects, XHProf UI and XHGui, provide an expanded visual interface, store multiple runs in a MySQL or MongoDB, and provide access for sorting and comparing multiple runs. These are a little more work to get installed and configured, but they provide a lot of flexibility if you are regularly profiling development code or profiling live code on production systems. For basic profiling to find obvious problems in development code, though, XHProf itself is a good place to start.

The leading commercial PHP profiling tool is Blackfire, which provides a fairly comprehensive profiling service and at the time of writing has a reasonable free tier. Do note that although the profiling client runs on your systems, data is reported to the Blackfire server back end and so may not be suitable for some uses.

Further Reading and Tools

- "The Need for Speed: Profiling PHP with XHProf and XHGui" by Matt Turland

  - https://www.sitepoint.com/the-need-for-speed-profiling-with-xhprof-and-xhgui/

- "XHProf PHP Profiling" by Adam Culp

  - www.geekyboy.com/archives/718

- "Profiling PHP Applications with XHGui" by Lorna Mitchell

  - https://inviqa.com/blog/profiling-xhgui

XHProf
Function-level hierarchical PHP profiler

- Main web site: https://github.com/phacility/xhprof

- Installation information: www.php.net/manual/en/xhprof.setup.php

- Main documentation: www.php.net/xhprof

- Tool for visual function graphs: http://graphviz.org/

XHProf UI
Expanded profiler based on XHProf

- Main web site and documentation: https://github.com/preinheimer/xhprof

XHGUI
A graphical interface for XHProf data built on MongoDB

- Main web site and documentation: https://github.com/perftools/xhgui

Xdebug
Comprehensive debugger with built-in profiler

- Main web site and documentation: https://xdebug.org/

KCachegrind
A tool for profile-data visualization. Use with Xdebug for visual profile information.

- Main web site and documentation: https://kcachegrind.github.io/html/Home.html

Webgrind

An alternative web-based profiling front end for Xdebug that implements a subset of KCachegrind's features

- Main web site and documentation: `https://github.com/jokkedk/webgrind`

Blackfire

Commercial PHP profiling service

- Web site: `https://blackfire.io/pricing`

Low-Level Profiling

When you really need to "go deep" into what's happening with your script, you sometimes need to look not at what your code is doing but at what PHP itself is doing instead. To be clear, most of us will never need to do this to solve performance problems, though it can be quite interesting and instructive to look at how PHP translates your code into calls to the system on which it's running. PHP itself is a C program compiled into a binary executable, which means you can use general-purpose tools like strace (shows system calls and signals), ltrace (shows library calls), and gdb (a debugger for C programs like PHP itself) to see what's going on under the hood. If this interests you, take a look at the following tutorial from Derick Rethans. As the author of Xdebug, he is somewhat of an expert on the mechanics of PHP.

So, now you've profiled your code, you know where your bottlenecks are, and you solved any simple rookie mistakes. You're already running the latest version of PHP, and you're on top-tier hardware. You're thus fairly confident that your problems are with particular parts of your code base, and you need to write some of your algorithms in a more efficient manner. Can functional programming offer any patterns to help speed up your code? Of course, it can; otherwise, this would be a very short chapter! The following sections cover some functional techniques that are applicable in many situations, even where your whole code base isn't functional.

Further Reading

- "What is PHP doing?" by Derick Rethans

- `http://derickrethans.nl/what-is-php-doing.html`

Memoization

If you've been programming for a while, particularly in the web sphere, you will have come across the concept of caching. *Caching* is the process whereby you take the results of an "expensive" computation, store the results, and then use the stored results the next time you call that computation instead of running the computation itself again. *Expensive* means things that take a long time to run, that take a lot of memory, that make a lot of external API calls, or that do any other action that you would like to minimize for cost or performance reasons. *Cache invalidation* is the process by which you choose to remove items from the cache. For instance, if it takes a lot of effort to generate the front page of your news web site, you'll want to cache that page so that you don't need to generate it each time a visitor comes to your site. However, as soon as the next breaking story happens, you'll want to update your front page, and you won't want your visitors hitting the cached version and getting old news, so you will "invalidate" the cache and regenerate the page. If you've been involved in writing or using caching systems, you'll no doubt be familiar with the following saying (or at least understand where it's coming from), based on quote by Phil Karlton:

"There are only two hard things in computer science: naming things, cache invalidation, and off-by-one errors."

You've already looked at how recursion can reduce off-by-one errors, and there's no hope of anyone ever solving the problem of naming things, so how about solving cache invalidation? Hands up if you think that function programming has a trick up its sleeve. Good, gold star for you! Indeed, it does, and the trick is to simply not invalidate the cache, ever. Problem solved!

I'm actually being serious. Functional programming offers a technique called *memoization*, which is rooted in the properties inherent in pure functions. In the earlier theory chapters, you looked at how pure functions are referentially transparent. Given a particular set of input parameters, a pure function will always produce the same return value, and (for that set of inputs) the function could be simply replaced by the return value. This should start to sound a bit like caching: for a given set of inputs (say, your news stories), you want to replace the (expensive to run) function with its return value (the cached output). The process of taking the output of a pure function and caching it is memoization and is just a special case of caching.

Let's say you are memoizing an expensive function and caching the result to disk. Each time you run the function with different parameters, you are likely to get different results. What you want to eliminate is the cost of running the function on the same parameters multiple times, as each time your (pure) function is guaranteed to give you the same results. So, you cache the results by, for instance, creating a hash representing the input parameters used and using that as the file name to store the return value of that run. The next time you run the function, you hash the input parameters again, see whether a cache file by that name exists, and return the contents if it does (rather than rerunning the expensive function).

So far, this is typical of caching. But how do you avoid ever having to invalidate the cache? The answer is you don't; memoization effectively does that for you. Your functions are pure, which means there are no side effects involved. So if on your fictional news web site a new story breaks, details of that story will only hit the (pure) function that creates your front page via the input parameters to that function. For instance, you may have an array of headlines as one parameter. Suddenly, the hash of your parameters has changed, so the memoized function won't be able to find a file on disk with that hash and so will run the full function and cache the new result to disk in a file named with the new hash value. To recap, as your only inputs are parameters, if none of the parameters has changed, you must be OK to use the cache. However, if the parameters *have* changed, then there will be no corresponding cache file, so there's no need to invalidate it. Of course, the old cache file will still be there, so when you accidentally publish a story falsely claiming this book is rubbish, you can immediately retract it, and the function will go back to using the old cached file because the hash will once again match the parameters.

So far, so good. Functional programming doesn't stop with its goodness there, though, oh no. If you're thinking about how to write your functions to do memoization, then stop. In general, you don't need to. You can simply wrap your function in another function that memoizes it for you automatically. Such a wrapper function is simple to write, as all you are concerned about are the inputs and outputs of your pure function and not what it does on the inside.

So, let's take a look at an example of a memoization. In Listing 5-3, you'll cache results of your pure function to disk. For brevity, you'll separate those impure disk functions into separate functions rather than cooking up some IO monads, but you can of course do so if you desire.

Listing 5-3. memoize.php

```php
<?php

# We're going to cache our results on disk, so let's
# define a directory and file prefix

define('CACHE_PREFIX', sys_get_temp_dir().'/memo-cache-');
```

```
# This is a helper function to read a cached file
# from disk. I've broken it out as a separate function
# as it is necessarily impure. You can replace it
# with an IO monad or similar in production if you wish

$get_value = function($hash) {

    # return null if the file doesn't exist

    if (!file_exists(CACHE_PREFIX.$hash)) { return null;  }

    # read the file into $value

    $value = file_get_contents(CACHE_PREFIX.$hash);

    # return null if the file exists but couldn't be read

    if ($value === false) { return null; }

    # return our value if all is good

    return $value;

};

# Likewise, this is an impure helper function to write
# the value to a cache file.

$store_value = function($hash, $value) {

    if (file_put_contents(CACHE_PREFIX.$hash, $value) === false) {

        $value = null;

    }

    # return the value that was stored, or null if the
    # storage failed

    return $value;

};

# Finally, this is our actual memoization function.
# It returns a closure which is a "memoized" version
# of the function you call it on, i.e. a version
# of your function which automatically caches return
# values and automatically uses those cached values
# without further coding from you.
```

```
# $func is the function (closure or other callable) that
# you want to memoize

$memoize = function($func) use ($get_value, $store_value)
{
        # We're returning a memoized function

    return function() use ($func, $get_value, $store_value)
    {
                # Get the parameters you (the end user) call
                # your memoized function with

        $params = func_get_args();

                # Get a unique hash of those parameters, to
                # use as our cache's key. We needs to convert
                # the params array to a string first, we use
                # json_encode rather than serialize here as
                # it is a lot faster in most cases

            $hash = sha1( json_encode( $params ) );

                # Check the cache for any return value that
                # has already been cached for that particular
                # set of input parameters (as identified by
                # its hash)

                $value = $get_value($hash);

                # If there was no pre-cached version available,
                # $value will be null. We check this with the ??
                # null coalescing operator, returning either :
                # a) the cached $value if it's not null, or
                # b) the results of actually calling the user
                # function. Note that we wrap the call in the
                # $store_value function to cache the results,
                # and $store_value passes the value back
                # through as its result and so it is also
                # returned to the user in this case

                return $value ?? $store_value(

                                $hash, call_user_func_array($func, $params)

                        );
    };

};
```

First, your memoize function makes a unique string representation of the input parameters by encoding them to JSON. If you're wondering why you didn't simply use implode("|", $params), for instance, think about the two following function calls:

```
func("Hello","|There");
func("Hello|","There");
```

This would lead to both being encoded as Hello||There and thus being treated as the same set of parameters when they are in fact different. You could use implode with a glue character if you can guarantee that character won't ever appear in your parameters, but usually it's a good idea to code defensively and use a proper serialization function, just in case. You can use PHP's serialize() function instead of json_encode because with some workloads it may be faster. Both have edge cases that you may want to familiarize yourself with before you choose one, such as the inability of serialize() to work with some types of objects. See the PHP Manual for more information on both.

Once you have your string representation of your inputs, you need to transform it into another string that is suitable for use as a file name. Your JSON string is likely to have characters that aren't valid for file names, so instead you'll create an SHA1 hash of it. An MD5 hash would be slightly faster to create but has a greater chance of a hash collision (where the same hash is generated for two different inputs). Even SHA1 can have collisions, although the risk is typically very low. If you definitely cannot ever cope with a collision, then you will need to write some code to parse the serialized string and substitute invalid characters, and so on, in a consistent way, ensuring that you stay within other limits for your cache medium (file name length for writing to disk, for example).

You now have your hash (or other unique way of describing the input parameters). You then try to load the contents of a file with the hash as the name, from your cache. If you fail to read it (usually because it doesn't exist as this is your first call with these parameters), you run your pure function with call_user_func_array(), grab its return value and create the cache file, and finally return that grabbed value as your return value. If you could read the file, you just return the contents as your return value and skip executing the function. You'll note that you're not using any form of strict typing here. If your return value from your pure function is an int (say), when you run the pure function for the first time, you'll write that to disk and return the int to the caller. However, on subsequent runs, you get the contents of the cached file as a string and return that, so your return value is then a string. If typing matters in your application, you can always serialize the value to disk and unserialize it again when you read it back.

Let's look at an example now of how to actually use this memoize function. You'll use another classic example task, an algorithm to generate the Fibonacci sequence. I'm using this as it's a short, easy-to-understand function that also happens to be recursive. Memoization works on any functions, recursive or not, but it is often particularly useful as recursive functions can frequently be resource heavy, as you've seen earlier. If you're not familiar with the Fibonacci sequence, it is a series of numbers where every number after the first two (or three if you start from zero) is the sum of the two preceding ones, so:

0, 1, 1, 2, 3, 5, 8, 13, 21, 34, 55, 89, 144, 233, 377, 610, 987, 1597, 2584, 4181, 6765, 10946 and so on...

This algorithm takes an integer *n* and calculates the *n*th number in the sequence. So, $fibonacci(7) would return 13 (13 being the 7th number in the previous sequence, starting from 0).

You'll create two functions: a standard version of the function and one wrapped in the earlier $memoize function. Normally you would create only one function and wrap it in $memoize. However, as I want to demonstrate a recursive version that recursively calls the memoized version (and contrast that to the unmemoized form), you'll create two here. And as Fibonacci is not a particularly taxing task for a modern PC, you'll add some artificial "expense" in the form of a usleep statement to make each computation take longer. This will demonstrate the effect memoization can have on genuinely longer-running functions. See Listing 5-4 and Listing 5-5.

Listing 5-4. memo_example.php

```php
<?php

# Get our memoize function and helpers

require('memoize.php');

# Define a plain old recursive fibonacci function

$fibonacci =

        function ($n) use (&$fibonacci) {

        usleep(100000); # make this time-expensive!

    return ($n < 2) ? $n : $fibonacci($n - 1) + $fibonacci($n - 2);

    };

# Define the same fibonacci function again in exactly the
# same way (except for the name), but this time wrap the
# function body in a call to $memoize to get a memoized version

$memo_fibonacci = $memoize(

        function ($n) use (&$memo_fibonacci) {

        usleep(100000);

    return ($n < 2) ? $n : $memo_fibonacci($n - 1) + $memo_fibonacci($n - 2);

        }

);

# Let's define a timer function, to time a run of a function,
# and return the parameters, results and timings.

$timer = function($func, $params) {

    $start_time = microtime(true);

    $results = call_user_func_array($func, $params);

    $time_taken = round(microtime(true) - $start_time, 2);

    return [ "Param" => implode($params),
                    "Result" => $results,
                    "Time" => $time_taken ];

};
```

```
# And now let's do a set of runs of both our
# ordinary function and it's memoized sister.
# I've added an extra * parameter to the
# non-memoized runs so that you can spot them
# easier in the output (the '*' isn't used
# by the fibonacci functions, it's just passed
# through to the output of the timer function)

print_r( $timer(  $fibonacci, [6, '*'] ) );

print_r( $timer(  $memo_fibonacci, [6] ) );

print_r( $timer(  $fibonacci, [6, '*'] ) );

print_r( $timer(  $memo_fibonacci, [6] ) );

print_r( $timer(  $memo_fibonacci, [10] ) );

print_r( $timer(  $memo_fibonacci, [11] ) );

print_r( $timer(  $memo_fibonacci, [8] ) );
```

Listing 5-5. memo_example-output.txt

```
Array
(
    [Param] => 6*
    [Result] => 8
    [Time] => 2.5
)
Array
(
    [Param] => 6
    [Result] => 8
    [Time] => 0.7
)
Array
(
    [Param] => 6*
    [Result] => 8
    [Time] => 2.5
)
Array
(
    [Param] => 6
    [Result] => 8
    [Time] => 0
)
Array
(
    [Param] => 10
    [Result] => 55
```

```
    [Time] => 0.4
)
Array
(
    [Param] => 11
    [Result] => 89
    [Time] => 0.1
)
Array
(
    [Param] => 8
    [Result] => 21
    [Time] => 0
)
```

If you look at the output of the first runs in Listing 5-5, you'll see that the standard function takes 2.5 seconds to compute the 6th Fibonacci number, while the memoized version takes only 0.7 seconds. Surely, they should operate the same the first time round, as nothing is cached yet. Well, because your functions are recursive, you're actually calling the function multiple times for each calculation, and as your memoized version will call itself with the same parameters multiple times, your cache will be used.

The third run demonstrates that calling your standard function again with the parameter 6 still takes 2.5 seconds the next time you call it, which is obvious as it does no caching. However, calling the memoized version on 6 takes 0 seconds (rounded down!) because the cache is being hit for each recursive call in the calculation.

Calculating the 10th number next, you take only 0.4 seconds. This is quicker than calculating the 6th number, because they share some steps (each one needs to calculate the 1st, 2nd, 3rd, and so on, numbers), which will already be cached, with the 10th number only requiring the actual calculation of the 7th, 8th, 9th, and finally 10th number. The next run demonstrates this further; calculating the 11th number now takes only 0.1 second (as it has only one uncached call to the function), and the last run to calculate the 8th number runs in 0 seconds as it is already in the cache from when you generated the 10th number.

If you call the script for a second time, you'll find that all the runs that use the memoized function complete in 0 seconds, as your cache is already there for all the values needed because you've generated them all before at least once. Unless someone changes the fundamental basis of math, you can leave your cache intact permanently because the cached results will always be correct for the given inputs. If you're wondering what the cache looks like, running more /tmp/memo-cache-* gives the output in Listing 5-6. As you can see, there are 12 files, which makes sense because you calculated the 11th Fibonacci number (counting from 0) and therefore called the memoized function with 12 different parameters.

Listing 5-6. cache_files.txt

```
::::::::::::::
/tmp/memo-cache-10ae24979c5028fa873651bca338152dc0484245
5
::::::::::::::
/tmp/memo-cache-1184f5b8d4b6dd08709cf1513f26744167065e0d
0
::::::::::::::
/tmp/memo-cache-1fb0856518ee0490ff78e43d1b6dae12ad6ec686
21
::::::::::::::
/tmp/memo-cache-2499831338ca5dc8c44f3d063e076799bea9bdff
1
```

```
::::::::::::::
/tmp/memo-cache-3ad009a144b1e8e065a75ca775c76b2fc2e5ff76
89
::::::::::::::
/tmp/memo-cache-4a0a63ce33cc030f270c607ea7bf90a6717572bb
8
::::::::::::::
/tmp/memo-cache-7a60554107407bfe358bedce2bfcb95c90a8ea0d
34
::::::::::::::
/tmp/memo-cache-8f4e345e7cd51e4e633816f5a52a47df465da189
3
::::::::::::::
/tmp/memo-cache-bd703dc0b11593277a5a82dd893f2880b8d0f32a
13
::::::::::::::
/tmp/memo-cache-e9310b0c165be166c43d717718981dd6c9379fbe
55
::::::::::::::
/tmp/memo-cache-f1e31df9806ce94c5bdbbfff9608324930f4d3f1
2
::::::::::::::
/tmp/memo-cache-f629ae44b7b3dcfed444d363e626edf411ec69a8
1
```

In these examples, you cached to disk, which allows you to create an enduring cache that can survive reboots and be used by multiple processes. However, sometimes the disk is too slow, and if your function parameters often change, you may only want to cache for the duration of a single script run. An alternative is to cache in memory, and in fact PHP offers a way to create variables that act like global variables but that are restricted to a given function and are ideal for caching within a single run of a script. These are called *static variables*, and if you're not familiar with them, Listing 5-7 (and Listing 5-8) is an example of a static variable ($sta), compared to global ($glo), parameters ($par), and normal function scope ($nor) variables.

Listing 5-7. static.php

```php
<?php

$my_func = function ($par) {

  static $sta;
  global $glo;

  var_dump( "static : ". $sta += 1 );
  var_dump( "global : ". $glo += 1 );
  var_dump( "param  : ". $par += 1 );
  var_dump( "normal : ". $nor += 1 );

  return $sta;

};
```

```
while ( $my_func(1) < 5) { echo "-----\n"; };

echo "*****\n";

var_dump( "static : ". $sta );
var_dump( "global : ". $glo );
var_dump( "param  : ". $par );
var_dump( "normal : ". $nor );
```

Listing 5-8. static-output.txt

```
string(10) "static : 1"
string(10) "global : 1"
string(10) "param  : 2"
string(10) "normal : 1"
-----
string(10) "static : 2"
string(10) "global : 2"
string(10) "param  : 2"
string(10) "normal : 1"
-----
string(10) "static : 3"
string(10) "global : 3"
string(10) "param  : 2"
string(10) "normal : 1"
-----
string(10) "static : 4"
string(10) "global : 4"
string(10) "param  : 2"
string(10) "normal : 1"
-----
string(10) "static : 5"
string(10) "global : 5"
string(10) "param  : 2"
string(10) "normal : 1"
*****
string(9) "static : "
string(10) "global : 5"
string(9) "param  : "
string(9) "normal : "
```

As you can see, even though you call my_func with the same parameter (1) each time, the value of $sta is different each time. So while you can't access it from any scope outside of the function, it is normally still considered a "side effect" because for any particular call of a function you can't determine what state it will be in (in this case, without knowing how many times the function has already been called). So, how can you use static variables in your functional programs? The answer is, carefully. Let's look at an example (see Listing 5-9). You'll create a version of your memoize function that uses a static array to hold your cache rather than writing to disk.

Listing 5-9. memoize-mem.php

```php
<?php

$memoize = function($func)
{

    return function() use ($func)
    {

            static $cache;

        $params = func_get_args();

            $hash = sha1( json_encode( $params ) );

            $cache["$hash"] = $cache["$hash"] ??
                                        call_user_func_array($func, $params);

            return $cache["$hash"];
    };
};
```

So, everything you put into the $cache array, and later read from it, is fully determined by the parameters you call your function with (via the hash), and what you put into it is the value of that function. Your use of the static variable is effectively referentially transparent, so in this case you aren't creating any potential side effects. If you call the same memoize-example.php script as before but using this memory-based memoize function instead, you get the output in Listing 5-10.

Listing 5-10. memo_mem_example-output.txt

```
Array
(
    [Param] => 6*
    [Result] => 8
    [Time] => 2.51
)
Array
(
    [Param] => 6
    [Result] => 8
    [Time] => 0.7
)
Array
(
    [Param] => 6*
    [Result] => 8
    [Time] => 2.51
)
Array
(
    [Param] => 6
```

```
        [Result] => 8
        [Time] => 0
)
Array
(
        [Param] => 10
        [Result] => 55
        [Time] => 0.4
)
Array
(
        [Param] => 11
        [Result] => 89
        [Time] => 0.1
)
Array
(
        [Param] => 8
        [Result] => 21
        [Time] => 0
)
```

As you can see, it's exactly the same output as the file-based example. It actually runs a tiny bit faster because you're not doing disk I/O, but you're rounding to the nearest 0.1 second here. The only other difference compared to the disk-based example is that if you run the script for a second time, you'll get this output again (rather than all zeros for the memoized calls), as the static variable used for the cache is destroyed when the script ends.

There is an alternative to disk and session-based memory caches, the humble RAM disk. On Linux type systems, a file system called tmpfs is available, which allows you to create and use files that are stored in memory rather than on disk. These virtual files act and operate like normal files on disk and can thus allow different PHP processes to read and write cache data in files as you would with normal "on-disk" files. The advantages tmpfs brings are twofold; first, it's fast, and second, everything is temporary. Because the files are held in memory, there is no mechanical hard disk to wait for, so I/O is very quick. And because they are held in memory, they are only temporary and will disappear upon a reboot if you haven't already deleted them. A further advantage is that, being normal files, they aren't a PHP-specific technology and so can be accessed from other software as needed. You can access files on a tmpfs file system in the same way as normal files and streams; the fact they are in memory is transparent to your PHP script. The earlier file-based example will work perfectly fine with RAM disks.

To create a tmpfs file system on Linux, first create a directory on disk to use to "attach" the memory device to your file system. Then mount the memory device at that location and start using it. The shell script in Listing 5-11 (with the output in Listing 5-12) gives an example of mounting and removing a tmpfs RAM disk.

Listing 5-11. ramdisk.sh

```bash
#!/usr/bin/env bash

mkdir /tmp/myMemoryDrive

sudo mount -t tmpfs /mnt/tmpfs /tmp/myMemoryDrive

php -r "file_put_contents('/tmp/myMemoryDrive/test.txt',\"Hello\n\");"
```

```
cat /tmp/myMemoryDrive/test.txt

sudo umount /mnt/tmpfs

cat /tmp/myMemoryDrive/test.txt
```

Listing 5-12. ramdisk-output.txt

```
Hello
cat: /tmp/myMemoryDrive/test.txt: No such file or directory
```

In Listing 5-11, you create a directory at /tmp/myMemoryDrive to attach the memory device and then mount it there. You execute a line of PHP to demonstrate creating a memory file as you would any other file and then cat the file, which should output Hello. Finally, you umount the device and try to cat the file again, but as you would expect, the file is gone; it is never saved to the physical disk. You can mount tmpfs devices using the mount command, as shown earlier each time you boot your system or whenever you want to use them, or you can add an entry into your fstab file to have it automatically created each time your system boots. Whichever way you mount it, when you shut down or reboot, always remember that it, and all of the files within it, will be destroyed.

As tmpfs operates in the same way as a normal file system, you need to make sure you set the relevant file permissions to allow all of your applications to access it (or prevent access by those that shouldn't be able to meddle with it). Also bear in mind that memory swapping to disk may occur if your system becomes short of memory, so your data may temporarily touch your hard disk in these cases and under certain conditions may be recoverable from disk after that. Always consider the security implications of any caching system you choose.

If you are considering using tmpfs instead of physical hard disks for performance reasons, you should also bear in mind that modern operating systems (including modern Linux) can use aggressive in-memory caching for disk access. This means the operating system transparently caches oft-read disk-based files to dynamically allocated unused memory (usually without you even knowing) to increase apparent physical disk performance. In these cases, you might not see the performance improvements that you may expect when reading some files from, and traversing directory trees on, a tmpfs memory disk. Writes to disk and less often accessed files aren't usually cached, so tmpfs may still give you the wins you are expecting in those cases.

In Windows there is no built-in way to create a memory-based file system. Assorted third-party software exists to create RAM disks, but it is not standardized, and most applications require a GUI to set up the disk manually on each system. The Wikipedia page listed next gives some more pointers for you to explore if you are still interested.

Further Reading

List of third-party RAM disk software on Wikipedia

- https://en.wikipedia.org/wiki/List_of_RAM_drive_software#Microsoft_Windows

The Downsides of Memoization

As you can see, caching via memoization is generally a Good Thing,™ but as my mother always said, "You can have too much of a good thing." The temptation to start memoizing all of your functions by default may creep in, but as with everything, there are some trade-offs to think through first. Your memoized function will come with a slight overhead for checking whether a cached version is available every time you run it and for fetching or storing any cached version generated. If you are memoizing to speed up execution of your script and your cache resides on disk as with the earlier main example, the extra time for disk I/O (which is usually *slow* in comparison to memory storage or indeed many compute-only functions) may be longer than it takes a low-to-medium complexity function to run. Of course, that may be an acceptable trade-off if you're caching to optimize a low memory system, reduce the number of calls to an external API, or minimize other non-time-related resource usage.

Another consideration to make when caching with memoization is whether the ephemeral nature of some data limits the value you get from it with respect to the cost. For instance, if one of the parameters to your function is a customer ID but your customers rarely make more than one visit/purchase to your online shop, any caching of that function is likely to be of benefit only during that one visit. One of the benefits of the memoization of pure functions, over the more general cases of caching, is that you never have to worry about cache invalidation because your cache is never invalid. However, this leads to the temptation to simply forget about the cache and leave it be, which is perfectly fine from a programming perspective; your code will continue to run fine with the correct outputs. However, your sysadmins may soon come along and start asking if you really do need all of that disk space on the expensive SAN. The cost of disk space may outweigh the limited speedups to scripts. In these situations, you have three options.

- *Drop the memoization*: Accept some longer-running scripts.

- *Cache to memory or per-session files on disk, rather than long-term disk storage*: This speeds up multiple calls in the same visit, at the temporary expense of some memory.

- *Perform some form of cache eviction*: Delete cached files that are, say, more than one month old.

Lazy Evaluation

Lazy evaluation is the art of only doing the minimum amount of work possible to get the result you need. This should come naturally to a PHP programmer! Consider the following pseudocode:

if (do_something_easy() OR do_something_hard()) { return }

This code says "if either do_something_easy() or do_something_hard() are true, then return." So, to find out whether you should return, you could call both functions, and if one of them returns true, then you know to return. However, consider that if do_something_easy() returns true, it doesn't matter what do_something_hard() returns, as you will be returning in any case. So, after running do_something_easy(), there is actually no point in running the second function call, and you can save yourself the overhead of doing so. If instead it had returned false, you would need to run the second one, but then you're no worse off than if you had automatically called both in the first place. This is called *lazy evaluation*; you only evaluate what you need to and not a statement more.

PHP uses a type of lazy evaluation called *short-circuit* evaluation when evaluation Boolean expressions, which depends on the precedent of the logical operator. So, there is nothing for you to do here, other than taking a note of the following pages in the manual if you are calling functions from within such expressions to make sure you aren't short-circuiting the short-circuiting!

Further Reading

PHP Manual:

- Logical operators: http://php.net/manual/en/language.operators.logical.php

- Operator precedence: http://php.net/manual/en/language.operators.precedence.php

Generators

However, you can take this concept of lazy evaluation and apply it to your functions to speed those up. In the examples of functional composition that you looked at in previous chapters, you usually take an array of data, do something to it, pass the array to the next function, do something else, and so on, down the chain. Even where you don't actually need all of the data in the array, you typically pass it along whole and apply your functions and transformations to the whole thing. You looked at `array_filter`, which does cut down the size of an array to certain elements using some filter function, but even then the filter function is applied to every single element of the array. If you need only the first 10 matching elements and there are 100 matching elements, you've wasted time applying the filter function after the first 10 have been found, and you need an additional step like using `array_slice` to cut the resulting 100 down to 10.

PHP has a useful language tool called *generators*, which were introduced in PHP 5.5. A generator allows you to create functions that return something that is a bit like an array but whose data is generated "in real time" as the elements are accessed. You can use generators to create lazy functions that do only the minimum necessary work.

When you chain generator functions together, execution takes place backward. Consider a pseudochain of three standard functions like this:

- `array_filter some_function();`
- `array_filter another_function();`
- `array_slice 0, 10;`

First the whole array would be filtered, then the whole result filtered again, and then the second result would be reduced to ten items. In a generator-based system, you can write a chain like this:

- `lazy_filter some_function();`
- `lazy_filter another_function();`
- `lazy_slice 0, 10;`

It looks the same, but when you execute it, the action effectively starts at `lazy_slice`, which pulls values up through the chain. The slice function requests values from the second filter until it has ten. Each time the second filter gets a request for a value, it requests values from the first filter and applies `another_function()` to them until it has a match. And each time the first filter gets a request for a value, it takes values from the array and applies `some_function()` to them until it gets a match. Thus, by the time `lazy_slice` has gotten its ten values, the two `lazy_filter` functions have called their (potentially expensive) filtering functions only enough times to generate those ten and not (necessarily) to all items of the original data.

In a moment you'll look at a basic example of a generator. But before you do, let's create a function to repeatedly call a function. When you look at timings, unrelated tasks on the same PC can temporarily slow down your script runs. Running the scripts or functions many times can limit the effect of such temporary blips on your benchmark timing numbers. See Listing 5-13.

Listing 5-13. repeat.php

```php
<?php

# For benchmarking results, it's best to repeatedly run the
# function to minimize the effect of any external slowdowns.
# The following function simply calls a function $func $n times
# with arguments $args, and returns the return value of the last
# call.
```

```php
$repeat = function ($func, $n, ...$args) {

    for ($i=0; $i < $n; $i++) {

        $result = $func(...$args);

    }

    return $result;

};
```

Now let's look at a simple example of a generator (see Listing 5-14, with the output shown in Listing 5-15). A generator is a function that has a `yield` statement instead of a `return` statement. Unlike a normal function that loses its state when it returns, a function that yields keeps its state until the next time it is called.

PHP has a native function called `range()` that returns an array of numbers from $start to $end, with an optional $step value. You'll create a generator version, `gen_range()`, which produces the same output but lazily. You'll call both with same parameters, to generate every fourth number between 1 and 10 million, and then exit your running function when you get a number that is divisible by 123.

Listing 5-14. generators.php

```php
<?php

# Get our repeat function

require('repeat.php');

# PHP's native function range() takes a
# $start int, $end in and $step value, and
# returns an array of ints from $start to $end
# stepping up by $step each time. We'll create
# a generator version that takes the same
# parameters and does the same task, called gen_range()

function gen_range($start, $end, $step) {

  for ($i = $start; $i <= $end; $i += $step) {

        # yield turns this function into a generator

    yield $i;

  }

};

# We'll create a function to run either range() or
# gen_range() (as specified in $func) with the
# same paramters, and to iterate through the
# returned values until we find a number exactly
# divisible by 123 (which in this case is 369)
```

```php
$run = function ($func) {

    # Get a range from 1 to ten million in steps of 4,
    # so 1,4,9,13,18,...,9999989,9999993,9999997

  foreach ( $func(1, 10000000, 4) as $n ) {

    if ($n % 123 == 0) {

                # exit the function once we've found one, reporting
                # back the memory in use (as it will be freed once
                # we have returned).

        return memory_get_usage();

    };

  };

};

# A function to get the time/memory use for the runs

$profile = function ($func, ...$args) {

    $start = ["mem" => memory_get_usage(), "time" => microtime(true)];

  $end = ["mem" => $func(...$args),  "time" => microtime(true)];

    return [
            "Memory" => $end["mem"] - $start["mem"],
            "Time" => $end["time"] - $start["time"]
        ];
};

# Finally let's run each of range() and gen_range() 100 times,
# and output the time taken for each and memory used

Echo "*** range() ***\n";

print_r ( $profile($repeat, $run, 100, 'range') );

Echo "*** gen_range() ***\n";

print_r ( $profile($repeat, $run, 100, 'gen_range') );
```

Listing 5-15. generators-output.txt

```
*** range() ***
Array
(
    [Memory] => 134222280
    [Time] => 8.9564578533173
)
```

```
*** gen_range() ***
Array
(
    [Memory] => 4952
    [Time] => 0.0016660690307617
)
```

So, as you can see, the amount of memory used by the lazy version is much less than the normal range() function. This is because range() has to generate the whole array of values before you start iterating through them with foreach, whereas gen_range() only holds the current value in the sequence. The time taken for gen_range() is also much less because as soon as you hit 369, you're done, whereas range() has to generate every single value in the sequence even before you get started.

Notice that the memory used is the value memory_get_usage returns when the $run function returns, which for your functions is likely to be just about the highest amount used in each function.

So, that's what a generator looks like. Now let's look at how to use them in functional composition to minimize the amount of work your chain of functions have to do. You'll create a script that takes the veritable (public domain) complete works of Shakespeare (as a plain-text file), gets the lines that mention the word *hero*, gets any of those that are more than 60 characters long, and then returns the first three matches.

Listing 5-16 shows how you would do it in a nonlazy fashion, with the output shown in Listing 5-17.

Listing 5-16. filter.php

```php
<?php

# Borrow some functions from Chapter 3,
# and our repeat function

require('../Chapter 3/compose.php');
require('../Chapter 3/partial_generator.php');
require('repeat.php');

# A helper function to fix parameters from the right,
# as we'll otherwise call partial(reverse()) a lot below.

$partial_right = function ($func, ...$params) {

    return partial(reverse($func), ...$params);

};

# Get the start time, to see how long the script takes

$start_time = microtime(true);

# A function to return true if $word is in $str
# (not comprehensive, but matches a word bounded
# by non-A-Z chars, so matches "hero" but not "heroes")

$match_word = function($word, $str) {

    return preg_match("/[^a-z]${word}[^a-z]/i", $str);

};
```

```
# A function to return true if $str is longer than $len chars

$longer_than = function($len, $str) {

    return strlen($str) > $len;

};

# A partial function, fixing hero as the word to search for

$match_hero = partial($match_word, 'hero');

# Another partial function, picking out strings longer than 60 chars

$over_sixty = partial($longer_than, 60);

# A partial function which uses array_filter to apply $match_hero
# to all elements of an array and return only those with 'hero' in

$filter_hero = $partial_right('array_filter', $match_hero );

# Similarly, we'll filter an array with the $over_sixty function

$filter_sixty = $partial_right('array_filter', $over_sixty );

# A function to grab the first 3 elements from an array

$first_three = $partial_right('array_slice', 3, 0);

# Let's now compose the function above to create a
# function which grabs the first three long
# sentences mentioning hero.

$three_long_heros = compose(

                                              $filter_hero,
                                              $filter_sixty,
                                              $first_three
                              );

# Finally, let's actually call our composed function 100 times
# on the contents of all_shakespeare.txt
# Note that calling file() as a parameter means that it is
# only evaluated once (and not 100 times), so the time for disk
# IO won't be a major element of our timings

$result = $repeat(
                        $three_long_heros,
                          file('all_shakespeare.txt'),
                          100
                    );
```

```
# Print out the result of the last call (which should be the
# same as all of the rest, as all of our composed functions are
# pure and are called on exactly the same input parameter)

print_r($result);

# and the time taken

echo 'Time taken : '.(microtime(true) - $start_time);
```

Listing 5-17. filter-output.txt

```
Array
(
    [0] =>      Enter DON PEDRO, DON JOHN, LEONATO, FRIAR FRANCIS, CLAUDIO, BENEDICK, HERO,
BEATRICE, and Attendants

    [1] =>      Sweet Hero! She is wronged, she is slandered, she is undone.

    [2] =>      Think you in your soul the Count Claudio hath wronged Hero?

)
Time taken : 6.2691030502319
```

This gives you the three lines you are looking for, and 100 runs take approximately 6 seconds on my wimpy laptop. Listing 5-18 rewrites this script in a lazy way, with the output shown in Listing 5-19.

Listing 5-18. lazy_filter.php

```php
<?php

# Again we'll borrow some functions from Chapter 3,
# and our repeat function

require('../Chapter 3/compose.php');
require('../Chapter 3/partial_generator.php');
require('repeat.php');

# and start timing

$start_time = microtime(true);

# We'll now define a lazy version of array_filter, using
# a generator (note the yield statement)

$lazy_filter = function ($func, $array) {

# Loop through the array

    foreach ($array as $item) {
```

```
        # Call the function on the array item, and
        # if it evaluates to true, return the item

        if ( $func($item) ) { yield $item; }

    };

};

# The following functions are exactly the same as
# in the non-lazy filter.php example

$match_word = function($word, $str) {

    return preg_match("/[^a-z]${word}[^a-z]/i", $str);

};

$longer_than = function($len, $str) {

    return strlen($str) > $len;

};

$match_hero = partial($match_word, 'hero');

$over_sixty = partial($longer_than, 60);

# Our $filter_hero function is almost the same,
# but note that it calls $lazy_filter instead of
# array_filter (and it uses partial() rather than
# $partial_right, as I've implemented $lazy_filter
# with the parameters in the opposite order to
# array_filter.

$filter_hero = partial($lazy_filter, $match_hero );

# Again $filter_sixty uses $lazy_filter rather than array_filter

$filter_sixty = partial($lazy_filter, $over_sixty );

# As the output from filter_sixty will be a generator object
# rather than an array, we can't use array_slice to
# get the first three items (as data doesn't exist in a
# generator until you call for it). Instead, we'll create
# a $gen_slice function which calls the generator $n times
# and returns the $n returned values as an array. We'll take
# advantage of that fact that a generator is an iterable object,
# and so has current() and next() methods to get each value.
# We'll practice our recursion, rather than just using
# a for loop!
```

```php
$gen_slice = function ($n, $output = [], $generator) use (&$gen_slice) {

    $output[] = $generator->current();

    $generator->next();

    if ($n > 1) {

        $output = $gen_slice(--$n, $output, $generator);

    }

return $output;

};

# $first_three uses $gen_slice rather than array_slice

$first_three = partial($gen_slice, 3, []);

# We'll compose them together, repeatedly call them
# and output the results using exactly the same
# code as in the non-lazy version

$three_long_heros = compose(

                                            $filter_hero,
                                            $filter_sixty,
                                            $first_three
                            );

$result = $repeat( $three_long_heros, file('all_shakespeare.txt'), 100 );

print_r($result);

echo 'Time taken : '.(microtime(true) - $start_time);
```

Listing 5-19. lazy_filter-output.txt

```
Array
(
    [0] =>     Enter DON PEDRO, DON JOHN, LEONATO, FRIAR FRANCIS, CLAUDIO, BENEDICK, HERO,
BEATRICE, and Attendants

    [1] =>     Sweet Hero! She is wronged, she is slandered, she is undone.

    [2] =>     Think you in your soul the Count Claudio hath wronged Hero?

)
Time taken : 2.1842160224915
```

You get the same results but in a paltry two seconds, which is roughly three times quicker. So, how does this work? Well, your `lazy_filter` doesn't return any data but instead "yields" a generator object. The object implements PHP's iterator interface, and so functions like `foreach` automatically know how to use it as if it were any other iterable data type. This becomes most apparent when you get to the `gen_slice()` function, which rather than pretending you're working with an array simply calls the `current()` and `next()` methods of the generator object to request the next three pieces of data. If you're not familiar with iterators, the following section in the PHP Manual will sort you out.

Further Reading

- The `Iterator` class in the PHP Manual

    - `http://php.net/manual/en/class.iterator.php`

As an aside, when I wrote the previous scripts, I started with the `compose` statement naming the three functions it chained together and then worked backward to work out what functions were needed to implement them. This is a pattern you'll often find yourself using when programming functionally; the declarative nature lends itself to a top-down approach to program design.

The Downsides of Lazy Evaluation

Generators are great, and lazy evaluation in general is a pretty useful tool. As you might expect, however, it's worth being aware that there can be downsides. If you run your `generators.php` example again, but this time instead of looking for a number divisible by 123 you instead use the value 9999989, Listing 5-20 and Listing 5-21 show what happens.

Listing 5-20. generators2-output.txt

```
*** range() ***
Array
(
    [Memory] => 134222280
    [Time] => 26.05708694458
)
*** gen_range() ***
Array
(
    [Memory] => 4952
    [Time] => 41.604923009872
)
```

The standard `range()` function takes 26 seconds, but your lazy `gen_range()` function nearly doubles that to 41 seconds. Why? Well, there is an overhead inherent in generators. Looking for a number divisible by 9999989 (which is, in this case, itself) means that you have to go all the way until virtually the end of your sequence of numbers to find it. But you're having to call a function (via `foreach`) on every number in the sequence, rather than one function call to `range()`, and every function call has a small amount of overhead. Additionally, the function you are calling is written by *you* in PHP, rather than a whole team of PHP core developers in C, and so is much less likely to be highly optimized code. So, often there will be a point at which a generator is less time efficient than doing the full evaluation first. It is normally minimal and toward the end of the evaluation process, and if you have an even "spread" of input values for your runs, you usually come out ahead overall even if a few do take longer than the full evaluation approach. It's always worth think about your use case, though, and profiling your code against real-world data to be sure.

It's not all bad news, though. If you take a look at the memory usage figures, you'll see that they are exactly the same as for the first example where you looked for a number divisible by 123. In cases like this, you may consider the reduction in memory caused by mutating the value each time (rather than generating them all up front) worth the occasional extra execution time, if you're working on memory-constrained devices.

Parallel Programming

During the long slog of writing a book, I've often wished that each of my hands could be writing a different chapter at the same time; that way I'd finish the book twice as fast. Unfortunately, my cunning plan is thwarted when I realize that my puny brain is only capable of keeping track of one set of words at a time. Luckily, modern computers aren't as limited as me and can carry out and keep track of many tasks at once. Computers do this in various ways (parallel computing, multitasking, multithreading, multiprocessing, etc.), but they all boil down to one thing: the more you do at the same time, the quicker you get things done.

It's not all roses, though, even with the smarts of the modern PC keeping things straight when you're doing different things at the same time. Resource contention, deadlocks, race conditions: these are all things that happen when multiple threads or processes try to access the same resources (variables, data, files, hardware, etc.) at the same time. Perhaps the hardest part of programming like this is thinking through all the possibilities that can occur when the execution of your script goes off on different paths.

Functional programming can make this easier. When your program needs to do parallel tasks, they will spin off some threads, child processes, or similar to complete the tasks, and they will often combine the results or take some action when the threads or processes return. If you write these task workers using the functional principles that you've looked at in this book, each can become a chain of pure functions where:

- The task depends only on its given inputs (like parameters to a function) and not any external state.

- The task can be reasoned about easily in isolation, as it is not affected by other tasks.

This means you don't have to worry (too much) about what other tasks are doing, which resources they may be using that you want, etc. Your task has everything it needs provided as part of the input when it is called, and it returns its output for the parent script to worry about processing/storing, etc. Even though it's not strictly a function, you can write your worker script as if it were, accepting input from the parent as if it were parameters and returning a single value to the parent at the end like a return value.

PHP does not come naturally to parallel programming, but there are a number of ways to implement parallel computation that can be pressed into action when the need arises. Perhaps the simplest is by using PHP's built-in process control functions to launch multiple PHP scripts in parallel to do the work. Let's look at an example of using process control in this way.

You're going to create a program to do some analysis of the complete works of Shakespeare. You're going to create a function that does the analysis in a normal linear manner, as well as a function that spawns multiple "client" PHP worker scripts to do the analysis in parallel. First you'll look at your main `parallel.php` controlling script, and then you'll look at the `client.php` script used in the parallel version, and finally you'll look at the `functions.php` script, which contains the various analysis and parallelization functions. Your script will pick out words from the text that meet certain criteria, sum the number of occurrences of such words throughout the text, and then report the top ten occurring words from this set. You'll repeat each function 100 times to benchmark them.

Listing 5-21. parallel.php

```php
<?php

# Get a set of functions that we'll look at shortly

require('functions.php');

# The text to work on.

$shakespeare = file_get_contents('all_shakespeare.txt');

# How many times we're going to run each function, for
# benchmarking purposes

$repeats = 100;

# Compose our single process "standard" function.

$analyze_single = compose(

                $only_letters_and_spaces, # simplify the text

                'strtolower', # all lowercase, please

                $analyze_words, # do the analysis

                $sort_results, # sort the results

                'array_reverse', # get the results in descending order

                $top_ten # return the top ten results
);

# Run the single process version $repeats time on $shakespeare input
# Time the runs

$checkpoint1 = microtime(true);

print_r( $repeat($analyze_single, $repeats, $shakespeare) );

$checkpoint2 = microtime(true);

# Now create a parallel process version

$analyze_parallel = compose (

                $launch_clients, # Launch a set of client processes to do
                                            # the analysis

                $report_clients, # Tell us how many clients were launched
```

```php
                $get_results, # Get the results back from the clients

                $combine_results, # Combine their results into one set

                $sort_results, # sort the combined results

                'array_reverse', # get the results in descending order

                $top_ten # return the top ten results
);

# Run the parallel version and time it

$checkpoint3 = microtime(true);

print_r ( $repeat($analyze_parallel, $repeats, $shakespeare) );

$checkpoint4 = microtime(true);

# Finally, dump the timings for comparison

var_dump( 'Single : '.($checkpoint2 - $checkpoint1));

var_dump( 'Parallel : '.($checkpoint4- $checkpoint3));
```

In the $analyse_parallel composition, the $launch_clients function will launch multiple runs of the script in Listing 5-22 in parallel.

Listing 5-22. client.php

```php
<?php

require('functions.php');

# Get the chunk of text for the client to analyze
# by reading the contents of STDIN which are piped to
# this script by the fwrite($clients[$key]["pipes"][0], $string)
# line in the $launch_clients function in the parent process

$string = stream_get_contents(STDIN);

# Compose a function to do the analysis. This is the same
# as the first three steps of the single process analysis
# function, with a step to encode the results as JSON at
# the end so we can safely pass them back

$client_analyze = compose(

                    $only_letters_and_spaces,

                    'strtolower',
```

```
                                        $analyze_words,

                                        'json_encode'

);

# Run the function and write the results to STDOUT,
# which will be read by the stream_get_contents($client["pipes"][1])
# line in the $get_results function in the parent process. In most cases
# you can use echo to write to STDOUT, but sometimes it can be
# redirected, and so explicitly writing like this is better practice

fwrite(STDOUT, $client_analyze($string) );
```

Finally, Listing 5-23 shows the functions.php script that implements all the functions you have composed in the previous scripts. I've separated these out to make the scripts clearer to read and also because many are accessed by both scripts.

Listing 5-23. functions.php

```php
<?php

# Borrow some utility functions from previous examples

require('../Chapter 3/compose.php');
require('repeat.php');

# To simplify our analysis, replace anything that's not
# a letter with a space.

$only_letters_and_spaces = function($string) {

    return preg_replace('/[^A-Za-z]+/', ' ', $string);

};

# This is the "expensive" deliberately un-optimized function
# that does our "analysis".

$analyze_words = function ($string) {

    # Split our text into an array, one word per element

    $array = preg_split('/ /i', $string, -1, PREG_SPLIT_NO_EMPTY);

    # Filter our array for words that...

    $filtered = array_filter($array, function ($word)  {

        return (

                            # ... contain any of the letters from the word shakespeare
```

```
                    preg_match('/[shakespeare]/', $word) != false)

                    # ... AND has at least 1 character in common with this sentence

                    && (similar_text($word, 'William is the best bard bar none') > 1)

                    # ... AND sound like the word "bard"

                    && (metaphone($word) == metaphone('bard'))

                    # ... AND have more than three characters in them

                    && ( (strlen($word) > 3 )

                );
    });

    # Finally, count up the number of times each of the filtered
    # words appears in the analyzed text, and return that

     return array_count_values($filtered);

};

# Slice the top 10 items off the top of the array

$top_ten = function ($array) {

    return array_slice($array, 0 ,10);

};

# Sort the results numerically

# asort mutates the array, so we wrap it in a function

$sort_results = function($array)  {

            asort($array, SORT_NUMERIC);

            return $array;

};

# The following functions manage the execution of parallel client scripts

# A function to split the text into chunks and launch the
# appropriate number of clients to process it

$launch_clients = function ($string) {
```

```php
    # Split the string into chunks of 1 million characters,
    # a value which I found by trial and error to give the
    # best results on this machine for this process

    $strings = str_split($string, 1000000);

    # An array to hold the resource identifiers for the client scripts

    $clients = [];

    # Descriptors for "pipes" to read/write the data to/from our client
    # scripts

    $descriptors = [
                                0 => ["pipe", "r"], #STDIN, to get data
                                1 => ["pipe", "w"]  #STDOUT, to send data
                    ];

    # Iterate through the chunks...

    foreach ($strings as $key => $string) {

        # $key will be the array index, 0, 1, 2, 3... etc.
        # We'll use it as a handy way to number our clients

        # Define the command that runs the client

        $command = "php client.php";

        # Open the clients with proc_open. This returns a resource identifier.
        # We'll store it, although our script won't actually use it.

        $clients[$key]["resource"] = proc_open( $command,

$descriptors,

$clients[$key]["pipes"]

                                                                            );
        # Note the third parameter above is a variable passed by reference.
        # This is used by proc_open to store an array of file pointers
        # identifying PHP's end of the pipes that are created.

        # We use that info here to write our text chunk to. This writes
        # it to STDOUT, and our client script reads it in through STDIN
        # at its end of the pipe.

        fwrite($clients[$key]["pipes"][0], $string);

        # Close the pipe now we're done writing to this client.

        fclose($clients[$key]["pipes"][0]);

    };
```

136

```php
    # Once all of the clients have been launched, return their
    # resource identifiers and pipe details

    return $clients;
};

# Simple impure function to report how many clients were
# launched. You could use a writer monad instead if you wanted

$report_clients = function ($clients) {

    # The escape code at the end minimizes our output when
    # when running the script many times, by going up one line
    # and overwriting the output each time.

    echo("Launched ".sizeof($clients)." clients\n\033[1A");

    return $clients;

};

# A function to get the results back from the clients.
# The clients will send a JSON encoded array back to us

$get_results = function ($clients) {

    # An array to gather the results. Each clients' result
    # will be stored as an element of the array

    $results = [];

    # Iterate through the client resource identifiers

    foreach ($clients as $key => $client) {

            # Clients write output to STDOUT, which corresponds to the
            # STDIN Pipe at our end. We'll read that JSON data and
            # decode it to a PHP array. Each client's results will be
            # stored as a separate element of the $results array.

            $results[] = json_decode(
stream_get_contents($client["pipes"][1]),

                                                true);

            # We've done reading from the client, so we can close the pipe.

            fclose($clients[$key]["pipes"][1]);

        };
```

```
            # And finally return all of the results from all of the clients

            return $results;

};

# This function takes the results array from $get_results above and
# combines it into a single array

$combine_results = function ($results) {

# Reduce and return the input array by...

 return   array_reduce($results, function($output, $array) {

        #... iterating over each individual clients results array
        # and either creating or adding the count for each word to
        # the output depending on whether that word already exists in
        # the output

        foreach ($array as $word => $count) {

            isset($output[$word]) ?
                                        $output[$word] += $count   :
                                        $output[$word] = $count ;
        }

        # return $output through to the next iteration of array_reduce

    return $output;

}, []); # starting with a blank array [] as output

};
```

Let's run parallel.php and see what happens (see Listing 5-24).

Listing 5-24. parallel-output.txt

```
Array
(
    [beard] => 76
    [bright] => 43
    [buried] => 43
    [bred] => 36
    [breed] => 35
    [bird] => 34
    [bride] => 30
    [broad] => 15
    [bread] => 15
    [board] => 15
)
```

```
Launched 4 clients
AArray
(
    [beard] => 76
    [bright] => 43
    [buried] => 43
    [bred] => 36
    [breed] => 35
    [bird] => 34
    [bride] => 30
    [broad] => 15
    [bread] => 15
    [board] => 15
)
string(24) "Single : 48.808692932129"
string(25) "Parallel : 25.10250711441"
```

As you can see, you get the same results from both the single process and parallel process versions of the analysis, but the parallel version takes roughly half the time to execute. Chunking the text as you did gave you four client processes in parallel to analyze all the text. Considering that both versions of the function used exactly the same expensive function ($analyze_words), you may be wondering why with four clients it didn't complete in a quarter of the time. The reason is that there is a nontrivial amount of setup to do to run in parallel, including the following:

- Dividing up the text into chunks

- Spinning up new PHP processes

- Writing to and reading from the process pipes

- Combining the results together at the end

So, if you want to speed it up some more, can't you simply spin up more clients in parallel? Let's give it a try, by chunking the text into blocks of 100,000 characters, which needs 38 clients to calculate in parallel (see Listing 5-25).

Listing 5-25. parallel-output2.txt

```
Array
(
    [beard] => 76
    [bright] => 43
    [buried] => 43
    [bred] => 36
    [breed] => 35
    [bird] => 34
    [bride] => 30
    [broad] => 15
    [bread] => 15
    [board] => 15
)
Launched 38 clients
Array
(
```

```
        [beard] => 76
        [bright] => 43
        [buried] => 43
        [bred] => 36
        [breed] => 35
        [bird] => 34
        [bride] => 30
        [broad] => 15
        [bread] => 15
        [board] => 15
)
string(24) "Single : 49.230798959732"
string(26) "Parallel : 145.74519586563"
```

In this case, you've gone from twice as quick to nearly three times as long! This is again because of the overhead of coordinating all the clients and bringing the results together. So, with this technique, there is often a sweet spot in the number of parallel processes that give the maximum results. This depends greatly on the task at hand, and for functions that have the following characteristics, you are likely to get better results:

- Functions where results don't need a lot of post-processing (e.g., where the order or content of results from different clients doesn't matter)

- Functions where the setup is inexpensive (e.g., minimal processing to split up the input data, minimal data transfers to clients)

- Longer-running functions (where the time overhead is minimal compared to function execution time)

As you can see, the speed improvements don't come without a lot of extra code to manage the parallelization. Before you got to the stage of parallelizing the code, there are a number of things you could do to speed up execution, including the following:

- Using lazy evaluation, by counting and ordering the words first (cheap operations) and then applying the analysis as part of a generator function

- Reordering the operations in array_filter to take advantage of PHP's lazy evaluation, paring down the data with cheap functions such as strlen first, before the more expensive preg_match is called

- Calculating metaphone('bard') in advance and storing in a variable rather than calculating it each time

- Replacing preg_match with the cheaper strpbrk PHP function

If that isn't enough to get you under your performance goals and you need to go parallel, there are a few other things you could do to speed up the parallel version (which I haven't done to keep the code simple and save space in the book).

- Include only the functions you need in each script, maybe using a build step to inline them.

- Pass data directly in shared memory rather than via pipes, which can be quicker.

- Don't wait for each client to send data before moving on to read from the next, repeatedly cycling through them in a nonblocking manner until each has data ready for you.

Lazy evaluation can be hard with parallel scripts because each script returns data in the order appropriate to its local input and not necessarily representative of the data as a whole. For instance, with this script, each client could calculate its own top results, but you couldn't just accept the first ten that you received as they might not be the top ten of the whole works of Shakespeare but merely of those chunks that have been analyzed and returned first. As you can see, parallelizing work takes some thinking about, even when functional programming helps you by eliminating the additional burden of considering side effects. Consider also that I haven't even touched on what to do if one of your clients fails to complete or hangs, and you'll see why you should only consider such techniques if really necessary.

Multithreaded Programming

Multithreaded programming works in a similar manner to the multiprocess example you looked at in the previous section. The key difference is that the parallel execution happens within the same process rather than separate processes. PHP isn't multithreaded; however, multithreading is possible with the use of the Pthreads extension. Pthreads is a robust OOP-based implementation, and performance can be significantly better than with multiprocess scripts; however, it is more complicated to implement than multiprocess code because of the nature of the threads coexisting within the same process. Also, note that the Pthreads extension can be used only with the "thread-safe" versions of PHP, which isn't compatible with many PHP extensions. Most package managers on Linux don't include the thread-safe version and so will require you to manually compile PHP (see Appendix A if you want information on compiling PHP yourself), or for Windows you will need to download the thread-safe executable from the PHP web site.

Still, employing the principles of functional programming as shown earlier will help you to bypass some of the problem areas common with multithreaded programming. More information about the extensions and examples of use can be found on the Pthreads web site.

Further Reading

- Pthreads web site: `http://pthreads.org/`

- Pthreads section in the PHP Manual: `http://php.net/manual/en/book.pthreads.php`

The Standard PHP Library (SPL)

At the beginning of this chapter, I discussed the fact that some of the apparent performance problems PHP has are because of the overhead necessary to provide users with easy-to-use and versatile data structures and functions. If you find this overhead starts limiting your scripts, one port of call is the Standard PHP Library (SPL), a core PHP extension that contains common and esoteric data structures and functions. These are designed to solve common programming problems, albeit with a little more thought needed to use than PHP's more common structures like the normal PHP array type. There's nothing exclusive to functional programming in the SPL, but rather there are useful functions and structures that can be used in the functional techniques that you've looked at in this book.

So, for instance, if you find that passing around large arrays of data is causing your script to hit memory limits, you might like to look at the `SplFixedArray` class. It has some restrictions (you can only use integers as indexes, and the length of the array must be specified in advance) but provides a faster implementation that uses less memory than a normal array. If you're not familiar with some of the data structures in the SPL (such as heaps, linked lists, etc.), then most basic introductions to computer science (or programming in more traditional languages) should help you out. The SPL also contains functions and classes for common iterator-based tasks, which you can use with the generators you looked at earlier.

The example script in Listing 5-26 gives you a taste of the iterator_to_array function, the SplFixedArray structure, and the FilterIterator class.

Listing 5-26. spl.php

```php
<?php

# Borrow our simple generator example

function gen_range($start, $end, $step) {

  for ($i = $start; $i <= $end; $i += $step) {

    yield $i;

  }

};

# Call the generator...

$gen_obj = gen_range(1,10,1);

# ... and check what we have is a generator object
print_r($gen_obj);

# Generators are iterators, so when we need a full array
# of data instead of a generator, we can convert
# it to an array using SPL's iterator_to_array function

$array = iterator_to_array($gen_obj);

print_r($array);

# An SplFixedArray is SPLs fixed size array data structure.
# Let's create an empty SPL fixed array and a standard PHP array.
# Note we need to specify a size for the SPL array

$spl_array = new SplFixedArray(10000);

$std_array = [];

# Let's create a function to fill an array with data. As both
# array types can be written to in the same way, we can
# use the same function here for both

$fill_array = function($array, $i = 0) use (&$fill_array) {

    # recursively fill the $array with data

    if ($i < 10000) {
```

```
        $array[$i] = $i * 2;

        return $fill_array($array, ++$i);

    };

    return ($array);

};

# Let's do some operations with the arrays. We'll measure
# the memory in use before and after each operation.

$mem1 = memory_get_usage();

# Fill the standard array with data

$std_array = $fill_array($std_array);

$mem2 = memory_get_usage(); # 528384 bytes

# Fill the SPL array with data

$spl_array = $fill_array($spl_array);

$mem3 = memory_get_usage(); # 0 bytes

# It took no memory to fill!
# This is because this type of array allocates all of its memory
# up-front when you create it

# Create a new SPL array and fill with data

$spl_array2 = new SplFixedArray(10000);

$spl_array2 = $fill_array($spl_array2);

$mem4 = memory_get_usage(); # 163968 bytes

# This time it did, as we declared it within the section we
# were measuring

# Create a new empty standard array

$std_array2 = [];

$mem5 = memory_get_usage(); # 56 bytes - a small amount

# Create a new empty SPL array

$spl_array3 = new SplFixedArray(10000);
```

143

```php
$mem6 = memory_get_usage(); # 163968 bytes - for an empty array!

# This shows that you need to use it with care. A Standard
# array may use more memory for the same amount of data, but
# the memory also shrinks with the array contents too.

echo "Filled Standard Array : ".($mem2 - $mem1). " bytes \n";

echo "1st Filled SPLFixedArray : ".($mem3 - $mem2). " bytes \n";

echo "2nd Filled SPLFixedArray : ".($mem4 - $mem3). " bytes \n";

echo "Empty Standard Array : ".($mem5 - $mem4). " bytes \n";

echo "Empty SPLFixedArray : ".($mem6 - $mem5). " bytes \n";

# The SPL provides various iterator classes that you can extend
# to work with iterable structures like the SPLFixedArray and
# generators

# Let's create a class to filter for values that are divisible by three

class by_three extends FilterIterator {

    # We extend the FilterIterator class, and implement the accept() class
    # with your filtering function

  public function accept()
  {

    $value = $this->current();

    if ($value % 3 == 0) {

            # return true to include the value in the output

      return true;

    }

        # or false to filter it out

    return false;
  }

};

# Let's use it to filter our previous SPL array

$nums = new by_three($spl_array);

var_dump(iterator_count($nums)); # int(3334) (~third of the array is returned)
```

There are many more classes, functions, and data structures available in the SPL. Check out the PHP Manual for more details.

Further Reading

- PHP SPL documentation

  - www.php.net/manual/en/book.spl.php

Conclusion

In this chapter, you looked at some common applications of functional programming in the area of performance improvement. Even if you don't go whole hog and write your application fully in functional code, picking out key functions that are causing bottlenecks and rewriting them with functional principles in mind can allow you to apply these performance-enhancing techniques to those sections of code. And of course if you do write your application from scratch in a functional style, applying techniques such as memoization when you find a problem function is quick and simple to do.

CHAPTER 6

■ ■ ■

Managing Business Logic with Functions

In this chapter, you'll look at some other common uses for functional programming. You'll start by looking at how functional code can help you to manage the business logic implemented in your programs. You'll then look at what event-based programming is and how functional programming can help you deal with the complexities of managing incoming events and keep your data flows straight. Finally, you'll take a quick look at asynchronous programming and see why functional programming is a useful tool in that domain too.

Managing Business Logic

Most (useful) programs perform a multitude of different operations, from talking to databases to generating pretty interface screens and much more. But the key thing that defines what a program *does* is its implementation of "business logic." *Business logic* (sometimes called *domain logic*) is the part of the program that encodes the real-world business rules into code. In an accounting program, for instance, the business rules include how to add, subtract, and round monetary values; how to deal with sales tax and depreciation; how to convert between currencies; and how to move money from one account or ledger to another. The PHP (or other language) code that implements these rules is the business logic. Functions such as creating the user interface, generating a PDF report, and so forth aren't usually considered business logic, although they can be if particularly important business rules (such as rounding precision, output formatting specified by regulators, etc.) are involved. Although it contains the word *business*, business logic doesn't just apply to commercial or financial applications. Take a program like Photoshop, for instance. There is a lot of code in Photoshop that deals with loading and saving images, creating the user interface, responding to user mouse and keyboard input, and so on. The business logic in Photoshop, however, consists of the algorithms that apply the transformations, filters, paint and tool operations, and so on. These are the "business" tasks of an artist, and an artist will have "rules" (or expectations) for what happens when you invert an image or apply a dither. A written specification for a piece of software will often start with the business rules that the software needs to implement.

Business logic, when compared to other code, has some particular needs that characterize it.

- *Business logic needs to be testable*: If your accounting web site accidentally uses the Arial font instead of Verdana, it's not likely to be a big deal. But if it rounds millions of transactions up to the nearest penny instead of down, someone is getting fired. Testing code carries an overhead, and if that's a problem, then identifying key business logic to focus limited testing time on is usually a smart move. Making that business logic easy to test maximizes the benefit you get from your limited testing resources.

© Rob Aley 2017
R. Aley, *Pro Functional PHP Programming*, DOI 10.1007/978-1-4842-2958-3_6

- *Business logic needs to be centralized and encapsulated into small single-purpose sections of code*: Take sales taxes like VAT and GST, which can have assorted percentages depending on the products in question and the location of the purchaser and seller. If the government of the United Kingdom decides that the VAT on computer books is going to be raised from 0 percent to 10 percent for EU citizens but not for non-EU citizens, a book retailer will need to ensure that the new rate is calculated and applied correctly on its web site product pages, basket page, checkout pages, e-mail confirmations, card-processing system, and back-end accounting system. Having the rate specified in one location and having single-purpose centralized functions to determine purchaser location and product type ensure both that changes are reflected in all parts of the system at the same time and that the chance of unintended effects on unrelated code (or tax rates, etc.) are minimized.

- *Business logic needs to map clearly onto real-world business rules so that it is clear how one relates to the other*: If you can read your English-language business rules and follow along in the code implementation at the same time, it makes it easier to verify that they are all being implemented.

- *Business logic needs to be resilient to failures*: If a web site fails to load a user's preferred text color from their settings, the default black text is usually only a minor annoyance for the user who was expecting muted charcoal-gray lettering. If the same web site fails to load the array of tax rates for its e-commerce pages, the application of null percent tax to all sales is going to make the tax department very unhappy.

Functional programming, as I hope you'll have feeling for by now, can help you to manage your business logic and meet these needs. Taking the previous three bullet points in reverse, here's how it can help:

- Eliminating side effects can improve resilience to some types of failure, and using constructs like the Maybe monad can help you deal with others.

- I talked about functional programming being a "declarative" coding style. This means that you code in a way that describes "what" you are doing, not "how" you are doing it (at least at the higher level of composing functions). This declarative style makes it easier to match real-world business rules to their corresponding code and keep an eye on both.

- As you've seen, functional programming encourages you to break your code down into single-purpose functions and then build up chains of functions and partial functions into easy-to-read (and reason about) blocks of code. This encourages code reuse, and encapsulating values (e.g., a tax rate) in a function helps encourage immutability.

- Functional programming makes testing (like unit testing) easy.

So, even when your whole program isn't written in a functional style, identifying your key business logic and implementing that using functional programming can still bring you benefits. I'll talk further in the next chapter about mixing and matching other programming paradigms with functional code. But for now let's look at a short example of encapsulating key business logic in pure functions.

The following example implements some (very simplified) key financial logic used by a hypothetical e-commerce web site. It is structured into three files: business_data.php, business_logic.php, and shopping.php. The first and second contain your centralized business logic. You may wonder why you've created functions in the business_data.php file to return your data (product prices, tax rates, etc.) rather than just providing static arrays or variables (given that is what the functions return anyway). Creating them as functions gives you the flexibility at a later date to replace them with functions that, for example, tweak the data based on more complex formula or otherwise generate or gather the data from other functions or sources.

"But you could just run such a function and replace the variable/array with the output," you cry, but that would preclude you from using gems such as generators (see Chapter 5 if you're not familiar with them) or other similar iterable structures. The code that uses the data is already set to call functions to get it, so you only need to alter the function's implementation in the future (unless you need to add new parameters, of course).

As you look through the functions, you'll notice that you've implemented most of them as closures, with functions "use"ing other functions. One advantage of using closures like this is that it helps retain the immutability of used functions. For instance, if in your calling code you accidentally assign another function (e.g., that always returns zero) to $get_tax_rate, closures that have already been created that use $get_tax_rate will not be affected because closures "close over" or encapsulate the "value" (function) that was assigned to $get_tax_rate at the time the closure was created, not when it is executed.

To simplify the example, I'll omit any error checking or sanitization code (as with most examples in this book), but in the real world it's often worth using "guard" functions to check for valid data coming in from the outside of your carefully tested and wholly pure business logic inner sanctum before you start processing the data. Structures like the Maybe monad can also be used to deal with common failure modes.

So, without further ado, let's look at the code. The first file, shown in Listing 6-1, contains some data for your business logic.

Listing 6-1. business_data.php

```php
<?php

# First let's create core business data.

# Rather than just define arrays, we're going to create functions
# that return arrays. We'll discuss why in the chapter.

# Every sale is either local, within our own country, or beyond

$locations = function () {
  return ['local', 'country', 'global'];
};

# Each category of products that we sell has a different tax rate,
# and that rate varies depending on where our purchaser is located

$rates = function () {
  return [
    'clothes' => ['local' => 0, 'country' => 5, 'global' => 10],
    'books' => ['local' => 0, 'country' => 5, 'global' => 5],
    'cheeses' => ['local' => 20, 'country' => 17.5, 'global' =>2]
  ];
};

# A list of our products, with their category and price

$products = function () {
  return [

    'T-shirt' => [ 'Category' => 'clothes', 'Price' => 15.99 ],
    'Shorts'  => ['Category' => 'clothes', 'Price' => 9.99 ],
    'The Dictionary'  => ['Category' => 'books', 'Price' => 4.99 ],
    'War and Peace' => ['Category' => 'books', 'Price' => 29.45 ],
```

```
    'Camembert'  => ['Category' => 'cheeses', 'Price' => 3.50 ],
    'Brie' => ['Category' => 'cheeses', 'Price' => 7.00 ]

  ];
};

# We only sell in dollars, but we format the prices differently
# depending on the location of the purchaser.

$price_formats = function () {
  return [
    'local' => ['symbol' => '$', 'separator' => '.'],
    'country' => ['symbol' => '$', 'separator' => '.'],
    'global' => ['symbol' => 'USD ', 'separator' => ',']
  ];
};
```

The next file, shown in Listing 6-2, contains some key business logic functions.

Listing 6-2. business_logic.php

```
<?php

# Now we're going to create a set of functions which describe our business
# logic. We're going to keep them as simple as possible, and reference
# other functions within this file where possible to keep a
# "single source of truth" for when we need to update them.

# Load our business data

require('business_data.php');

# Fetch the details of a single product from the list of products

$get_product_details = function ($product) use ($products) {

  return  $products()[$product];

};

# Get the category name from the details of a single product

$get_category = function ($product_details)  {

  return $product_details['Category'];

};

# Get the tax rate for a category of products based on the location
# of the purchaser

$get_tax_rate = function ($category, $location) use ($rates) {
```

```php
    return $rates()[$category][$location];

};

# Get the net (tax exclusive) price of a product by name.

$get_net_price = function ($product) use ($get_product_details) {

    return $get_product_details($product)["Price"];

};

# Roll the above functions together to create a function that gets
# the gross (tax inclusive) price for a certain quantity of products
# based on the location of our purchaser.
# Note that the tax is rounded using the PHP_ROUND_HALF_DOWN constant
# to indicate the particular rounding method.

$get_gross_price = function ($product, $quantity, $location) use
    ($get_net_price, $get_tax_rate, $get_category, $get_product_details)    {

        return round(
                    $get_net_price($product) *
                    $quantity *
                    ( 1 + (
                            $get_tax_rate(
                              $get_category(
                                $get_product_details($product)
                              ),
                              $location)
                            /100
                        )
                    ),
                    2, PHP_ROUND_HALF_DOWN) ;

};

# A function to get the actual amount of tax charged. Note that this doesn't
# simply use the tax rate, as the actual amount charged may differ depending on
# the rounding performed and any future logic added to $get_gross_price.
# Instead we call $get_net_price and $get_gross_price and return the difference.

$get_tax_charged = function ($product, $quantity, $location) use
                            ($get_gross_price, $get_net_price) {

    return $get_gross_price($product, $quantity, $location) -
            ( $quantity * $get_net_price($product) );

};
```

```php
# Finally, a function to format a string to display the price, based
# on the purchasers location.

$format_price = function ($price, $location) use ($price_formats) {

  $format = $price_formats()[$location];

  return $format["symbol"] . str_replace('.',
                                  $format["separator"],
                                  (string) $price
                                  );
};
```

Finally, Listing 6-3 shows a set of common business tasks that use the business logic. In reality, these may be split up over a number of different scripts and systems, although all of them would "require" the same business logic scripts.

Listing 6-3. shopping.php

```php
<?php

# Import our set of pure functions which encapsulate our business logic.

require('business_logic.php');

# Now we can use them in our not so pure, not so functional code, safe in the
# knowledge that they (should) provide us with consistent, correct results
# regardless of what we do to the global or external state here.

# Let's generate a shopping cart of products for a user in Bolivia

$cart = ['Brie' => 3, 'Shorts' => 1, 'The Dictionary' => 2 ];
$user = ["location" => 'global'];

# One common function is to list the contents of the cart. Let's do
# that here

echo "Your shopping cart contains :\n\n";

echo "Item - Quantity - Net Price Each - Total Price inc. Tax\n";
echo "=========================================================\n\n";

foreach ($cart as $product => $quantity) {

  $net_price = $get_net_price($product);

  $total = $get_gross_price($product, $quantity, $user["location"]);

  echo "$product - $quantity - $net_price - $total \n";

};
echo "=========================================================\n\n";
```

```php
# In a confirmation e-mail we may want to just list a (formatted) total price...

$total_price = array_reduce( array_keys($cart),

                # loop through the cart and add gross price for each item

                function ($running_total, $product) use
                ( $user, $get_gross_price, $cart ) {

                    return $running_total +
                        $get_gross_price( $product,
                                        $cart[$product],
                                        $user["location"]);
}, 0);

echo "Thank you for your order.\n";
echo $format_price($total_price, $user["location"]).' will ';
echo "be charged to your card when your order is dispatched.\n\n";

# And on the backend system we may have a routine that keeps details of
# all the tax charged, ready to send to the Government. Let's create a
# summary of the tax for this order.

$tax_summary = array_reduce( array_keys($cart),

    # Loop through each item and add the tax charged to the relevant category

    function ($taxes, $product) use
    ( $user, $get_tax_charged, $cart, $get_category, $get_product_details ) {

        $category = $get_category($get_product_details($product));

        $tax = $get_tax_charged($product, $cart[$product], $user["location"]);

        isset($taxes[$category]) ?
                $taxes[$category] =+ $tax : $taxes[$category] = $tax;

        return $taxes;

}, []);

echo "Tax Summary for this order :\n\n";

var_dump($tax_summary);
```

Listing 6-4 shows the output.

Listing 6-4. shopping-output.txt

```
Your shopping cart contains :

Item - Quantity - Net Price Each - Total Price inc. Tax
=========================================================

Brie - 3 - 7 - 21.42
Shorts - 1 - 9.99 - 10.99
The Dictionary - 2 - 4.99 - 10.48
=========================================================

Thank you for your order.
USD 42,89 will be charged to your card when your order is dispatched.

Tax Summary for this order :

array(3) {
  ["cheeses"]=>
  float(0.42)
  ["clothes"]=>
  float(1)
  ["books"]=>
  float(0.5)
}
```

Structuring your business logic like this makes extending it easier as well. The example is for a fictional U.S.-based retailer (you can tell from the currency symbols!) that sells to the whole world from a single web site. However, after doing some market research, the retailer discovers that it could increase its European sales by crafting a dedicated European web site, pushing sales of Brie (for the cheese-loving French), and dictionaries (because the British can't spel). Given that all the transactions on the new site will fall under the "global" tax rates, they can simplify their code by creating a partial function called $get_eu_tax_rate, fixing the location to global. Extending the logic like this, rather than rewriting it, means that they still get close integration with the rest of their existing back-end systems that use this common business logic, and when they extend their cheese range in the United States to include Monterey Jack, it's simple to promote it to Europeans as the Choix Du Jour for garnishing the modern cheeseburger.

Event-Based Programming

When you are writing PHP-based web pages, your scripts are called by the web server in response to requests from users. These requests are *events*, and you never know when they will come and what pages will be requested, in what order, and from which user. You write your scripts to deal with a single particular page request, and the web server (Apache, Nginx, etc.) deals with managing the full range of incoming events, calling the relevant scripts for each one and returning the output to the correct browser. Your script only "sees" the current request it is being called for and doesn't (for instance) need to work out which of the potentially many concurrent visitors it needs to send the output back to. It doesn't need to keep the state of each script separate from other scripts (or instances of the same script) that may be called before, during, or after its own execution. Your script runs in a simple "top-to-bottom" procedural fashion, and after the event/request is handled, your script is finished. In this scenario, the web server deals with the event-based programming problems, and your life is simple!

PHP, being the versatile language that it is, does let you step out of this comfort zone and write your own event-based scripts. You can write long-running scripts that react to and handle an ongoing set of events, in a similar manner to software like Apache. There are numerous ways to do this, but one of the easiest ways to get started with event-based programming in PHP is to use the PECL "event" extension. This extension is a wrapper for the mature cross-platform libevent library. At its core, libevent provides a way to attach a callback function to events. Events it can respond to include signals, file and network events, timeouts, and any event that can be built on top of one of those base types. One of the event types that libevent supports natively and that the PHP event extension wraps fully is the HTTP event. You'll use HTTP events to write a simple web server that you'll use to perform some math functions so you can see a functional approach to managing events and of course to serve up cute cat pictures like any good web server does.

So, why use functional programming to write event-based programs? The previous description outlines why event-based programming is hard. You don't know what order your callback functions will be called in (i.e., in what order events will arrive at your program), you need to keep events from different users separate, but you still need to manage the state applicable to each user, potentially across multiple events. And you need to do all of this from within the same long-running script (not separate instances that terminate after each event). I'm sure you can envisage why managing such state transitions with global or external sate/variables would quickly become a tangled nightmare to keep your data straight. In contrast, functional programming teaches you to pass state "along the chain" from function call to function call, eschewing the use of mutable or impure external data. Your (functional programming) functions don't need to try to divine whose request/event they are handling or what the state of that users' current session is, they are handed all of this information as their input parameters. For HTTP requests, you can carry such information along a sequence of HTTP requests by encoding the return values of your functions in your HTML output and receiving such values back as input parameters via the URI parameters supplied with each HTTP request. And having small, single-purpose functions makes it easier to reason about what your program will do even when it's not clear in advance which functions will be called in what order.

Two PECL extensions are available for wrapping libevent: the aptly named libevent extension and the newer event extension. I would advise using the latter only because it is more comprehensive than the libevent extension and is still being actively maintained. To use the event extension, you will need to install it using PECL, but first you'll need libevent and its headers installed on your system. The installation steps in Listing 6-5 are for Debian/Ubuntu-based operating systems; instructions for other operating systems can be found in the "Further Reading" section that follows.

Listing 6-5. install_event.txt

```
# Install the libevent library and it header files

sudo apt-get install libevent-2.0-5 libevent-dev

# Ensure that PECL (which comes as part of the PEAR package)
# and the phpize command which PECL needs are installed

sudo apt-get install php-pear php-dev

# Install the event extension

sudo pecl install event

# Finally make the extension available to the PHP CLI binary
# by editing php.ini

sudo nano /etc/php/7.0/cli/php.ini
```

```
# and adding the following line in the section where other .so
# extensions are include

extension=event.so
```

Further Reading

- The event extension in the PHP Manual

    - http://php.net/manual/en/intro.event.php

- Requirements and installation information

    - http://docs.php.net/manual/en/event.setup.php

- Main libevent web site

    - http://libevent.org/

Now that you have libevent and the event extension installed, you can write a program to act as an HTTP server and handle incoming HTTP request events. You'll break this down into two scripts, one that contains your business logic functions and another to set up the server and connect the functions as callbacks to incoming request events. You're going to create some simple math functions (like add() and subtract()) that are mapped to URIs (like /add and /subtract) that operate on a value that is carried along from request to request. Listing 6-6 shows your function's script.

Listing 6-6. server_functions.php

```php
<?php

# We'll create a set of functions that implement the logic that should
# occur in response to the events that we'll handle.

# Use our trusty partial function generator

require('../Chapter 3/partial_generator.php');

# A generic function to output an HTTP header. $req is an object representing
# the current HTTP request, which ensures that our function deals with the
# right request at all times.

$header = function ($name, $value, $req) {

    $req->addHeader ( $name , $value, EventHttpRequest::OUTPUT_HEADER );

};

# We are going to be serving different types of content (html, images etc.)
# so we need to output a content header each time. Let's create a
# partial function based on $header...

$content_header = partial($header, 'Content-Type' );

# and then make it specific for each type of content...
```

```php
$image_header = partial($content_header, "image/jpeg");

$text_header  = partial($content_header, "text/plain; charset=ISO-8859-1");

$html_header = partial($content_header, "text/html; charset=utf-8");

# The following function creates a "buffer" to hold our $content and
# then sends it to the browser along with an appropriate HTTP status
# code (Let's assume our requests always work fine so send 200 for everything).
# Note that it's a pure function right up until we call sendReply. You could
# return the EventBuffer instead, and wrap it all into an IO or Writer monad to
# put the impure sendReply at the end if you wish.

$send_content = function($req, $content) {

    $output = new EventBuffer;

  $output->add($content);

  $req->sendReply(200, "OK", $output);

};

# The input parameters for our maths functions are held in the URI parameters.
# The URI is held in the $req request object as a string. Let's get the
# URI and parse out the parameters into an associative array.

$parse_uri_params = function ($req) {

    $uri = $req->getUri();

    parse_str(

        # Grab just the parameters (everything after the ?)

        substr( $uri, strpos( $uri, '?' ) + 1 ),

        # and parse it into $params array

        $params);

    return $params;

};

# Get the URI "value" parameter

$current_value = function($req) use ($parse_uri_params) {

    return $parse_uri_params($req)["value"];

};
```

```
# Get the URL "amount" parameter

$amount = function($req) use ($parse_uri_params) {

    return $parse_uri_params($req)["amount"];

};

# A function to send the results of one of our maths functions which follow.

$send_sum_results = function($req, $result) use ($html_header, $send_content) {

  # Create some HTML output, with the current result, plus some links
    # to perform more maths functions. Note the uri parameters contain
    # all of the state needed for the function to give a deterministic,
    # reproducable result each time. We also include some links to
    # the other utility functions. When you visit them, note that you
    # can use your browser back button to come back to the maths functions
    # and carry on where you left off, as the parameters the functions
    # need are provided by the URI parameters and no "state" has been
    # altered of lost

    $output = <<<ENDCONTENT

    <p><b>The current value is : $result</b></p>

    <p><a href="/add?value=$result&amount=3">Add 3</a></p>
    <p><a href="/add?value=$result&amount=13">Add 13</a></p>
    <p><a href="/add?value=$result&amount=50">Add 50</a></p>
    <p><a href="/subtract?value=$result&amount=2">Subtract 2</a></p>
    <p><a href="/subtract?value=$result&amount=5">Subtract 5</a></p>
    <p><a href="/multiply?value=$result&amount=2">Multiply by 2</a></p>
    <p><a href="/multiply?value=$result&amount=4">Multiply by 4</a></p>
    <p><a href="/divide?value=$result&amount=2">Divide by 2</a></p>
    <p><a href="/divide?value=$result&amount=3">Divide by 3</a></p>
    <p><a href="/floor?value=$result">Floor</a></p>

    <p><A href="/show_headers">[Show headers]</a> 
    <a href="/really/cute">[Get cat]</a> 
    <a href="/close_server">[Close down server]</a></p>

ENDCONTENT;

  # Send the content header and content.

    $html_header($req);

    $send_content($req, $output);

};
```

```
# These are our key maths functions. Each one operates like a good Functional
# function by only using the values supplied as input parameters, in this
# case as part of $req. We call a couple of helper functions ($current_value
# and $amount) to help extract those values, $req isn't necessarily
# immutable (we could alter values or call methods), but we'll use
# our discipline to keep it so right up until we're ready to send_contents.
# While we don't formally "return" a value, $send_sum_results effectively
# acts a return statement for us. Any return value would simply go back to
# libevent (which is the caller, and it just ignore it).
# If we want to keep to strictly using explicit return statements, we could
# wrap this in another function that does the same as $send_sum_results, (and
# for the same reason wouldn't have a return statement) or we could create an
# Writer monad or similar to gather the results and only output to the browser
# at the end. For this simple example we'll go with using $send_sum_results
# though for simplicity and clarity.

$add = function ($req) use ($send_sum_results, $current_value, $amount) {

  $send_sum_results($req, $current_value($req) + $amount($req) );

};

$subtract = function ($req) use ($send_sum_results, $current_value, $amount) {

  $send_sum_results($req, $current_value($req) - $amount($req) );

};

$multiply = function ($req) use ($send_sum_results, $current_value, $amount) {

  $send_sum_results($req, $current_value($req) * $amount($req) );

};

$divide = function ($req) use ($send_sum_results, $current_value, $amount) {

  $send_sum_results($req, $current_value($req) / $amount($req) );

};

$floor = function ($req) use ($send_sum_results, $current_value) {

  $send_sum_results($req, floor($current_value($req)) );

};

# Now we'll define some utility functions

# Grab the HTTP headers from the current request and return them as an array

$get_input_headers = function ($req) {

    return $req->getInputHeaders();

};
```

```php
# A recursive function to loop through an array of headers and return
# an HTML formatted string

$format_headers = function ($headers, $output = '') use (&$format_headers) {

    # if we've done all the headers, return the $output
    if (!$headers) {

        return $output;

    } else {

        # else grab a header off the top of the array, add it to the
        # $output and recursively call this function on the remaining headers.

        $output .= '<pre>'.array_shift($headers).'</pre>';

        return $format_headers($headers, $output);

    };

};

# Use the function above to format the headers of the current request for
# viewing

$show_headers = function ($req) use ($html_header, $send_content, $format_headers) {

    $html_header($req);

    $send_content($req, $format_headers( $req->getInputHeaders() ) );
};

# Let's handle all requests, so there are no 404's

$default_handler = function ($req) use ($html_header, $send_content) {

    $html_header($req);

    $output = '<h1>This is the default response</h1>';

    $output .= '<p>Why not try <a href="/add?value=0&amount=0">some math</a></p>';

    $send_content($req, $output);

};

# Ensure that there are sufficient supplies of cat pictures available
# in all corners of the Internet

$send_cat = function($req) use ($image_header, $send_content) {
```

```php
    # Note we send a different header so that the browser knows
    # a binary image is coming

    $image_header($req);

    # An impure function, you could alway use an IO monad or

    $send_content($req, file_get_contents('cat.jpg'));
};

# A function to shut down the web server script by visiting a particular URI.

$close_server = function($req, $base) use ($html_header, $send_content) {

    $html_header($req);

    $send_content($req, '<h1>Server is now shutting down</h1>');

    $base->exit();

};
```

Listing 6-7 shows your script that actually runs the HTTP server and connects the earlier functions to the URIs.

Listing 6-7. web_server.php

```php
<?php

# Let's get all of our functions that implement our
# business logic

require('server_functions.php');

# Now we're ready to build up our event framework

# First we create an "EventBase", which is libevent's vehicle for holding
# and polling a set of events.

$base = new EventBase();

# Then we add an EventHttp object to the base, which is the Event
# extension's helper for HTTP connections/events.

$http = new EventHttp($base);

# We'll choose to respond to just GET  HTTP requests

$http->setAllowedMethods( EventHttpRequest::CMD_GET );

# Next we'll tie our functions we created above to specific URIs using
# function callbacks. We've created them all as anonymous/closure functions
```

```
# and so we just bind the variable holding them to the URI. We
# could use named functions if we want, suppling the name in "quotes".
# with the EventHttpRequest object representing the current request as
# the first paramter. If you need other parameters here for your callback,
# you can specify them as an optional third parameter below.

# Our set of maths functions...

$http->setCallback("/add", $add);

$http->setCallback("/subtract", $subtract);

$http->setCallback("/multiply", $multiply);

$http->setCallback("/divide", $divide);

$http->setCallback("/floor", $floor);

# A function to shut down the server, which needs access to the server $base

$http->setCallback("/close_server", $close_server, $base);

# A utility function to explore the headers your browser is sending

$http->setCallback("/show_headers", $show_headers);

# And a compulsory function for all internet connected devices

$http->setCallback("/really/cute", $send_cat);

# Finally we'll add a default function callback to handle all other URIs.
# You could, in fact, just specify this default handler and not those
# above, and then handle URIs as you wish from inside this function using
# it as a router function.

$http->setDefaultCallback($default_handler);

# We'll bind our script to an address and port to enable it to listen for
# connections. In this case, 0.0.0.0 will bind it to the localhost, and
# we'll choose port 12345

$http->bind("0.0.0.0", 12345);

# Then we start our event loop using the loop() function of our base. Our
# script will remain in this loop indefinitely, servicing http requests
# with the functions above, until we exit it by killing the script or,
# more ideally, calling $base->exit() as we do in the close_server()
# function above.

$base->loop();

# We'll only hit this point in the script if some code has called
# $base->exit();

echo "Server has been gracefully closed\n";
```

To start your HTTP server, simply type php web_server.php at the command line. You can now visit http://localhost:12345 in your web browser, and you'll see the default response. Click the link to start using some of the math functions and to access links to the utility functions. Now try opening another browser tab (or indeed another browser) and visiting the same URL; try clicking through some of the math functions and the stunningly cute picture of my cat. Switch between your browser tabs/browsers and check that each page keeps the correct state no matter what you are doing in the other tabs/browsers. Because you're passing state around as input/URL parameters and "return values" in the HTML output, your state follows each separate event flow, and you don't need to explicitly keep track of users and their individual state.

Now, of course, this is a toy problem to illustrate the idea, but ideally you can see how the properties inherent in functional programming can help remove the need for convoluted methods to keep track of state when writing event-based programs. These need not be web servers; any event-based model (a program that responds to system events or file system changes, for example) can benefit from functional-style programming.

Asynchronous PHP

Asynchronous (async) programming is a way of writing code to fully utilize the processor in single-threaded applications (like PHP scripts) by executing code while waiting for external I/O (such as database calls and disk I/O) to complete. For much the same reasons that functional programming is well-suited to event-based programming, it is also a good bet for managing the related complexities of out-of-order processing inherent in async programming. PHP doesn't natively support async programming, so I won't cover it in this book, but there are a couple of libraries that do implement async capabilities, which are detailed next. These libraries are more or less limited to running I/O type functions asynchronously, rather than arbitrary code (which would require multitasking or multithreading capabilities). Facebook's Hack language, an extended but mostly compatible implementation of PHP, has native I/O async capabilities (see the following link), but these aren't compatible with the main PHP VM or any of the PHP libraries. Whichever route you choose, using the functional principles outlined in this book will help you to reason about the execution of your code.

Further Reading

- ReactPHP is perhaps the main event-driven async library for PHP. Initially modeled after NodeJS in the JavaScript world, it is also the base for other async and event libraries.

  - http://reactphp.org

- ReactPHP provides an implementation of Promises, which are based on the JavaScript promise model.

  - http://reactphp.org/promise/

- Hack provides an async interface to optionally execute certain I/O-type operations asynchronously.

  - https://docs.hhvm.com/hack/async/introduction

- Amp is an asynchronous concurrency framework for PHP.

  - http://amphp.org/

- GitHub has a list of resources, code, libraries, and other material related to asynchronous processing in PHP.

  - https://github.com/elazar/asynchronous-php

CHAPTER 7

■ ■ ■

Using Functional Programming in Objected-Oriented and Procedural Applications

So far in this book you've looked at the fundamentals of what functional programming is and how to use it to solve some common programming issues. In this chapter, you'll look at how to put that functional code into your existing or new applications. Specifically, you'll look at the following:

- How to structure a functional application and whether to make it *fully* functional

- How and when to mix and match paradigms like functional and object-oriented programming

By the end of this chapter, I hope you will have the confidence to start exploring or even implementing basic functional strategies within your own applications.

History of PHP Paradigms

To understand where functional programming fits in your application, it's handy to understand where it fits in PHP in general. When it comes to programming paradigms, PHP is a mixed bag, which is both a blessing and a curse. And to understand how PHP got into the shape it is now, you'll first need to understand its history. Back in 1994 when Rasmus Lerdorf first created PHP, it was a purely procedural language. As time went on and PHP became more and more widespread, people started using it for bigger and bigger web-based systems. Bigger systems, particularly those with teams of developers rather than a single coder, demand ever-increasing code discipline, and so in came the academics and professional coders who demanded object-oriented language features. The delivery of OO features began in version 3; however, at the same time, there was a push for more powerful and consistent language syntax on the procedural side, and so version 3 delivered both.

The basic OO features at that stage were derided by many (particularly those coming from other languages like Java and C++), which dissuaded many procedural PHP programmers from trying the OOP capabilities. Proper OO features didn't appear until version 5, with the implementation of a new object model in Zend Engine 2. Even then, object-related syntax and feature support didn't reach the kind you currently have until the later releases in the version 5 series. That, combined with the PHP developers' (perfectly reasonable) reluctance to break backward compatibility, mean that PHP's procedural chops remain finely honed alongside its newer OO features.

© Rob Aley 2017

R. Aley, *Pro Functional PHP Programming*, DOI 10.1007/978-1-4842-2958-3_7

If you look at the "History of PHP" page in the PHP Manual, you won't find a mention of functional programming anywhere. Functional programming, as a concept, has never been part of the formal development road maps for PHP. The fact that you can do (some form of) functional programming in PHP is thanks to people who have spotted elements of it (like closures) in other languages and brought them over to PHP to spice up the procedural and OO models.

All of this means that you can pick and choose your programming paradigm in PHP, and PHP does very little to stand in your way of mixing them together as you see fit. Far from being a cheerleader for functional programming, this book aims to highlight both the benefits and the disadvantages of each paradigm. To that end, the "Further Reading" section covers the downsides of each in more detail.

Further Reading

- The history of PHP in the PHP Manual

    - http://php.net/manual/en/history.php.php

- Limitations of procedural-oriented programming

    - www.extropia.com/tutorials/java/procedural_programming_limits.html

- "All evidence points to OOP being bullshit" by John Barker

    - https://content.pivotal.io/blog/all-evidence-points-to-oop-being-bullshit

- "What are some limitations/disadvantages of functional programming?" response by Tikhon Jelvis

    - https://www.quora.com/What-are-some-limitations-disadvantages-of-functional-programming/answer/Tikhon-Jelvis

PHP Is Not a Functional Language

PHP is not a functional language. Let me say that one more time, just in case it's not clear: PHP is not a functional language. Sure, you can do functional-style programming in PHP. This would be a very short book if you couldn't. But PHP is not a functional language. PHP is a very versatile, almost paradigm-agnostic, general-purpose programming language. But it still isn't a functional language.

You can write your whole program, application, or system using the functional code you've explored in this book. But if you do that, here's what you'll be missing out on:

- Access to libraries and other third-party code written in OO or procedural PHP

- Access to your own existing nonfunctional PHP code

- Unfettered access to I/O (in the ways that PHP makes so easy)

- Support and understanding from other programmers around you (unless they're keen on functional programming too!)

To hone in on I/O in particular, you can use the IO or Writer monad to deal with I/O in a functional way, but this usually means pushing script execution right to the end of the script, and while functional scripts are usually easier to reason about and follow, most people find code flow with monads the opposite. With third-party libraries, you may find that they have nice functions or object methods that you use in a functional style, but (unless you carefully scrutinize and potentially rewrite their code), you can't be sure that the implementation of those functions adhere to the functional principles such as immutability and referential transparency.

My advice? Mix and match the paradigms as you see fit. Functional programming is just another tool in your toolbox; use it where and when it looks like it will provide a solution to the problem at hand. That said, don't go overboard! The best way to keep things straightforward is to segregate your code into blocks of functional and nonfunctional code. An obvious arrangement is to write your business logic, high-performance algorithms, and such in functional code, sandwiching this between impure OO or procedural code to deal with input and output, as demonstrated in Figure 7-1.

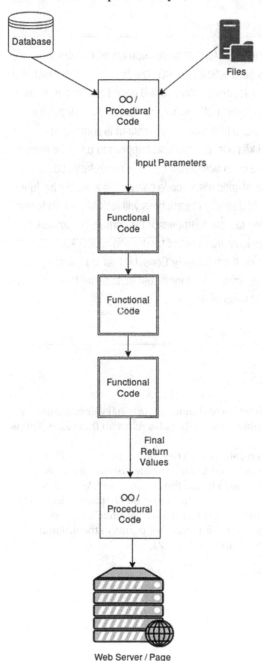

Figure 7-1. *Example of mixed architecture*

With an arrangement like this, you have clean blocks of functional code to reason about and test, and when problems do occur, it's easier to work out where they are likely to be located. When you're faced with updating an existing code base using functional techniques, a good approach is to first identify the sections of code that would fit neatly into the middle of Figure 7-1 and prioritize them first.

This is all good in theory, but things often get messier in the real world, and your code paradigms start to overlap. In the next few sections you'll look at some potential gotchas when mixing OO and procedural code with purely functional code.

■ **Aside**   Don't use monads in PHP. Really, don't use monads in PHP. Monads were popularized by purely functional code that had no other way to deal with potentially impure actions like I/O. PHP is not a purely functional language, and there are plenty of other ways of minimizing the deleterious effects of I/O gone bad. They may seem like a neat trick, the sense of well-being that you feel when you finally "get" monads is nice, and the dopamine rush when your code finally passes your tests and the correct values trickle out of your script is something to cherish. There are times when you'll accidentally write monad-like code, or code that happens to pass the monad laws. And as long as that style is part of your normal coding style or an accidental trait of a necessary code structure, that's OK. But keeping on top of monads-for-the-sake-of-monads as code changes is a headache, junior developers will look at your code and start to cry, and your semitechnically literate boss will look at your code and say, "Back to pure OOP everyone." Keep them as toys, something to wow members of the same or opposite sex, for academic research, or to scare interns, but for heaven's sake keep them out of production code. I know I've introduced them to you, shown you how they work, and mentioned them liberally. Consider that to be like a parent talking to their kids about drugs: you need to make sure your kids know about them, get facts about them from you and not their "friends," and understand them. But you don't want them to use them.

To summarize, don't use monads in PHP.

Objects and Mutability

When you pass a value into a function, you don't want the function to mutate the original value. If it does, it will make it much, much harder to reason about any code going forward that also relies on that value. This is easier said than done when you are passing objects about.

Objects in PHP are not actually stored in variables. When you create a new object using code like `$my_object = new some_class();`, the object isn't actually assigned to the variable. Instead, an object identifier is assigned to the variable, which allows accessing code to locate the actual object. What this means is that if you pass an object variable to a function as a parameter, the value you are passing in is the object identifier, not the object itself. When the code inside the function uses that identifier, it is working with the original object, not a copy (the identifier is a copy but a faithful copy that points to the original object). Let's look at an example of this in action (see Listing 7-1 and Listing 7-2).

Listing 7-1. passing_objects.php

```php
<?php

# Create a class to encapsulate a value

class my_class
{

        # The value we want to encapsulate

    private $value = 0;

        # Constructor to set the value (or default to -1)

        public function __construct($initial_value = -1) {

            $this->value = $initial_value;

        }

        # Method to get the value

    public function get_value() {

        return $this->value;

    }

        # Method to set the value

        public function set_value($new_value) {

        $this->value = $new_value;

    }
}

# Let's create a new object with a value of 20

$my_object = new my_class(20);

# Check the value

var_dump ($my_object->get_value()); # int(20)

# Demonstrate we can mutate the value to 30

$my_object->set_value(30);

var_dump ($my_object->get_value()); # int (30)
```

```php
# Now let's create a function which doubles the value
# of the object. Note that the function parameter
# doesn't have a "&" to indicate it's passed by reference

function double_object ($an_object) {

    # Get the value from $an_object, double it and set it back

    $an_object->set_value( $an_object->get_value() * 2 );

    # return the object

    return $an_object;

}

# Now we call the function on our $my_object object from
# above, and assign the returned object to a new variable

$new_object = double_object($my_object);

# Check that the returned object has double the value (30)
# of the object we passed in as a parameter

var_dump( $new_object->get_value() ); # int(60)

# Let's just check the value on the original object

var_dump( $my_object->get_value()); # int(60)

# It's also changed. Let's var_dump the original object
# and returned object, and check their object reference number
# (look for the number after the #)

var_dump ($my_object); # #1

var_dump ($new_object); # #1

# They're both the same. Just for clarity, create a new
# object from scratch and check it's reference number

$last_object = new my_class();

var_dump ($last_object); # #2
```

Listing 7-2. passing_objects-output.txt

```
int(20)
int(30)
int(60)
int(60)
```

```
object(my_class)#1 (1) {
  ["value":"my_class":private]=>
  int(60)
}
object(my_class)#1 (1) {
  ["value":"my_class":private]=>
  int(60)
}
object(my_class)#2 (1) {
  ["value":"my_class":private]=>
  int(-1)
}
```

So, what do you do when you want to pass objects about as parameters in a bit of functional code? There are several options. The first is easy: don't do it. Do you really need to pass whole objects about? In many cases, you can grab a value (or two) from the object, pass it into a composed stack of functions (which could include methods from the class you are working with), and then set the result of the functional code back into your object. This ensures that your object is not mutated during the functional part of your code. Listing 7-3 shows a simple example.

Listing 7-3. static_methods.php

```php
<?php

# use our trusty compose function

include('../Chapter 3/compose.php');

# The same class as before, but with an added static method

class new_class
{

    private $value = 0;

        public function __construct($initial_value = -1) {

            $this->value = $initial_value;

        }

    public function get_value() {

        return $this->value;

    }

        public function set_value($new_value) {

        $this->value = $new_value;

    }
```

```php
        # a static method to halve the provided value

        public static function halve($value) {

            return $value / 2;

        }

}

# Let's create a new object with an initial value of 25

$my_object = new new_class(73.4);

# Let's stack some math functions together including our
# static method above

$do_math = compose (

                        'acosh',
                        'new_class::halve',
                        'floor'
    );

# Now let's actually do the math. We set the object value
# to the result of $do_math being called on the original value.

$my_object->set_value(

                        $do_math(

                                $my_object->get_value()

                        )

                );

# Show that our object value has been changed. Note that nothing changed
# while we were in our functional (compose) code.

var_dump ( $my_object->get_value() ); # float(2)
```

If your object contains multiple values that your functions need to work with, you can of course extract them first into a data structure like an array.

If you really do need to pass the whole object to your functions, then you will need to clone it first because there is no direct way to pass the contents of an object by value to a function. You will need to ensure that nothing else in your code tries to access those cloned objects, and each function that returns the object will need to clone it before returning for exactly the same reasons. Listing 7-4 demonstrates the mechanics of this process, with the output shown in Listing 7-5.

Listing 7-4. clones.php

```php
<?php

# use our trusty compose function

include('../Chapter 3/compose.php');

# The same class as previously

class my_class
{

    private $value = 0;

        public function __construct($initial_value = -1) {

            $this->value = $initial_value;

        }

    public function get_value() {

        return $this->value;

    }

        public function set_value($new_value) {

        $this->value = $new_value;

    }

}

# A function to triple the value of the object

$triple_object = function ($an_object) {

    # First clone it to make sure we don't mutate the object that
    # $an_object refers to

    $cloned_object = clone $an_object;

    # Then set the value to triple the current value

    $cloned_object->set_value( $cloned_object->get_value() * 3 );

    # and return the new object

    return $cloned_object;

};
```

```
# A function to multiply the value of the object by Pi.
# Again we clone the object first and return the mutated clone

$multiply_object_by_pi = function ($an_object) {

    $cloned_object = clone $an_object;

    $cloned_object->set_value( $cloned_object->get_value() * pi() );

    return $cloned_object;

};

# Let's create an object encapsulating the value 10.

$my_object = new my_class(10);

# We'll compose the above functions together

$more_math = compose(

                                    $triple_object,
                                    $multiply_object_by_pi,
                                    $triple_object

    );

# and then call that composition on our object.

var_dump ( $more_math($my_object) );

# Let's check our original object remains unchanged

var_dump ($my_object);
```

Listing 7-5. clones-output.txt

```
object(my_class)#4 (1) {
  ["value":"my_class":private]=>
  float(282.74333882308)
}
object(my_class)#3 (1) {
  ["value":"my_class":private]=>
  int(10)
}
```

Objects #1 and #2 are the closure objects that hold the $triple_object and $multiply_object_by_pi functions. Object #3 is the original object, and object #4 is the returned object. The cloned objects in each function exist only while the variable $cloned_object refers to them. As soon as the function is returned, $cloned_object (like all variables in the scope of a function) is destroyed and PHP automatically removes objects that are no longer referred to. Thus, the #4 identifier is freed to be used by the object that was created by calling the $more_math function (although it too would have been destroyed after the var_dump statement as it is not assigned to any variable).

As you can see from the previous code, it can get cumbersome to do this, and the type of cloning that you are doing is a "shallow" copy, so there are limitations depending on how your class/object is structured. If you have implemented a __clone method for other purposes, note that it would also be automatically used in these circumstances. And if another object is accessed by methods in your object, cloning it will *not* clone the other object. For these reasons, I advise you to keep your functional code separate from your objects, at least where value passing is concerned.

As a final note, it's worth mentioning that PHP resource variables (such as file pointers and database handles) are, like objects, just references to the external resource. As with objects, this means that when you pass them into a function as a parameter, the actual resource is not copied, just the variable value. You've already looked at why resources like files are considered to be external state and can introduce side effects into your function. However, if you were thinking that a particular resource was stable and guaranteed enough for your particular purposes (for instance, an output file for logging), do consider that the resource being pointed to could be changed from under your feet by another part of the script because your variable is pointing to a shared resource, rather than your own distinct copy.

Further Reading

- Objects and references in the PHP Manual, outlining the relationship between the object variable and object itself

    - http://php.net/manual/en/language.oop5.references.php

- Object cloning in the PHP Manual, detailing the level to which objects are cloned by the clone keyword

    - http://php.net/manual/en/language.oop5.cloning.php

Immutable Data with Objects

Having looked at why objects are inherently mutable in some senses, let's now look at the other side of the coin and see how objects can help you keep other data structures immutable.

As I discussed earlier in the book, the only real immutable construct that PHP has are constants, declared using define or const. There are some drawbacks, though. Only scalars and, recently, arrays can be defined as constants; objects cannot. Constants are also defined globally (like superglobals) rather than in normal variable scope, which I've talked about avoiding previously because of it being considered external state that you can't reason about (and therefore a side effect of your functions). It may not seem much of a problem in this case because each constant is immutable once it's defined and so you can rely on its value. However, consider that the define statement allows you to conditionally create constants and set their value based on variables or other calculated values, rather than a hard-coded value. This means you cannot rely on the constant having a value at all, let alone to an expected value, so if it isn't passed in as one of the parameters of your function, you can't reliably reason about the output of your function.

One way around these issues is to create a class that encapsulates values and forcibly keeps them constant (or unmutated). An object of such a class can be constructed over a given value and then can ensure that the value doesn't get changed during the lifetime of the object by eschewing methods such as setters. As a normal object variable, the usual variable scoping rules will apply. The concerns expressed in the previous section about passing objects around are less applicable here as you're deliberately minimizing the mutability of the object.

So, let's look at a way of creating a constant array as an immutable object (see Listing 7-6 and Listing 7-7).

Listing 7-6. const_array.php

```php
<?php

# Create a class to represent an immutable array

# Make the class "final" so that it can't be extended to add
# methods to mutate our array

final class const_array {

  # Our array property, we use a private property to prevent
  # outside access

  private $stored_array;

  # Our constructor is the one and only place that we set the value
  # of our array. We'll use a type hint here to make sure that we're
  # getting an array, as it's the only "way in" to set/change the
  # data, our other methods can be sure they are then only dealing
  # with an array type

  public function __construct(array $an_array) {

    # PHP allows us to call the __construct method of an already created
    # object whenever we want as if it was a normal method. We
    # don't want this, as it would allow our array to be over written
    # with a new one, so we'll throw an exception if it occurs

    if (isset($this->stored_array)) {

        throw new BadMethodCallException(
                'Constructor called on already created object'
            );

    };

    # And finally store the array passed in as our immutable array.

    $this->stored_array = $an_array;

  }

  # A function to get the array

  public function get_array() {

        return $this->stored_array;

  }
```

```php
# We don't want people to be able to set additional properties on this
# object, as it de facto mutates it by doing so. So we'll throw an
# exception if they try to

public function __set($key,$val) {

    throw new BadMethodCallException(
            'Attempted to set a new property on immutable class.'
        );

}

# Likewise, we don't want people to be able to unset properties, so
# we'll do the same again. As it happens, we don't have any public
# properties, and the methods above stop the user adding any, so
# it's redundant in this case, but here for completeness.

public function __unset($key) {

            throw new BadMethodCallException(
                    'Attempted to unset a property on immutable object.'
                );

}

}

# Let's create a normal array

$mutable_array = ["country" => "UK", "currency" => "GBP", "symbol" => "£"];

# and create an const_array object from it

$immutable_array = new const_array($mutable_array);

var_dump ($immutable_array);

# Let's mutate our original array

$mutable_array["currency"] = "EURO";

# our const_array is unaffected

var_dump ($immutable_array);

# We can read the array values like normal

foreach ( $immutable_array->get_array() as $key => $value) {

    echo "Key [$key] is set to value [$value] \n\n";

};
```

```php
# And use dereferencing to get individual elements

echo "The currency symbol is ". $immutable_array->get_array()["symbol"]."\n\n";

# Need to copy it? Just clone it like any other object, and the methods
# which make it immutable will be cloned too.

$new_array = clone $immutable_array;

var_dump ($new_array);

# The following operations aren't permitted though, and will throw exceptions

# $immutable_array->stored_array = [1,2,3];
#    BadMethodCallException: Attempted to set a new property on immutable class

# $immutable_array->__construct([1,2,3]);
#    BadMethodCallException: Constructor called on already created object

# unset($immutable_array->get_array);
#    BadMethodCallException: Attempted to unset a property on immutable object.

# $immutable_array->new_prop = [1,2,3];
#     BadMethodCallException: Attempted to set a new property on immutable class

# $test = new const_array();
#    TypeError: Argument 1 passed to const_array::__construct()
#    must be of the type array, none given

# class my_mutable_array extends const_array {
#
#    function set_array ($new_array) {
#
#        $this->stored_array = $new_array;
#
#    }
#
# };
#    Fatal error:  Class my_mutable_array may not inherit from final
#    class (const_array)

# Unfortunately, there is no practical way to stop us overwriting the object
# completely, either by unset()ing it or by assigning a new value to the
# object variable, such as by creating a new const_array on it

$immutable_array = new const_array([1,2,3]);

var_dump($immutable_array); # new values stored
```

Listing 7-7. const_array-output.txt

```
object(const_array)#1 (1) {
  ["stored_array":"const_array":private]=>
  array(3) {
    ["country"]=>
    string(2) "UK"
    ["currency"]=>
    string(3) "GBP"
    ["symbol"]=>
    string(2) "£"
  }
}
object(const_array)#1 (1) {
  ["stored_array":"const_array":private]=>
  array(3) {
    ["country"]=>
    string(2) "UK"
    ["currency"]=>
    string(3) "GBP"
    ["symbol"]=>
    string(2) "£"
  }
}
Key [country] is set to value [UK]

Key [currency] is set to value [GBP]

Key [symbol] is set to value [£]

The currency symbol is £

object(const_array)#2 (1) {
  ["stored_array":"const_array":private]=>
  array(3) {
    ["country"]=>
    string(2) "UK"
    ["currency"]=>
    string(3) "GBP"
    ["symbol"]=>
    string(2) "£"
  }
}
object(const_array)#3 (1) {
  ["stored_array":"const_array":private]=>
  array(3) {
    [0]=>
    int(1)
    [1]=>
    int(2)
    [2]=>
    int(3)
  }
}
```

You can see at the end that it's not entirely immutable; you can overwrite the object variable completely with a new value or object. You *could* add a __destruct method to the class, which throws an exception if the object is destroyed (by being unset or overwritten), but this has two issues. First, when your script terminates, all objects are destroyed and so the exception will be thrown at that point each time your script runs, which may be a problem if you have other destructors on other objects that then don't get called. Second, as I described earlier, object variables are just references to the actual objects. This means if you create one of these immutable objects as $a and then do $b = $a and finally unset($a), your __destruct method won't fire as the actual object still lives on as it is referred to by $b. For these reasons, throwing an exception on __destruct probably isn't pragmatic in most cases. Nevertheless, creating *mostly* immutable objects like this can be a useful way to prevent accidental mutation of values in most kinds of data structures, including objects themselves.

Object Properties As External State

Object methods are functions, which is great, and you can use them as such in your functional compositions. Objects also have properties (values), which are encapsulated into the object. Encapsulation is fine as a concept; you've looked at how it helps in closures where you encapsulate a value into your scope through the use clause on your functions. But an object property isn't the same as a value that is pulled into a closure function; it is only internal to the *object* and not the individual method. Sure, private properties are accessible only to the methods within the object, but *any* method (private or public) within the object can access and alter the property. Effectively, the property is in a "global" type scope within the class, at least as far as the methods are concerned, so you should be able to see why this can be a problem when using them in functional programming. The example that follows demonstrates how a property can effectively become external state, and when you don't explicitly pass it in as a parameter to your function (method) calls, you can't always reason about the output the function will give you for a particular input. See Listing 7-8 and Listing 7-9.

Listing 7-8. properties.php

```php
<?php

# Get our compose function
require '../Chapter 3/compose.php';

# This class will provide a set of methods to work with tax

class tax_functions {

  # Store the rate of tax

  private $tax_rate;

  # Our constructor sets the tax rate initially

  public function __construct($rate) {

    $this->tax_rate = $rate;

  }
```

```php
  # Provide a method to set the tax rate at any point

  public function set_rate($rate) {

    $this->tax_rate = $rate;

  }

  # A method to add tax at the $tax_rate to the $amount

  public function add_tax($amount) {

    return $amount * (1 + $this->tax_rate / 100);

  }

  # A method to round the $amount down to the nearest penny

  public function round_to($amount) {

    return floor($amount * 100) / 100;

  }

  # A function to format the $amount for display

  public function display_price($amount) {

    return '£'.$amount.' inc '.$this->tax_rate.'% tax';

  }

}

# So let's create an object for our program containing the
# methods, with the tax rate set at 10%

$funcs = new tax_functions(10);

# Now let's compose our methods into a flow that adds tax, rounds
# the figure and then formats it for display.

# Note that to pass a method of an object as a callable, you need
# to give an array of the object and method name. If you are using
# static class methods, you can use the class::method notation instead

$add_ten_percent = compose (

    [$funcs, 'add_tax'],

    [$funcs, 'round_to'],
```

```
    [$funcs, 'display_price']

  );

# We've composed our $add_ten_percent function, but we may not want to use it
# until much later in our script.

# In the mean-time, another programmer inserts the following line in our
# code in between...

$funcs->set_rate(-20);

# and then we try to use our $add_ten_percent function to add
# tax to 19.99, hopefully getting the answer £21.98 inc 10% tax

var_dump( $add_ten_percent(19.99) ); # £15.99 inc -20% tax
```

Listing 7-9. properties-output.txt

```
string(20) "£15.99 inc -20% tax"
```

As you can see, object properties can be considered external state for your functions. The side effect in this example caused by someone changing the property value (albeit in the very contrived and obvious example!) outside of your function flow gave you a result you didn't expect.

So, what can you do about this? There are several strategies.

- Don't use properties! Wrap values up into functions/methods that return the value.

- Use const to declare properties as constants where possible.

- Use static class methods rather than instantiated objects; then there are no properties or $this to worry about.

In short, treat object properties in the same way (or with the same caution) that you would any other state that is external to your functions.

Inline Impurities

Earlier you looked at how to structure your programs so that you separate problematic impure sections of code from your sections of functional code. You also looked earlier in the book at monads, which allow you to neatly separate these impurities (typically pushing execution to the end of the code definition). From a pragmatic point of view, both of these methods can be problematic. Monads are complex to write and work with. And structuring code to separate I/O from the functional code can be undesirable, for instance, when you need to log data or update a user on progress in a long-running script.

One possible solution (which will get the functional purists screaming) are pass-through type functions. These are functions that you can compose into your normal chain of functions, which do the following:

- Take the return value from the previous function as its parameter

- Do some impure actions (e.g., logging)

- Return the original parameter (unmutated) as its return value

The key here is that the function is not just referentially transparent but completely transparent to the chain of functions. So, it could be added or removed anywhere in a chain of functions at any time without affecting the output of the chain.

Listing 7-10 shows an example of logging as you go, using a wrapper function called $transparent to create a transparent version of the impure logging function. Listing 7-11 shows the output.

Listing 7-10. transparent.php

```php
<?php

# Grab our compose function

require('../Chapter 3/compose.php');

# Define some math functions

$add_two = function ( $a ) {

        return $a + 2;

};

$triple = function ( $a ) {

    return $a * 3;

};

# Now we're going to create a "dirty" function to do some logging.

$log_value = function ( $value ) {

    # Do our impure stuff.

    echo "Impure Logging : $value\n";

    # Oops, we mutated the parameter value...

    $value = $value * 234;

    # ...and returned it even more mutated

    return $value.' is a number';

};

# Now we're going to create a higher-order function which returns a
# wrapped function which executes our impure function but returns
# the original input parameter rather than any output from our impure
# function. Note that we must pass $value to $impure_func by value and
# not by reference (&) to ensure it doesn't mess with it. Also see
# the sections on the mutability of objects if you pass those through,
```

183

```
# as the same concerns will apply here.

$transparent = function ($impure_func) {

    return function ($value) use ($impure_func) {

            $impure_func($value);

            return $value;

    };

};

# Compose the math functions together, with the $log_value impure function
# made transparent by our wrapper function

$do_sums = compose(
            $add_two,
            $transparent($log_value),
            $triple,
            $transparent($log_value)
    );

# We should get the expected result

var_dump( $do_sums(5) ); # 21
```

Listing 7-11. transparent-output.txt

```
Impure Logging : 7
Impure Logging : 21
int(21)
```

A key point to note is that the $transparent wrapper function doesn't make the $log_value function pure. The impure function can still affect the code by throwing exceptions or errors, and while you can reason about your functional code, ignoring the impure function for the most part, you can't (necessarily) reason about the impure function itself. However, it is a useful tool for minimizing the potential impact of impure functions that, for pragmatic reasons, you want to include midstream in your code. It is most suitable for performing output, as typically the main reason for doing input is to get values to process in your functions, which this method does not permit. Figure 7-2 shows how such a transparent function can fit into the normal flow of mixed functional and nonfunctional code.

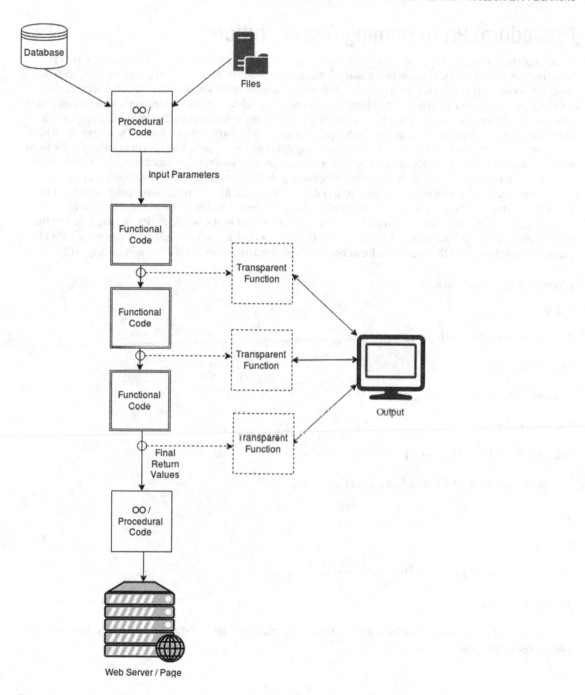

Figure 7-2. *Mixed architecture with transparent functions*

Procedural Programming Considerations

Mixing functional programming with procedural programming is less problematic usually; after all, most of the syntax and constructs you use in functional programming are borrowed from standard procedural code. As described previously in this chapter, it's worth keeping the two separate where possible; however, with the fewer mutability concerns you looked at with objects, it's common to see chunks of procedural code wrapped up inside functions rather than bookending it. If you do this, just keep half an eye on what you're doing with state external to the function, and try not to let it affect your functions' return value. You'll most commonly see procedural code wrapped into a function when it's "necessary" (read: pragmatic) to do things such as output or writing to file from within a flow of functions. Finally, always remember that just because you're using functions in your procedural code, it doesn't necessarily mean you're writing functional code (or mutating functions such as array_walk).

When you need to mix existing procedural code in, you can include or require scripts and treat them as a kind of function. When you include or require a file, PHP executes that script in the current scope (e.g., global or function scope). If you add a return value statement to the script, PHP will return that as the return value of the include or require statement. This means that, if you're careful, you can wrap a file of procedural code up into the scope of a function. Consider the procedural code shown in Listing 7-12.

Listing 7-12. procedural.php

```php
<?php

# This is some typical procedural code

echo ("a is $a\n");

$number = $a + 5;

$number = $number * 2;

for ($i = 0; $i < 5; $i++) {

    echo "We're doing procedural stuff here\n";

};

$b = 50;

# Note the addition of a return statement.

return $number;
```

Now consider Listing 7-13, which pulls in the procedural file twice but does it in slightly different ways. Listing 7-14 shows the output.

Listing 7-13. procedural2.php

```php
<?php

# First set some variables in global scope

$a = 25;
$b = 0;

# Do a simple require of the file.

$return_value =  require "procedural.php";

var_dump ( $return_value ); #60 - the script operated on our $a value of 25
var_dump ( $a ); # 25
var_dump ( $b ); # 50 - the script has mutated $b in the global scope

# Reset $b

$b = 0;

# This function executes the file as if it were a function, within the
# scope of the function. You can pass in a set of parameters as an array,
# and the extract line creates variables in the function scope which
# the code in the file can access. Finally, it requires the file and
# returns the files return value as its own.

$file_as_func = function ($filename, $params) {

        extract ($params);

        return require $filename;

};

# We'll call it on our procedural.php file, with a couple of parameters
# that have the same name but different values to our global $a and $b

var_dump ( $file_as_func( 'procedural.php', ['a'=>50, 'b'=>100] ) ); # 110
# this clearly operated on our parameter "a" and not the global $a

var_dump ( $a ); # 25
var_dump ( $b ); # 0 - unchanged this time
```

Listing 7-14. procedural2-output.txt

```
a is 25
We're doing procedural stuff here
We're doing procedural stuff here
We're doing procedural stuff here
We're doing procedural stuff here
We're doing procedural stuff here
int(60)
int(25)
int(50)
a is 50
We're doing procedural stuff here
We're doing procedural stuff here
We're doing procedural stuff here
We're doing procedural stuff here
We're doing procedural stuff here
int(110)
int(25)
int(0)
```

As you can see, this method provides you with a handy way to limit the scope of a section of procedural code but still push data in in a parameterized way and draw a return value back out. This doesn't particularly increase your ability to reason about the procedural code or limit the scope of many types of side effects, but it does minimize the chances of some kinds of errors and helps you to mentally compartmentalize the code.

Summary

You've looked at various methods and pitfalls when mixing coding paradigms but also explored why it's often a good idea to find a place within your application for functional code, rather than trying to construct completely functional code bases. PHP is a pragmatic language, so be a pragmatic PHP programmer!

CHAPTER 8

■ ■ ■

Using Helper Libraries in Your Application

So far in this book you've mostly seen how to write your own functional code from scratch (although you did use a couple of libraries in the monad sections). In this chapter, you'll look in more depth at some of the more popular libraries available to help you turn your applications into functional powerhouses. These can help you reduce development time, implement tricky or extensive functions, or marshal your code into a consistent style.

How to Choose a Library

Unfortunately, there is no single go-to function library to recommend in PHP. As you've discovered, unlike some other languages, PHP has no formal thoughts on functional programming and how to structure it, so the functional libraries I'll cover encompass different ways of implementing functional structures and procedures. Which you choose to use in your own projects will depend on your own coding style, your general level of PHP experience, and, in some cases, which libraries provide the particular constructs you would like to use. As you look at each library in turn, I'll comment on any particular strengths or weaknesses it has; you'll look at some sample code; and I'll list the official downloads, web sites, and documentation for that library. The following are aspects of each library you may want to explore before settling on one:

- Does the library contain all the functions you need?

- Is the library still maintained? (This may matter less if it is compatible with current PHP versions and is stable.)

- Are the functions you need well implemented (consistent, performant, extensible) in this library?

- Are features such as autocurrying present (if you need them)?

- How "pure" is the library?

That last item is worthy of further explanation. Many of the libraries available take the pragmatic approach to impure, side-effect-inducing operations like file I/O that I've been advocating and simply partition them off into separate functions. Others strictly enforce side-effect-free code and implement their own takes on strict typing and immutable values. Make sure you are happy with the level of functional purity your library imposes (or doesn't) before you build your app around it.

© Rob Aley 2017
R. Aley, *Pro Functional PHP Programming*, DOI 10.1007/978-1-4842-2958-3_8

Pick Libraries Apart

It's often less than ideal to use a whole library for a single function, wasting resources by including the whole code base just to use a small part of it. Functional programming libraries, if they're built in the functional way you've looked at in this book, are often composed of small, single-purpose, composable functions. Assuming you are happy the library is at a stable release point, dive into the source code, pull out the function you need, and paste/reimplement it into your code (respecting any copyrights, of course!). That said, if you're expecting your project to grow to use many more functions or the library is not yet stable, the overhead of including (and updating) the library may be worth it.

Libraries Based on Ramda

Ramda is a popular JavaScript library for functional programming. The following PHP libraries are inspired by features and syntax of the Ramda library.

Pramda

- *Download*: https://github.com/kapolos/pramda

- *Documentation*: https://github.com/kapolos/pramda#pramda

- *Key points*: Pramda features extensive lazy evaluation and autocurrying. The documentation gives a good basic introduction to functional programming concepts using the library but has limited documentation of the functions provided.

- *Example code*: In Listing 8-1, you're going to reprise your Shakespeare analysis functions to grab three long sentences containing the word *hero*. Note that the library functions are exposed as static methods of the P class (e.g., P::compose). To use the library, simply require it or install it via Composer and require the autoloader. Listing 8-2 shows the output.

Listing 8-1. pramda-example.php

```php
<?php

# Require the library

require('pramda/src/pramda.php');

# Start timing

$start_time = microtime(true);

# The same $match_word function

$match_word = function($word, $str) {

    return preg_match("/[^a-z]${word}[^a-z]/i", $str);

};
```

```
# we'll replace str_len with a composition of P::size and str_split.
# it provides no advantage here, other than to demostrate the composition
# of functions (and the fact that there's more than one way to skin a cat).
# Note that Pramda's compose method operates "right to left", i.e. it
# executes functions in the opposite order to the compose function
# we've used up to this point. Also note that we call the composed function
# immediately upon creation on the $str.

$longer_than = function($len, $str) {

    return P::compose(
                        'P::size',
                        'str_split'
                      )($str) > $len;

};

# Create a function to get lines with the word hero in. Pramda doesn't have
# a simple partial function, so instead we curry the function.

$match_hero = P::curry2($match_word)('hero');

# Ditto with a function to get lines with more than 60 chars

$over_sixty = P::curry2($longer_than)(60);

# Pramda's own functions are mostly auto-currying (where it make sense),
# and so we can simply call the P::filter method (similar to array_filter)
# with just a callback, which creates a partial/curried function that
# just needs an array to be called with. We don't need to explicitly
# call a currying function on it.

$filter_hero = P::filter($match_hero);

$filter_sixty = P::filter($over_sixty);

$first_three = P::slice(0,3);

# Now we'll compose these together. Note that we use P::pipe and not P::compose,
# as mentioned above P::compose operates right-to-left, whereas it's easier
# to read left-to-right (or top-to-bottom as we've laid the code out here).
# If you look at the Pramda source code, P::pipe simply reverses the arguments
# and calls P::compose on them!

$three_long_heros = P::pipe(
                            'P::file', //lazy file reader
                            $filter_hero,
                            $filter_sixty,
                            $first_three
                        );
```

```
# We call the composed function in the normal way

$result = $three_long_heros('../Chapter 5/all_shakespeare.txt');

print_r($result);

echo 'Time taken : '.(microtime(true) - $start_time);
```

Listing 8-2. pramda-example-output.txt

```
Array
(
    [0] =>      Enter DON PEDRO, DON JOHN, LEONATO, FRIAR FRANCIS, CLAUDIO, BENEDICK, HERO,
BEATRICE, and Attendants

    [1] =>      Sweet Hero! She is wronged, she is slandered, she is undone.

    [2] =>      Think you in your soul the Count Claudio hath wronged Hero?

)
Time taken : 1.4434311389923
```

As you can see, the output sentences are the same as those you got in Chapter 5. In Listing 8-3, you'll do some work on a restaurant menu (because I'm getting hungry again) to see some more of the functions available to work with arrays. Listing 8-4 shows the output.

Listing 8-3. pramda-example2.php

```php
<?php

# Get the library

require('pramda/src/pramda.php');

# Define our menu data

$menu = [

    [   'Item' => 'Apple Pie',
        'Category' => 'Dessert',
        'Price' => 4.99,
        'Ingredients' => ['Apples' => 3, 'Pastry' => 1, 'Magic' => 100]
    ],

    [   'Item' => 'Strawberry Ice Cream',
        'Category' => 'Dessert',
        'Price' => 2.22,
        'Ingredients' => ['Strawberries' => 20, 'Milk' => 10, 'Sugar' => 200]
    ],

    [   'Item' => 'Chocolate and Strawberry Cake',
        'Category' => 'Dessert',
```

```
        'Price' => 5.99,
        'Ingredients' => ['Chocolate' => 4, 'Strawberries' => 5, 'Cake' => 4]
    ],

    [   'Item' => 'Cheese Toasty',
        'Category' => 'Main Courses',
        'Price' => 3.45,
        'Ingredients' => ['Cheese' => 5, 'Bread' => 2, 'Butter' => 6]
    ]
];

# Let's get a list of all the distinct ingredients used in the menu

$all_ingredients = P::pipe(

                                            # get just the ingredient array from
                                            each element

                                            P::pluck('Ingredients'),

                                            # reduce them into a single array

                                            P::reduce('P::merge', []), #

                                            # grab just the keys (the ingredient
                                            names)
                                            # which will be unique due to the
                                            merge above

                                            'array_keys'
                                    );

var_dump( $all_ingredients($menu) );

# This time we want to count the quantity of fruit used in our menu, if
# we were making one of each dish

$fruit = ['Apples' => true, 'Strawberries' => true, 'Plums' => true];

# A function to get only items who contain fruit

$get_only_fruit = function($item) use ($fruit) {

        # P::prop returns an array element with a particular key, in this
        # case the element holding an array of Ingredients, from which
        # we get the elements which intersect with the keys in $fruit

        return array_intersect_key(P::prop('Ingredients', $item), $fruit);

};
```

```
$count_fruit = P::pipe ( # compose a function which...

                                     P::map( # ... maps a function onto the input
                                     which

                                             P::pipe(

                                                     $get_only_
                                                     fruit, # gets
                                                     the fruits and

                                                     'P::sum' #
                                                     sums the
                                                     quantities

                                                     ) # for each
                                                     element/item

                                     ),

                                     'P::sum' # ...and then sums all the quantities

                             );

var_dump( $count_fruit($menu) ); #28 (3 apples, 20 strawberries, 5 strawberries)

# Now let's say we want to get a dessert menu, ordered by price,
# starting with the most expensive to increase our profits

$dessert_menu = P::pipe(

                                 # First, sort the data by price

                                 P::sort( P::prop('Price') ),

                                 # Reverse the results so the most expensive is
                                 first

                                 'P::reverse',

                                 # Filter the results so that we only have
                                 # desserts

                                 P::filter(

                                     function ($value, $key) {

                                                 return P::contains
                                                 ('Dessert', $value);

                                     }

                                 ),
```

```
                            # P::filter returns a generator, but because we
                            need
                            # to iterate over it twice below, we need to
                            convert
                            # to an array first

                            'P::toArray',

                            # Now let's pick out just the information we
                            want to
                            # display in our menu

                            function ($items) {

                                    # Get an array of Item names to use
                                    as keys,
                                    # and an array of Prices to use as
                                    values,
                                    # and array_combine them into a
                                    single array.
                                    # Again, P:pluck returns a
                                    generator, we want
                                    # an array.

                                    return array_combine(

                                            P::toArray( P::pluck
                                            ('Item',$items) ),

                                            P::toArray( P::pluck
                                            ('Price',$items) )

                                    );

                            }

    );

print_r( $dessert_menu($menu) );
```

Listing 8-4. pramda-example2-output.txt

```
array(11) {
  [0]=>
  string(6) "Apples"
  [1]=>
  string(6) "Pastry"
  [2]=>
  string(5) "Magic"
  [3]=>
  string(12) "Strawberries"
  [4]=>
  string(4) "Milk"
```

```
  [5]=>
  string(5) "Sugar"
  [6]=>
  string(9) "Chocolate"
  [7]=>
  string(4) "Cake"
  [8]=>
  string(6) "Cheese"
  [9]=>
  string(5) "Bread"
  [10]=>
  string(6) "Butter"
}
int(28)
Array
(
    [Chocolate and Strawberry Cake] => 5.99
    [Apple Pie] => 4.99
    [Strawberry Ice Cream] => 2.22
)
```

Phamda

- *Download*: https://github.com/mpajunen/phamda

- *Documentation*: http://phamda.readthedocs.io/en/latest/

- *Key points*: Phamda is similar to Pramda (aside from the single-character difference in names!). For many tasks, though, Phamda is faster than Pramda, and it does offer some additional functions that Pramda doesn't yet.

- *Example code*: In Listing 8-5, you'll use the menu data again and explore some of the functions that Pramda doesn't have, such as ifElse, not, and evolve. To use the library, simply require it as you do here or install it via Composer. Listing 8-6 shows the output.

Listing 8-5. phamda-example.php

```php
<?php

# Load via composer, or require the four files below

require('phamda/src/CoreFunctionsTrait.php');
require('phamda/src/Exception/InvalidFunctionCompositionException.php');
require('phamda/src/Collection/Collection.php');
require('phamda/src/Phamda.php');

use Phamda\Phamda as P;

# Same data as before

$menu = [
```

```
    [   'Item' => 'Apple Pie',
        'Category' => 'Dessert',
        'Price' => 4.99,
        'Ingredients' => ['Apples' => 3, 'Pastry' => 1, 'Magic' => 100]
    ],

    [   'Item' => 'Strawberry Ice Cream',
        'Category' => 'Dessert',
        'Price' => 2.22,
        'Ingredients' => ['Strawberries' => 20, 'Milk' => 10, 'Sugar' => 200]
    ],

    [   'Item' => 'Chocolate and Strawberry Cake',
        'Category' => 'Dessert',
        'Price' => 5.99,
        'Ingredients' => ['Chocolate' => 4, 'Strawberries' => 5, 'Cake' => 4]
    ],

    [   'Item' => 'Cheese Toasty',
        'Category' => 'Main Courses',
        'Price' => 3.45,
        'Ingredients' => ['Cheese' => 5, 'Bread' => 2, 'Butter' => 6]
    ]
];

# A function to mark an item as a "special" if it's price is over 5. The
# Phamda functions we use here are :
# P::ifElse - If the first parameter is true, call the second parameter, else
#    call the third
# P::lt - If the first parameter (5) is less than the second, then return true
#    Note that due to auto currying the $price will be supplied as the second
#    parameter, which is why we use lt rather than gt
# P::concat - add the "Special: " string to the price, (called if P::lt returns
#       true)
# P::identity - the identity function returns the value passed in, so if P::lt
#    returns false this is called, and the price is returned unchanged.
#
# Note that we add ($price) on the end to execute the function straight away

$specials = function ($price) {

        return P::ifElse(P::lt(5), P::concat('Special: '), P::identity())($price);

};

# A function to format the menu item for our menu

$format_item = P::pipe(
                                            # Get just the fields that we want for the
                                            menu
```

```
                                        P::pick(['Item','Price']),

                                          # "Evolve" those fields, by applying
                                          callbacks to them.
                                          # Item is made into uppercase letters, and
                                          Price
                                          # is passed through our $specials function
                                          above
                                          # to add Special: to any item that costs
                                          over 5

                                          P::evolve(['Item'=>'strtoupper',
                                          'Price'=>$specials])

                                          );

# A function to parse our menu data, filter out non-desserts,
# and format the remaining items

$new_dessert_menu = P::pipe(

                                        # It would be more robust to use
                                        P::contains('Dessert')
                                        # on the P::prop('Category') lest we introduce
                                        # entrées at a later date, but for now to
                                        demonstrate
                                        # P::not and the scope of P::contains, we'll do
                                        this:

                                        P::filter( P::not ( P::contains('Main Courses') ) ),

                                        # Map the $format_item function above onto the
                                        remaining
                                        # (hopefully only Dessert) items

                                        P::map($format_item)

);

# Finally, create our menu

print_r( $new_dessert_menu( $menu ) );
```

Listing 8-6. phamda-example-output.txt

```
Array
(
    [0] => Array
        (
            [Item] => APPLE PIE
            [Price] => 4.99
        )
```

198

```
    [1] => Array
        (
            [Item] => STRAWBERRY ICE CREAM
            [Price] => 2.22
        )

    [2] => Array
        (
            [Item] => CHOCOLATE AND STRAWBERRY CAKE
            [Price] => Special: 5.99
        )

)
```

You may be wondering why you use the not function, rather than PHP's native ! (exclamation mark) operator. Indeed, if you look at Phamda's source code, you'll see that ! is used to implement the not function. However, on its own, ! is not easily composable, does not feature autocurrying, and is easy to miss in what should be easy-to-read declarative code. Phamda's not function is simply a wrapper around the native ! operator to turn it into a first-class function.

Libraries Based on Underscore

Underscore is a popular JavaScript functional programming library, and several libraries have attempted to port it to PHP or have been inspired by its syntax and features. Note there are two libraries here with identical names, so I've marked them (1) and (2).

Underscore.php (1)

- *Download*: https://github.com/brianhaveri/Underscore.php

- *Documentation*: http://brianhaveri.github.io/Underscore.php/

- *Key points*: Underscore.php (1) is a fairly straightforward port of the JavaScript library. While perfectly functional, it hasn't been updated in some six years at the time of writing.

- *Example code*: To use this library, simply require it as shown here. In Listing 8-7, you'll use the Fibonacci example from Chapter 5 to create a memoized version, using Underscore's memoize function. Check back to Chapter 5 to see how this works and to compare the results there to the results here.

Listing 8-7. undersore-memoize-output.txt

```php
<?php

# Get the library

require('Underscore.php/underscore.php');

# The code below is exactly the same as in Chapter 5, except where noted
```

```
$fibonacci =

        function ($n) use (&$fibonacci) {

        usleep(100000);

    return ($n < 2) ? $n : $fibonacci($n - 1) + $fibonacci($n - 2);

    };
# Here we memoize using the underscore memoize function rather than our own

$memo_fibonacci = __::memoize($fibonacci);

$timer = function($func, $params) {

    $start_time = microtime(true);

    $results = call_user_func_array($func, $params);

    $time_taken = round(microtime(true) - $start_time, 2);

    return [ "Param" => implode($params),
                        "Result" => $results,
                        "Time" => $time_taken ];

};

print_r( $timer(  $fibonacci, [6, '*'] ) );

print_r( $timer(  $memo_fibonacci, [6] ) );

print_r( $timer(  $fibonacci, [6, '*'] ) );

print_r( $timer(  $memo_fibonacci, [6] ) );

print_r( $timer(  $memo_fibonacci, [10] ) );

print_r( $timer(  $memo_fibonacci, [11] ) );

print_r( $timer(  $memo_fibonacci, [8] ) );

# We'll add an extra call with parameter 8

print_r( $timer(  $memo_fibonacci, [8] ) );
underscore-memoize.php
Array
(
    [Param] => 6*
    [Result] => 8
    [Time] => 2.5
)
```

```
Array
(
    [Param] => 6
    [Result] => 8
    [Time] => 2.5
)
Array
(
    [Param] => 6*
    [Result] => 8
    [Time] => 2.5
)
Array
(
    [Param] => 6
    [Result] => 8
    [Time] => 0
)
Array
(
    [Param] => 10
    [Result] => 55
    [Time] => 17.72
)
Array
(
    [Param] => 11
    [Result] => 89
    [Time] => 28.73
)
Array
(
    [Param] => 8
    [Result] => 21
    [Time] => 6.71
)
Array
(
    [Param] => 8
    [Result] => 21
    [Time] => 0
)
```

If you compare these results with those in Chapter 5, you'll notice some differences. Specifically, there is only a reduction in time taken when the parameters match exactly. For instance, calculating the 11th number takes a long time even though you've just calculated the 10th. The memoization function in this library only memoizes the outer function call and not the inner recursive calls. Thus, the function either takes the full amount of time to run or takes 0 in the case of the second call for the 6th and 8th Fibonacci numbers.

The lesson here is to always check the implementation details of functions that you rely on, even when they are named the same. You'll find a dozen different memoization functions available in different libraries, with many different ways of operating.

In Listing 8-8, you'll look at the library's throttle function. This is a higher-order function that creates a self-throttling function, which can be successfully called only once every *x* milliseconds. Listing 8-9 shows the output.

Listing 8-8. underscore-throttle.php

```php
<?php

# Get the library

require('Underscore.php/underscore.php');

# Create a simple function to output a dot

$write = function ($text) { echo '.'; };

# create a new function which is a throttled version of
# $write. It will execute at a maximum once per 1000ms.
# Any other calls during that 1000ms will be ignored.

$throttled_write = __::throttle( $write, 1000);

# Let's call $throttled_write 10 million times. On my
# system that takes a little over 7 seconds, but as it will
# only *actually* execute once every 1000ms (1sec) we
# will get a line of 7 dots printed.

__::times(10000000, $throttled_write);
```

Listing 8-9. underscore-throttle-output.txt

```
.......
```

Underscore

- *Download*: https://github.com/Im0rtality/Underscore

- *Documentation*: https://github.com/Im0rtality/Underscore/wiki/Intro

- *Key points*: Underscore is a more recent and more comprehensive port of the JavaScript library. It offers built-in chaining of functions but little in the way of documentation. When you need to know more about a particular function, you'll need to dive into the source code, although it's reasonably well written and easy to follow. Note that various changes mean that the examples in the documentation don't work (for instance, the pick function has been renamed to pluck).

- *Example code*: To use this library, you need to install it via Composer. Listing 8-10 shows how to chain function calls together. Listing 8-11 shows the output.

Listing 8-10. underscore-chain.php

```php
<?php

# Autoload the library

require __DIR__ . '/vendor/autoload.php';

use Underscore\Underscore;

# Run a set of chained functions. Note that we're *not* composing
# a function to be run later, but executing the series of functions
# right here.

# Some data to work with

$foods = [ 'Cheese' => 'Cheddar',
           'Milk' => 'Whole',
           'Apples' => 'Red',
           'Grapes' => 'White'
         ];

# The ::from function "loads" an array of data into the chain

$result = Underscore::from($foods)

            # Let's map a function to uppercase each value and prepend the
            # array key to it.

            ->map(function($item,$key) {

                    return strtoupper
                    ($key.' - '.$item);

            })

            # Invoke invokes a function over each element like map

            ->invoke(function($item) { var_dump($item);})

            # Shuffle the order of the array

            ->shuffle()

            # Finally generate the return value for the function chain which
            # is the array returned by shuffle()

            ->value();

# Output the final array

var_dump($result);
```

Listing 8-11. underscore-chain-output.txt

```
string(16) "CHEESE - CHEDDAR"
string(12) "MILK - WHOLE"
string(12) "APPLES - RED"
string(14) "GRAPES - WHITE"
array(4) {
  ["Grapes"]=>
  string(14) "GRAPES - WHITE"
  ["Cheese"]=>
  string(16) "CHEESE - CHEDDAR"
  ["Apples"]=>
  string(12) "APPLES - RED"
  ["Milk"]=>
  string(12) "MILK - WHOLE"
}
```

Underscore.php (2)

- *Download*: https://github.com/Anahkiasen/underscore-php

- *Documentation*: http://anahkiasen.github.io/underscore-php/

- *Key points*: Underscore.php (2) is probably the most flexible library of the Underscore clones you've looked at, and it also the best documented. It's not a direct port but inspired by the JavaScript library's style while deploying the best PHP has to offer.

- *Example code*: To use this library, you need to install it via Composer. Listing 8-12 shows the flexible ways you can call and chain methods and shows the integration with native PHP functions. Listing 8-13 shows the output.

Listing 8-12. underscore-flexible.php

```php
<?php

# Autoload the library

require __DIR__ . '/vendor/autoload.php';

# We're going to use the Arrays type

use Underscore\Types\Arrays;

# Some data

$data = [10, 25, 38, 99];

# A helper function, returns true if $number is Equivalent

$is_even = function ($number) {
```

```
    return $number % 2 == 0;

};

# We can call the library functions as static methods

var_dump( Arrays::average($data) ); # 43

# We can chain them together, here we load our data with from(),
# filter out the odd number (25 & 99) with our $is_even function,
# and then sum the remaining even numbers

var_dump ( Arrays::from($data)
                                            ->filter($is_even)
                                            ->sum()
              ); #10+38 = 48

# We can also instantiate an object to encapsulate our data,
# and call the methods directly on that (which is effectively what the
# static methods do in the background.

$array = new Arrays($data);

var_dump( $array->filter($is_even)->sum() ); #48 again

# The following chain contains a "reverse" function. However no such
# function exists in the library. The library will attempt to use
# native PHP functions for such calls, for arrays it tries to find
# a native function with the same name prefixed by array_, so in
# this case it will use the native array_reverse function.

var_dump( Arrays::from($data)->reverse()->obtain() );
```

Listing 8-13. underscore-flexible-output.txt

```
float(43)
int(48)
int(48)
array(4) {
  [0]=>
  int(99)
  [1]=>
  int(38)
  [2]=>
  int(25)
  [3]=>
  int(10)
}
```

Miscellaneous Libraries

The following libraries aren't clones like those you've looked at so far, and they try to stand on their own two feet and do things their own way.

Saber

- *Download*: https://github.com/bluesnowman/fphp-saber

- *Documentation*: https://github.com/bluesnowman/fphp-saber#saber

- *Key points*: Saber attempts to bring strong typing and immutability to PHP using its own object-based type system. While it succeeds in these goals, it fails (in my opinion) to be easy to develop with and leads to patches of hard-to-read code. Ironically, while one of the ideas of strong typing like this is to make it easier to reason about your code, the departure from PHP standard variables means the average PHP programmer is more likely to misunderstand the code. The lack of full documentation compounds the issue. That said, if those traits being enforced by your library are important for your use case, this is one of your only choices.

- *Example code*: To use this library, you need to install it via Composer. Listing 8-14 shows how to create strongly typed values and apply chains of functions to them. Listing 8-15 shows the output.

Listing 8-14. sabre-example.php

```php
<?php

# Autoload the library

require __DIR__ . '/vendor/autoload.php';

# You will need to use the Saber datatypes for all data

use \Saber\Data\IInt32;

# Ordinary PHP variable

$start = 20;

# To work with the value, we need to "box" it into a Saber object
# which encapsulates it in a "strictly typed" object

$boxed_value = IInt32\Type::box($start);

# We can chain functions onto the boxed value (note that the parameters
# for those functions also need to be the correct boxed types)

$boxed_result = $boxed_value -> increment() # 21

                            -> increment() # 22
```

```
                              -> multiply( IInt32\Type::box(3) ) # 66

                   -> decrement(); # 65

# To get the value back out into a standard PHP variable we need to "unbox" it

var_dump( $boxed_result->unbox() ); # 65

# And check that the original boxed value object that we chained the
# functions on is unmutated

var_dump( $boxed_value->unbox() ); # 20
```

Listing 8-15. sabre-example-output.txt

```
int(65)
int(20)
```

Functional PHP

- *Download*: https://github.com/lstrojny/functional-php

- *Documentation*: https://github.com/lstrojny/functional-php/blob/master/docs/functional-php.md

- *Key points*: Functional PHP is a set of functional primitives aimed at easing functional programming. It is relatively well maintained, and although Underscore is listed as one of its inspirations, it also draws on Scala, Dojo (a JavaScript toolkit), and other sources. It has good documentation, and the GitHub home page even has an XKCD comic about tail recursion, so what's not to like? Well, while it is strong on functional primitives (functions such as map, pluck, sort, etc.), it is less well-endowed in features for functional composition.

- *Example code*: To use this library, you need to install it via Composer. Listing 8-16 shows a smattering of the provided functions used on your menu data. Listing 8-17 shows the output.

Listing 8-16. functionalphp-example.php

```php
<?php

# Autoload the library

require __DIR__ . '/vendor/autoload.php';

# The recommended way to use the library (only in PHP 5.6+) is to
# import the individual functions as function names so that you
# don't need to qualify them in the code

use function Functional\select;
use function Functional\reject;
```

```
use function Functional\contains;
use function Functional\map;
use function Functional\pick;
use function Functional\sort;
use function Functional\drop_last;
use function Functional\select_keys;

# Our trusty menu data

$menu = [

    [   'Item' => 'Apple Pie',
        'Category' => 'Dessert',
        'Price' => 4.99,
        'Ingredients' => ['Apples' => 3, 'Pastry' => 1, 'Magic' => 100]
    ],

    [   'Item' => 'Strawberry Ice Cream',
        'Category' => 'Dessert',
        'Price' => 2.22,
        'Ingredients' => ['Strawberries' => 20, 'Milk' => 10, 'Sugar' => 200]
    ],

    [   'Item' => 'Chocolate and Strawberry Cake',
        'Category' => 'Dessert',
        'Price' => 5.99,
        'Ingredients' => ['Chocolate' => 4, 'Strawberries' => 5, 'Cake' => 4]
    ],

    [   'Item' => 'Cheese Toasty',
        'Category' => 'Main Courses',
        'Price' => 3.45,
        'Ingredients' => ['Cheese' => 5, 'Bread' => 2, 'Butter' => 6]
    ]
];

# Define a function to check if a food is a dessert, using the contains
# function. Returns true if it's a dessert

$is_dessert = function ($food) {
    return contains($food, 'Dessert');
};

# Using the function above, we can apply it in two different ways to our menu
# data using the select and reject functions.

$desserts = select($menu, $is_dessert);

$mains = reject($menu, $is_dessert);

# A helper function using map and pick to return an array of just item names
```

```
$list_foods = function ($foods) {

    return map($foods, function ($item) {

        return pick($item, 'Item');

    });

};

# Output the results of the select and reject statements above, using our
# helper function so we don't dump the whole array contents

echo "Desserts:\n";

print_r ( $list_foods( $desserts ) );

echo "Main Courses:\n";

print_r ( $list_foods( $mains ) );

# Our restaurant is struggling, so we want to dump our cheapest dishes.
# First, we need to use the libraries sort function (with a custom callback # function) to
sort our $menu based on $price.

$sorted = sort($menu, function($item1,$item2) {

    return $item1["Price"] < $item2["Price"];

}, true);

# Now we want to drop any items that cost less than 3. We use the drop_last
# function to drop the last elements of our sorted array that are >=3

$expensive_items = drop_last($sorted, function ($item) {

    return $item["Price"] >= 3;

});

# Let's see what we're left with :s

echo "Expensive Items:\n";

print_r( $list_foods( $expensive_items ) );

# To create our menu, we want to pick out just the Item and Price, so # we'll map the
select_keys function against each element to pick those out.

$new_menu = map($expensive_items, function ($item) {
```

```
        return select_keys($item, ['Item','Price']);

 });

echo "New menu:\n";

print_r($new_menu);
```

Listing 8-17. functionalphp-example-output.txt

```
Desserts:
Array
(
    [0] => Apple Pie
    [1] => Strawberry Ice Cream
    [2] => Chocolate and Strawberry Cake
)
Main Courses:
Array
(
    [3] => Cheese Toasty
)
Expensive Items:
Array
(
    [2] => Chocolate and Strawberry Cake
    [0] => Apple Pie
    [3] => Cheese Toasty
)
New menu:
Array
(
    [2] => Array
        (
            [Item] => Chocolate and Strawberry Cake
            [Price] => 5.99
        )

    [0] => Array
        (
            [Item] => Apple Pie
            [Price] => 4.99
        )

    [3] => Array
        (
            [Item] => Cheese Toasty
            [Price] => 3.45
        )

)
```

Other Libraries

The libraries you've explored in this chapter are (perhaps) the most common libraries for functional programming in use in PHP at the moment. There are others out there, and you'll find some of these listed in Appendix C of this book for you to explore. These libraries are also all general-purpose collections of functions, and there are other libraries available that focus on a particular type of function or functional concept. Again, you'll find them listed in the appendix.

CHAPTER 9

■ ■ ■

Processing Big Data with Functional PHP

Big Data is a hot topic today, with promises that it can cure cancer, automate away your jobs, and most importantly provide accurate movie suggestions on Netflix. When reading about Big Data, however, you'll rarely hear PHP mentioned. In this chapter, you'll look at what, exactly, Big Data is and see why it's perfectly possible to process Big Data using PHP. And of course, given the topic of this book, you'll look at how functional programming is a perfect way to structure your Big Data–crunching programs to help you reason about and manage the processes necessary to deal with data on a massive scale.

What Is Big Data?

Big Data is more than just "a lot of data." For years, the amount of data organizations have been collecting has been increasing exponentially. With the average desktop computer currently being able to store multiple terabytes of data, quantity alone is not a good qualifier of a data set being "Big Data." As a general rule of thumb, I tend to call a data set Big Data if it cannot be stored and processed on a single machine (at least not within a reasonable time frame). Another common trait of Big Data is that the data set is not tightly defined; it often encompasses a whole range of data (commonly everything possible that could be collected about a subject) and often is collected before the end goal of its analysis is known. On occasion, even where the data can fit on a single machine, it can often be called Big Data if it is a truly comprehensive data set covering all recordable aspects of the population being studied.

Data analysis research in the Big Data field usually focuses on methods for processing data that can't be done on a single machine. Discovery and analysis of previously unknown trends in the data is also another topic common in Big Data research and use.

Many organizations use Big Data to help meet their business goals. Companies use Big Data to identify purchasing trends, customer behavior, financial patterns, and many other interesting and useful metrics and bits of information. Research scientists use Big Data techniques to analyze ever larger data sets produced by experiments and obtained by the ever-increasing monitoring of the population. Politicians use Big Data to work out who is most likely to vote for them, and why, to allow them to target their messages with ever-increasing granularity.

One technique for processing Big Data, called MapReduce, was first formalized by Google in its early days. Faced with the problem of how to calculate information like page rank (a metric that demonstrates how well connected a given web page is) across billions of web pages using (what are now considered) underpowered commodity machines, Google engineers came up with a way to break down the task into smaller functions that could be distributed across many machines, the results of which could then be

© Rob Aley 2017
R. Aley, *Pro Functional PHP Programming*, DOI 10.1007/978-1-4842-2958-3_9

combined into a single set of answers. While Google has since moved onto other more advanced Big Data techniques, MapReduce remains a good starting point for the rest of us when getting into the world of processing huge data sets. A popular open source framework for implementing MapReduce and similar algorithms is called Hadoop, and luckily for you, its language-agnostic nature means that you can use PHP with Hadoop to join the world of Big Data analysts.

Introducing Hadoop

Hadoop is an Apache project that provides a language-agnostic framework for massive distributed parallel processing of large data sets. It can scale from a single machine to clusters of thousands of servers, and it takes care of managing the processing across all of the machines (including dealing with reliability issues such as processes or machines failing midrun). Hadoop aims to let you easily create the component parts of the processing task, point them at some data, and then sit back while it runs your task and delivers your results. It was first created to provide an implementation of the MapReduce algorithm, but it can also be used to implement numerous other distributed tasks.

About MapReduce

MapReduce takes a data set, breaks it down into small chunks against which some algorithm is run (usually in parallel), and then reduces the results of those individual tasks into the final results. In Google's version of MapReduce, the algorithm applied to the data maps it into sets of key-value pairs, before being reduced by grouping data by key and mapping a further reduction function against those groups. MapReduce as described in Google's seminal paper on the subject, "MapReduce: Simplified Data Processing on Large Clusters," is more nuanced and structured than this and offers features that ensure consistency, allow for failures and retrys, and so forth. MapReduce isn't a functional programming concept per se, and it can be implemented in all programming paradigms.

You should recall the terms *map* and *reduce* from previous chapters where you looked at array_map and array_reduce, and from these a more informal version of MapReduce has become common, particularly among practitioners of functional programming. An application that splits data into chunks, maps some function(s) against those in parallel, and then provides a reduction function to generate the final output is considered to be a generalized class of MapReduce. You will be using this more general understanding to build a simple functional app without the use of key-value pairs and so forth; however, if you want to more fully explore "proper" MapReduce in Hadoop, then you can find more details in the "Further Reading" section at the end of this chapter.

If this task sounds a little like the parallel programming job that you wrote in Chapter 5, that's because it is! If you haven't read that chapter yet, I suggest you go do so now, before you continue here. In the parallel example, you split the complete works of Shakespeare down into chunks, "mapped" a set of analysis functions to get some results for each chunk, and then "reduced" those individual sets of results back down into a single set of results representative of the text as a whole. This is essentially what this kind of MapReduce task does, and you'll use exactly the same example analysis to learn how to use Hadoop to implement MapReduce in PHP.

As mentioned previously, Hadoop is language-agnostic. As a developer, you can write and implement your map and reduce jobs in any way you want. Hadoop simply provides a framework to fire up processes, pass data between them, collect output from them, and manage and monitor the processes. You will write your processes as PHP scripts that accept data in from Hadoop via STDIN streams, work on it, and then spit results back out to STDOUT.

Installing Hadoop

Hadoop is officially supported only on Linux and Windows, although some have had success getting it running on Macs. While official support for Windows is strong, the best performance in real-world applications is usually to be found on streamlined Linux clusters. Hadoop is designed to run jobs across a cluster of servers, which is why it is used for Big Data. However, luckily for you, it can also run on a single desktop machine and operate on "small data," which is useful for learning and development.

Installing Hadoop can be quite involved depending on your system and what you want to do with Hadoop. The following are some guides to basic installation. For the purposes of this book, though, you're going to shortcut the full installation process and use a virtual machine that has already been set up with a minimal installation of Ubuntu and has Hadoop pre-installed and mostly configured for use as a single-machine cluster. The virtual machine is provided by Bitnami and can be downloaded for free. You'll need a suitable hypervisor; Bitnami VMs will run in VirtualBox and VMware and KVM hypervisors. If you're not familiar with virtualization software, I suggest using VirtualBox, which is a simple free desktop application and easy to get going with.

Tools

- Main Hadoop web site
    - `http://hadoop.apache.org/`
- Installing Hadoop on Windows
    - `https://wiki.apache.org/hadoop/Hadoop2OnWindows`
- Installing Hadoop on Linux
    - `https://wiki.apache.org/hadoop/GettingStartedWithHadoop`
- Main Hadoop documentation
    - `https://wiki.apache.org/hadoop/`
- Bitnami Hadoop VM download page
    - `https://bitnami.com/stack/hadoop/virtual-machine`
- Bitnami Hadoop VM documentation
    - `https://docs.bitnami.com/virtual-machine/apps/hadoop/`
- Bitnami VM FAQ
    - `https://docs.bitnami.com/virtual-machine/faq/`
- Download VirtualBox
    - `https://www.virtualbox.org/wiki/Downloads`
- Main VirtualBox documentation
    - `https://www.virtualbox.org/manual/UserManual.html`

At the time of writing, Bitnami offer two versions of the VM, one based on Debian and one on Ubuntu. You'll use the Ubuntu version here, although the Debian version operates in a similar manner. Download the Bitnami Ubuntu VM from the link given previously and import it into VirtualBox or your preferred hypervisor and start the new VM. Once booted, you should see the screen shown in Figure 9-1.

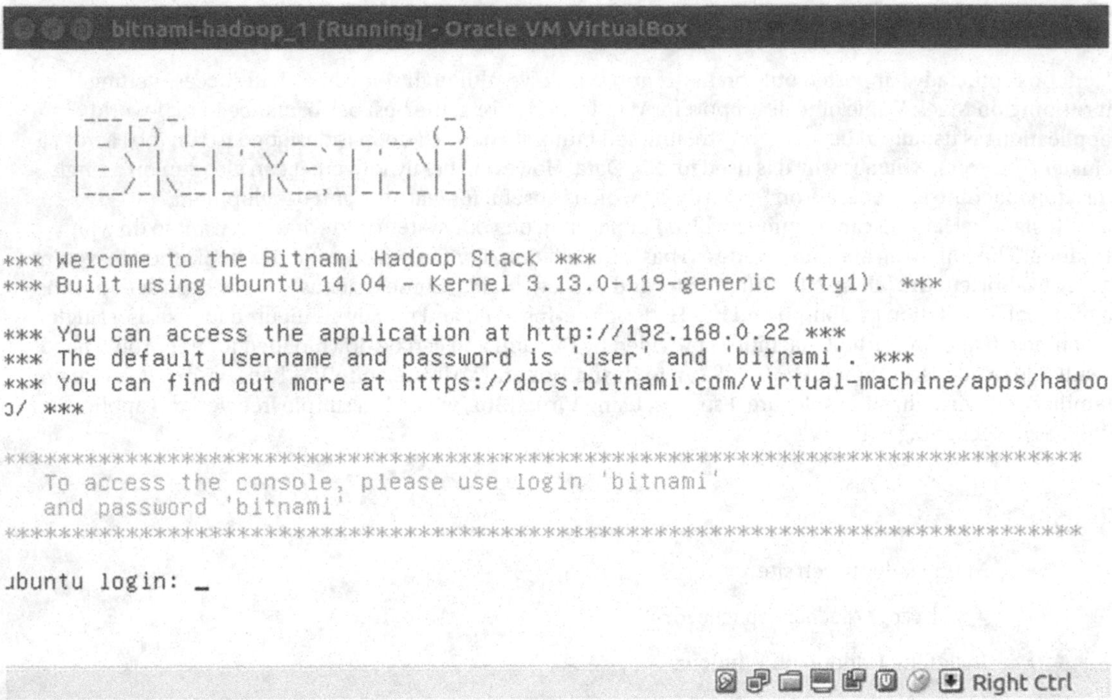

Figure 9-1. *vm_console.png*

Make a note of the IP address it shows (192.168.0.22 in my case) because you'll need it shortly. As you can see, the default username is *bitnami* and the password is also *bitnami*, so log in with those details. You'll configure the VM to enable you to ssh into it, which will allow you to more easily copy and paste commands and data in. Run the commands in Listing 9-1.

Listing 9-1. enable_ssh.txt

```
# Log in at the console, the default credentials are:
# bitnami:bitnami
# you will be prompted to change your password the first
# time you log in. You should change it, as everyone on your
# local network will be able to access your VM and hence
# able to SSH into it once SSH is enabled.

# We need to move the SSH config into place

sudo mv /etc/init/ssh.conf.back /etc/init/ssh.conf

# and then start SSH.

sudo start ssh

# SSH will now be started automatically each time the VM is
# started.
```

216

If you didn't make a note of the IP address previously, you can type `ifconfig` at the command line to view it. You can log out from the VirtualBox console now if you like, but don't shut down the VM. The Bitnami VM is based on Ubuntu 14.04 LTS (Long Term Support) and so only comes with PHP5 as standard. You want version 7.1, so let's `ssh` into the VM and install it, as shown in Listing 9-2.

Listing 9-2. install_php.txt

```
# SSH into the VM. Change the xxx's for your VM's IP address

ssh xxx.xxx.xxx.xxx -l bitnami

# Install the commands that will let us add a software repository

sudo apt-get install software-properties-common

# Now add the repository containing PHP and install PHP 7.1

sudo add-apt-repository ppa:ondrej/php

sudo apt-get update

sudo apt-get install php7.1

#  Check that we have the right version now

php -v
```

Hadoop operates on data that resides on its own file system, HDFS. HDFS is designed as a scalable file system that can span clusters of machines. You're going to write a Hadoop MapReduce job that works on the complete works of Shakespeare, but first you need to get it into the HDFS instance on your VM, and before that you need to get it onto the normal file system in the VM. It is possible to use VirtualBox to set up shared folders to move data between the host operating system and the Bitnami VM, and it is also possible to install and configure Samba or other network file store software on the VM to enable access to its file system. However, for this simple example, you'll go with a simple approach, which is to open a text editor (nano) and copy and paste the text/data that you want directly into your SSH session. See Listing 9-3.

Listing 9-3. hdfs_commands.txt

```
# By default the "namenode" in Hadoop is in safemode so
# we can't work with the file system. Let's turn that off.

hadoop dfsadmin -safemode leave

# We'll make a directory to put our data in

hadoop fs -mkdir shakespeare

# We can list the files to see where we're at

hadoop fs -ls /user/hadoop/
```

```
# The quickest way to get data onto the server is to copy and
# paste it into a text file, so open one, copy the contents
# from your local machine and paste it in.

nano all_shakespeare.txt

# The file we just created exists only on the VM's ordinary
# file system.

# Let's copy it into the HDFS directory we created above.

hadoop fs -copyFromLocal all_shakespeare.txt shakespeare/

# If we want to check the contents, we can "cat" the file

hadoop fs -cat shakespeare/all_shakespeare.txt
```

Creating Hadoop Jobs in PHP

Hadoop is written in Java, and there are numerous ways to create jobs in that language. For PHP users, Hadoop provides a "streaming" service to allow your PHP scripts to interact with it. You write your map and reduce jobs as PHP scripts, which take input as text via STDIN and write their output to STDOUT. Hadoop manages splitting up the data, spinning up the necessary concurrent map jobs, giving them bits of data, receiving their partial output, and then providing that to the reduce job and writing its output to disk. So, first you'll look at the PHP scripts you're going to use and then how to run them with Hadoop. You're going to run the same analysis on Shakespeare as you did in the parallel programming example in Chapter 5, so if you've skipped that part, go have a quick read so we're all on the same page.

As with the parallel programming example, you split your task into two scripts. The worker script, the "map" in MapReduce, is similar to the client.php script you wrote previously. Because Hadoop does the heavy lifting of spinning up worker (map) processes, controlling data flows, and so on, your other script simply has to implement the reduce function and so is a lot simpler than the previous version. Again, you'll bundle functions into a helper script. Let's take a look at those now (see Listing 9-4, Listing 9-5, and Listing 9-6).

Listing 9-4. map_job.php

```
#!/usr/bin/env php
<?php

require('job_functions.php');

# Compose our analysis function

$hadoop_analyze = compose(

                         $get_stream,

                         $only_letters_and_spaces,

                         'strtolower',

                         $analyze_words,

                         'json_encode'

);
```

218

```php
# Run the analysis function on the input from Hadoop on STDIN
# and write the results to STDOUT

fwrite( STDOUT, $hadoop_analyze(STDIN) );
```

Listing 9-5. reduce_job.php

```php
#!/usr/bin/env php
<?php

require('job_functions.php');

# Compose our reduce function

$reduce = compose (

                $get_stream_results,

                $combine_results,

                $sort_results,

                'array_reverse',

                $top_ten
);

# Call our reduce function on the results of the map jobs which Hadoop
# provides on STDIN, and print out the final result which Hadoop will
# save to disk

print_r( $reduce(STDIN) );
```

Listing 9-6. job_functions.php

```php
<?php

# All functions in this file are the same as in the Parallel example in
# Chapter 5, except for $get_stream and $get_stream_results

# Hadoop splits our input and provides it to each instance of the map job as
# a stream of text. Let's grab that text.

$get_stream = function ($stream) {

    return stream_get_contents( $stream );

}

# Hadoop sends the results from our map jobs (in no particular order) to
# the reduce job as a stream of lines of text. This function reads the
```

```php
# stream and formats it into an array suitable for our combine_results
# function

$get_stream_results = function ($stream) {

    # Map...

    return array_map(

                # ...json_decode...

                function ($string) { return json_decode($string, true); },

                # ... onto the contents of the stream which have been
                # exploded into an array to make it easier to parse by
                # the following functions

                explode( PHP_EOL , stream_get_contents( $stream ) )

            );

};

# All of the following functions are unchanged from the parallel script

$analyze_words = function ($string) {

    $array = preg_split('/ /i', $string, -1, PREG_SPLIT_NO_EMPTY);

    $filtered = array_filter($array, function ($word) {

        return (

                    preg_match('/[shakespeare]/', $word) != false)

                    && (similar_text($word, 'William is the best bard bar none') > 1)

                    && (metaphone($word) == metaphone('bard'))

                    && ( (strlen($word) > 3 )

                );
    });

    return array_count_values($filtered);

};

$only_letters_and_spaces = function($string) {

    return preg_replace('/[^A-Za-z]+/', ' ', $string);

};
```

```php
$sort_results = function($array)  {

        asort($array, SORT_NUMERIC);

        return $array;

};

$top_ten = function ($array) {

    return array_slice($array, 0 ,10);

};

$combine_results = function ($results) {

  return   array_reduce($results, function($output, $array) {

        foreach ($array as $word => $count) {

        isset($output[$word]) ?
                                $output[$word] += $count  :
                                $output[$word] = $count ;
        }

    return $output;
    }, []);

};

function identity ($value) { return $value; };

function compose(...$functions)
{
    return array_reduce(

        $functions,

            function ($chain, $function) {

                return function ($input) use ($chain, $function) {

                    return $function( $chain($input) );
                };

            },

            'identity'

        );
}
```

Note the #! "hashbang" first line of map_job.php and reduce_job.php. If you're not familiar with command-line scripting, this tells the shell what program to use to run the script. However, instead of a direct path to the PHP executable, you instead supply an environment variable that (if PHP has been correctly installed) will point to the PHP executable. This means if you run your script on another machine where PHP is installed into a different location, it should still run OK without change.

Overall, you've structured your scripts somewhat like a big pseudofunction, with STDIN as the parameters and STDOUT as the return value. If you assume that these standard streams are "pure" and guaranteed to work correctly each time, keeping your scripts structured in this manner means that Hadoop can deal with all the impure I/O, and you can reason about your scripts in a functional way. In fact, Hadoop handles many of the possible side effects that cause scripts to hang, fail, or behave unpredictably, and it can handle rerunning them where necessary to get the output you expect (or at least warn you when that's not possible).

Hadoop will happily run your scripts without them being moved into HDFS, so all you need to do make them executable. See Listing 9-7.

Listing 9-7. setup_scripts.txt

```
# Create a directory for our scripts

mkdir scripts

# Edit the files and copy/paste the scripts into them

nano scripts/map_job.php

nano scripts/reduce_job.php

# Make sure both we and Hadoop can run them by adding
# execute permissions for everyone. If you install Hadoop on
# another system, depending on the sensitivity of your system
# and scripts, and which user you run Hadoop as, you may want
# to change who has execute permission here.

chmod a+x scripts/*.php

# Add the functions file. This is "require"'d by the scripts
# and not exectued directly, so does not need execute permission

nano scripts/job_functions.php

# We can test that it all works by using the Standard Streams
# that are available to all shell scripts, using redirection
# and piping.

php scripts/map_job.php < all_shakespeare.txt | php scripts/reduce_job.php
```

If you run that last command, you should find that your scripts run and you get the output you were expecting (see Chapter 5 to confirm this). But as you can see, there is no Hadoop involved. This works because the streams that Hadoop uses are the standard streams available to any shell script. In the previous command, the < character sends the contents of all_shakespeare.txt to STDIN for map_job.php, the results of which are printed to STDOUT, and the | symbol pipes them into the STDIN for reduce_job.php. So, why bother with Hadoop at all?

In this command, you've run only one copy of `map_job.php`, which has processed the whole of Shakespeare in one go. While it works on a data set this small, it wouldn't work well on a data set that was too big to fit in memory (let alone one that was too big to fit on the disks of a single machine!). Hadoop deals with splitting the data into manageable chunks, spinning up multiple concurrent map jobs, and managing/ monitoring them as they work. Let's take a look at how to run the scripts with Hadoop (see Listing 9-8).

Listing 9-8. hadoop_commands.txt

```
# We need to know the location of the Hadoop streaming service.jar
# file. The path I've used below works at the time of writing,
# but if the version or path have changed when you try you'll need
# to locate it yourself. To do that, install and run the locate command.

sudo apt-get install locate

sudo updatedb

locate hadoop-streaming

# Once you've got the location, we're ready to run hadoop. The following
# command is split over several lines using the \ character, make sure
# you include all parts when you run it.

#The first line tells Hadoop what type of application we want to run.

# The -input line specifies the HDFS directory where our data resides
# (it will assume all files in that directory contain input data).

# The -output line specifies an HDFS output directory for the results, it
# must not already exist.

# The -mapper and -reduce lines specify
# our map and reduce scripts. Use the full directory path/filename.

hadoop jar /opt/bitnami/hadoop/share/hadoop/tools/lib/hadoop-streaming-2.8.0.jar \
-input shakespeare \
-output job_output \
-mapper /home/bitnami/scripts/map_job.php \
-reducer /home/bitnami/scripts/reduce_job.php

# Once Hadoop has run, you can examine the output directory

hadoop fs -ls /user/hadoop/job_output

# The main output is stored in part files, for us there is only one.

hadoop fs -cat /user/hadoop/job_output/part-00000
```

While your Hadoop job is running, it logs various details to the shell so that you can try to follow along with what it's doing. If you want a saner way to keep an eye on things, you're in luck. Hadoop has a web interface at http://xxx.xxx.xxx.xxx/cluster/apps (where the xxx's are the IP address of your Bitnami VM), which allows you to see the status of any jobs you are running. The default username is *user*, and the password is *bitnami*. Figure 9-2 shows what the web interface looks like with your job running. The Hadoop developers are still learning about responsive design, so a wide-screen monitor is a plus!

Figure 9-2. hadoop_web_interface.png

If Hadoop encounters any problems when it is trying to run your jobs, it tries to be helpful by spewing error messages, stack info, and other text to the shell. This can make finding the actual error a little tricky. The key is to scroll up until you come across routine output and then look at the first line of the error; this is usually the most informative line.

If all goes well, you should see output that looks something like Listing 9-9, with a set of stats about your job at the end.

Listing 9-9. hadoop_output.txt

```
packageJobJar: [/tmp/hadoop-unjar3885899711350629262/] [] /tmp/streamjob5472160291450525372.
jar tmpDir=null
17/06/14 19:45:56 INFO client.RMProxy: Connecting to ResourceManager at /0.0.0.0:8032
17/06/14 19:45:57 INFO client.RMProxy: Connecting to ResourceManager at /0.0.0.0:8032
17/06/14 19:45:57 INFO mapred.FileInputFormat: Total input files to process : 1
17/06/14 19:45:57 INFO mapreduce.JobSubmitter: number of splits:2
17/06/14 19:45:58 INFO mapreduce.JobSubmitter: Submitting tokens for job:
job_1497468403783_0001
17/06/14 19:45:58 INFO impl.YarnClientImpl: Submitted application
application_1497468403783_0001
17/06/14 19:45:58 INFO mapreduce.Job: The url to track the job: http://localhost:8088/proxy/
application_1497468403783_0001/
17/06/14 19:45:58 INFO mapreduce.Job: Running job: job_1497468403783_0001
17/06/14 19:46:08 INFO mapreduce.Job: Job job_1497468403783_0001 running in uber mode :
false
17/06/14 19:46:08 INFO mapreduce.Job:  map 0% reduce 0%
17/06/14 19:46:19 INFO mapreduce.Job:  map 100% reduce 0%
17/06/14 19:46:25 INFO mapreduce.Job:  map 100% reduce 100%
17/06/14 19:46:26 INFO mapreduce.Job: Job job_1497468403783_0001 completed successfully
17/06/14 19:46:26 INFO mapreduce.Job: Counters: 49
    File System Counters
        FILE: Number of bytes read=353
        FILE: Number of bytes written=417495
        FILE: Number of read operations=0
```

```
            FILE: Number of large read operations=0
            FILE: Number of write operations=0
            HDFS: Number of bytes read=3767109
            HDFS: Number of bytes written=203
            HDFS: Number of read operations=9
            HDFS: Number of large read operations=0
            HDFS: Number of write operations=2
        Job Counters
            Launched map tasks=2
            Launched reduce tasks=1
            Data-local map tasks=2
            Total time spent by all maps in occupied slots (ms)=16341
            Total time spent by all reduces in occupied slots (ms)=3773
            Total time spent by all map tasks (ms)=16341
            Total time spent by all reduce tasks (ms)=3773
            Total vcore-milliseconds taken by all map tasks=16341
            Total vcore-milliseconds taken by all reduce tasks=3773
            Total megabyte-milliseconds taken by all map tasks=16733184
            Total megabyte-milliseconds taken by all reduce tasks=3863552
        Map-Reduce Framework
            Map input records=157244
            Map output records=2
            Map output bytes=341
            Map output materialized bytes=359
            Input split bytes=234
            Combine input records=0
            Combine output records=0
            Reduce input groups=2
            Reduce shuffle bytes=359
            Reduce input records=2
            Reduce output records=13
            Spilled Records=4
            Shuffled Maps =2
            Failed Shuffles=0
            Merged Map outputs=2
            GC time elapsed (ms)=261
            CPU time spent (ms)=1610
            Physical memory (bytes) snapshot=599236608
            Virtual memory (bytes) snapshot=5641613312
            Total committed heap usage (bytes)=460849152
        Shuffle Errors
            BAD_ID=0
            CONNECTION=0
            IO_ERROR=0
            WRONG_LENGTH=0
            WRONG_MAP=0
            WRONG_REDUCE=0
        File Input Format Counters
            Bytes Read=3766875
        File Output Format Counters
            Bytes Written=203
17/06/14 19:46:26 INFO streaming.StreamJob: Output directory: job_output
```

And if you cat the part-00000 file, you should get the output shown in Listing 9-10.

Listing 9-10. part-00000.txt

```
Array
(
    [beard] => 76
    [buried] => 43
    [bright] => 43
    [bred] => 36
    [breed] => 35
    [bird] => 34
    [bride] => 30
    [board] => 15
    [broad] => 15
    [bread] => 15
)
```

As you can see, it's the same as your native PHP parallel version in Chapter 5, although note that the ordering of words with the same score (e.g., buried and bright, or board, broad, and bread) is different. This is a result of the fact that when running parallel tasks, you can't always be sure which process will return first and therefore in which order results will be delivered to your reduce job. If exact replication of the format/ordering of output results between runs is important, with a task like this you could normalize the results (for instance by ordering keys alphabetically) before or after reducing them (as appropriate).

From the "number of splits" and "launched map task" lines in Hadoop's output, you can see that it decided (based on the default settings) to break your data into two chunks and run two jobs in parallel. You can of course tinker with Hadoop's configuration to make it create smaller or large chunks and different numbers of map workers.

What you'll also notice is that Hadoop is a *lot* slower than your PHP parallel version. In fact, it's a lot slower than when you tested out your scripts earlier by executing them directly (and that was running the whole text through a single instance of map_job.php). Why? Because Hadoop comes with a *lot* of overhead. It's definitely overkill for a toy problem like this. No matter how prolific a writer Shakespeare was in his time, his life's output (well, the best bits anyway) can be concatenated into a couple of megabytes of text. Hadoop is designed to work on much, much larger data sets, and its overhead only starts to pay off when you get into complex calculations running on many hundreds of gigabytes of data. Indeed, simpler problems often require several terabytes of data before Hadoop pays off. But if you've got that much data and you've got PHP, then Hadoop is definitely worth looking at as a useful tool. If you don't have that much data, it's still a great way to learn about cluster-based processing.

As you may have guessed, you have barely scratched the surface of Hadoop (or indeed MapReduce). Let's recap the reasons I've included a chapter on Hadoop and Big Data in a book on functional programming. When you're dealing with quantities of data that mean you need to process it in a nonsequential manner (often across disparate machines), you need to be able to do the following:

- Reason about your code in an abstract manner

- Get control over side effects and manage clean flows of code

- Partition code into widely reusable and highly optimizable packages

Those are traits you should now be associating with functional programming after getting this far in the book. To be clear, you don't need to use functional programming to work with Hadoop or other distributed data processing systems; indeed, MapReduce isn't a functional concept (although its basic traits map nicely onto functional structures). But functional programming is increasingly being used to handle large data processing and flows by companies like Twitter, where keeping the basic business logic straight at scale is *hard*. They may not use PHP, but you do, and the same principles apply.

If this simple example has tantalized you, the following resources will let you learn more about MapReduce, Hadoop, and using PHP with HDFS.

Further Reading

- An article setting out my view as to why MapReduce is *not* functional programming per se

    - `https://medium.com/@jkff/mapreduce-is-not-functional-programming-39109a4ba7b2`

- A tutorial outlining how to implement the full MapReduce algorithm in Hadoop

    - `https://hadoop.apache.org/docs/r1.2.1/mapred_tutorial.html`

- PHDFS, a library to help you access HDFS directly from PHP

    - `https://github.com/yuduanchen/phdfs`

- Further details of the Hadoop streaming app that you use to work with PHP scripts

    - `https://hadoop.apache.org/docs/r1.2.1/streaming.html#How+Streaming+Works`

CHAPTER 10

■ ■ ■

Afterword

Where to Now?

If you've read this far, thank you. I sincerely hope that this book has held your interest and at the very least informed some areas of your future PHP programming. If it has, I encourage you to start some coding right now based on one or more topics in this book while they are still fresh in your mind. People far smarter than me have shown that the sooner relevant activity occurs after learning, the easier it is to retain information and techniques over the longer term.

If you haven't already headed for the keyboard, don't forget to glance through the appendixes that follow. There may be something interesting or useful in there for you (either to use now or to be aware of for the future).

If you're feeling a little "stuck," how about considering doing one or more of the following exercises:

- Take a look through the resources in Appendix C. Make yourself a "to learn" list of topics that interest you, and extend your knowledge of functional programming. You could also look at the non-PHP topics and try your hand at implementing some of the concepts in PHP.

- Do you have some buggy or problematic code you've been putting off fixing? Or perhaps there's a tired old application hanging around just begging for a rewrite? Why not try reimplementing that code (or just key/problematic parts) in functional PHP?

- Try entering online code contests, solving online puzzles, or practising "interview tasks" using the functional techniques you've learned from this book.

- Had a "side project" in mind for a while but no motivation to get going on it? Why not get started on it now using functional programming? Learning something while completing a defined, worthwhile task can both help you to learn quicker and help you to increase your motivation for the task.

- If you've only ever programmed in PHP using one paradigm (e.g., procedural programming), don't assume that functional programming is the bee's knees and will suit your use cases perfectly. Pick up a book or read a web tutorial on other paradigms used in PHP (like object-oriented programming) or even outside of PHP (such as aspect-oriented or constraint-based programming). You'll add to your skills toolbox, it will help you to see the drawbacks as well as the benefits of functional programming, and you may even come up with ways to better blend different paradigms to suit the tasks at hand.

© Rob Aley 2017
R. Aley, *Pro Functional PHP Programming*, DOI 10.1007/978-1-4842-2958-3_10

If you've tried some programming, you're not sure if you're on the right track, and you have no one to ask directly, one of the best ways to get feedback is by posting your code on the Internet. If you get no response, you're probably on the right track. But put one semicolon out of place online and somewhere someone will just be waiting to correct you! Alternatively, buy a copy of this book for a colleague or friend and get them to pair-program with you.

Giving Feedback and Getting Help and Support

E-mail: author@active-net.co.uk

Your feedback on this book—good or bad, fundamental or trivial—is solicited and very much welcomed. Don't just restrict it to how cute my cat is in the photo in the sample code bundle for Chapter 6 (as if you haven't already set it as your desktop wallpaper!). I want to know the following:

- What you thought about the book, overall or in regard to particular sections

- If there were any areas that weren't covered in enough depth (or in too much detail)

- If any topics you were expecting weren't present or any of the information wasn't clear

- If you use any of the techniques presented in the book in "real life" (I would be very interested to know!)

Likewise, if you have any problems getting the sample code to run or issues implementing the techniques discussed, please do drop me a line and I'll see whether there is any way I can help.

If you have found the book useful, and I hope you have, you can help others get the same satisfying dose of functional goodness by tweeting your thoughts about the book, mentioning it at PHP groups and meetups, or blogging about your new functional skills (with a cheeky mention of where you found them).

APPENDIX A

■ ■ ■

Installing PHP and Libraries

This book is aimed at programmers with at least some basic experience using PHP, so it is likely you already have access to a machine or two with PHP installed. However, many programmers use the versions already preinstalled in web hosting accounts or the default versions provided by package managers and so are unaware of how to compile, install, and tweak PHP and its ecosystem of extensions and libraries directly. Throughout this book you've looked at a number of extensions and libraries that provide functional programming structures and helper functions, and I've discussed features unique to PHP 7–like type declarations. Your web host or package manager may not have these extensions or versions available for automatic installation, so it's good to know how to install them yourself. In this appendix, you'll look at the various ways to change the PHP base upon which your programs are developed and run.

Compiling and Installing PHP

There are a dozen different ways to get PHP, including downloading and compiling it yourself, downloading precompiled binaries, using package managers and software repositories, and finding it preinstalled by a forward-thinking administrator. On most Linux distributions, PHP can be installed with a one-line command such as `sudo apt- get install` php or through graphical package managers such as the Synaptic Package Manager or the Ubuntu Software Center. Many common PHP extensions and add-ons are likewise available as prebuilt packages or alternatively available for easy installation through the PECL and PEAR systems. However, sometimes it is necessary to do a little more work to install PHP, such as in the following cases:

- When your project has requirements for a specific version of PHP that is different from the one shipped with your OS

- When you need extensions not available as packages

- When you want to compile a customized version of PHP specific to your needs

Like anything related to computers and software development, compiling PHP can take you down a rabbit hole of options, customizations, compatibility issues, libraries, and dependencies. A whole book could be written about the different possibilities (and possible headaches) involved. Luckily, in most use cases, the basics of compiling a standard version are quite straightforward. And like most things in life, it gets easier after you have done it once. In this section, I will go over the steps necessary for getting, compiling, and installing PHP and its core extensions. PHP is written in C, and because you might not be familiar with the process of compiling C programs, I have tried to explain each step to give you an idea of what is happening. This makes the process seem a little more verbose, but in reality it is quite straightforward. Go ahead and try it if you don't believe me! The rest of the appendix is also worth a read; it covers installing extras such as libraries and extensions from the PECL, PEAR, and Packagist repositories.

© Rob Aley 2017
R. Aley, *Pro Functional PHP Programming*, DOI 10.1007/978-1-4842-2958-3

The process for compiling and installing PHP varies depending on the operating system you are deploying to. The following sections deal with the main OSs that PHP is available on.

Microsoft Windows

For Windows, the proprietary Visual Studio compiler is required, and the steps are somewhat complicated and thus beyond the scope of this book. You can find the Windows source code, prebuilt binaries, and instructions for compiling at `http://windows.php.net/download/`, with older versions in the archive at `http://windows.php.net/downloads/releases/archives/`.

macOS/OS X

One of the easiest ways to get different versions of PHP on your Mac is by using the Homebrew or MacPorts software repository.

Here are resources for Homebrew, a popular macOS software repository and package manager system:

- *The Homebrew PHP repository, which has more than 700 "formulas" available covering various versions of PHP, extensions, applications, and related tools*: `https://github.com/Homebrew/homebrew-php/tree/master/Formula`

- *Main web site*: `https://brew.sh/`

- *Installation information and documentation*: `http://docs.brew.sh/Installation.html`

- *List of all software available*: `https://github.com/Homebrew/homebrew-core/tree/master/Formula`

Here are resources for MacPorts, an easy-to-use system for compiling, installing, and upgrading open source software on macOS:

- *Main web site, which has more than 700 PHP "portfiles" available covering various versions of PHP, extensions, applications, and related tools*: `https://www.macports.org/`

- *Installation information and documentation*: `https://www.macports.org/install.php`

- *Directory of software available (click "php" for the relevant software)*: `https://www.macports.org/ports.php`

Homebrew aims to be easier to use than MacPorts, but one of the downsides is that it tries to use macOS's shipped libraries where possible, which sometimes limits the versions of software available. MacPorts, on the other hand, maintains its own full tree of dependencies so tends to track the current mainline versions of most software well.

PHP also comes installed by default with recent OS X and macOS versions, although it's not always up-to-date. If you need to compile from scratch, you can follow the instructions for Linux/Unix systems. There are some issues you may run into depending on the version of OS X/macOS you are using and the version of PHP you are trying to compile. The following are the two main issues that may trip you up:

- *File/dependency locations*: These are sometimes different on a Mac and may vary between versions. Where possible, always try to explicitly specify the full location path for dependencies and installation.

- *Dependency versions*: The default versions of libraries that come with a Mac that core PHP and various extensions require aren't always in step with those that various versions of PHP require. Check any error messages produced during compilation (usually the first error message) for any hints as to version requirements or check the documentation for PHP or the extension in question. Then check the documentation for the dependency to see whether it can be safely upgraded/downgraded or whether you need to install another version in parallel.

Linux/Unix

Many *nix-based operating systems have package repositories containing not just the current version of PHP but often older versions (albeit usually just the major versions). Third-party repositories can also sometimes offer an easier route to getting particular versions or configurations, so check these out before starting to compile things yourself to see whether you can save yourself some time.

On *nix machines, the first step is to download the PHP source code from the PHP web site at www.php.net/downloads.php. This page lists the current stable release and the previous supported stable release. Older end-of-life versions are available at http://museum.php.net/, all the way back to version 1 if you're curious! Git users can also pull the source code for past, current, and future development versions down from the official mirror at https://github.com/php.

When you have identified which version you want, make a note of the URL of the .tar.gz source code file because you will need that in a moment. In your terminal, execute the following commands:

```
~$ mkdir php7.1
~$ cd php7.1
~$ wget http://uk1.php.net/get/php-7.1.4.tar.gz/from/this/mirror -o php-7.1.4.tar.gz
~$ tar zxvf php-7.1.4.tar.gz
~$ cd php-7.1.4
```

The first two lines create a directory for your work and step into it. The directory holds the source code and intermediate files and can be deleted once PHP is installed if you want. However, it is often a good idea to keep it in case you need/want to reinstall or check what version of the file you downloaded later. The third line downloads a copy of the source code file into your directory. Change the URL in the third line to that of the .tar.gz file you want to use, and change the -o option to the name of the file (otherwise, in the previous example, wget will simply call your file mirror). The fifth line unpacks the archive into a directory containing the individual source code files and changes the name of the file to the one you used on line 3. Finally, the last line steps you into the source code directory.

Now you can start the actual compilation process by issuing the following command:

```
~$ ./configure
```

The configure command creates the "setup" for compilation. You use it to provide the settings and arguments you want for your compilation session. For instance, you can specify which core extensions you want to include in your build. If you don't specify any arguments, the defaults provided by the PHP dev team are used. This is a good choice if you don't have any particular needs and want a version that is fairly similar/compatible with the versions included with most distributions. You can also install extensions at a later date either individually or by recompiling PHP from scratch, which I will discuss in the next section. If you want to include an extension at this stage that's not included in the default settings, then this is the place to do it. For example, if you wanted to include the LDAP extension, then you would change the previous command to ./ configure --with-ldap[=DIR], where [=DIR] is the base installation directory of ldap on your system. You can find the exact option to use and any necessary dependencies in the PHP manual, under the "Installing/Configuring" section for the extension in question. For example, you can find details for the LDAP extension at www.php.net/manual/en/ldap.setup.php. You can find a (not necessarily complete) list of options that you can pass to the `configure` command at `www.php.net/manual/en/configure.about.php`; for a full list of options supported on your system in the current version you are trying to compile, you can issue the command `autoconf` followed by `./configure --help`. You can find more information about the `configure` command at `www.airs.com/ian/configure/`. Now you will actually compile PHP by issuing the following commands:

```
~$ make clean
~$ make
~$ sudo make install
```

You compile the binary PHP files using the `make` tool. The first line removes any previously created files and resets you to the start of the make process. This is not strictly necessary on your first run at compiling, but it can help if your attempt fails for some reason (such as because of missing dependencies, incorrect settings, unintended interruptions to the process, and so on), so including it by default is often a good choice. The second line does the actual building and compiling of the files. The third line then takes those files and installs them on the system. By default, PHP will usually be installed in the `/usr/bin` directory on Linux. However, you can choose where to install it by specifying a prefix directory at the `./configure` stage. Simply add the switch `--prefix=/path/to/dir`, where `/path/to/dir` is the directory into which you want PHP to be installed. This is often useful if you want to install multiple versions on the same machine (although be aware that there are other considerations when doing so). Note that the `make install` line must be run with higher permissions (`sudo`) to allow it to copy files into "privileged" locations.

If all goes well, congratulations! You have installed PHP. To check that the correct version is installed and available, use `php -v` at the command line and PHP will display the current version number. If you have installed PHP in a location outside of your search path, you will need to specify the full path name, as in `/path/to/dir/php -v`. To check which extensions and other options were installed, use `php -i` at the command line to run the `phpinfo()` function. As well as extension information (and a lot more besides), this returns a list of the options used with the `./configure` command. This can be useful when reinstalling PHP or when trying to clone an installation on another machine (where the same binaries cannot just be reused).

If all doesn't go well, take a close look at the errors produced. The most common type of errors happen when your system doesn't have the relevant dependencies installed for a particular extension. Often the error message will say this explicitly, but even if it just gives you an obscure error message mentioning the name of an extension, the best advice is to double-check the installation section for that extension in the PHP Manual to find out exactly what dependencies are required. Missing dependencies can often be installed using your system's package manager rather than having to manually compile them. You should also check that you have provided the location of any dependencies at the configure stage if required.

If all else fails, copy and paste the exact error message into your favorite Internet search engine, probably starting with the first error message shown if multiple errors appear. Many people have compiled PHP, and most errors have been encountered and documented online. Don't let all this talk of errors put you off trying to compile PHP. Errors are more likely to occur the more complicated you make your configuration, and if you're careful about dependencies, you can often avoid them altogether. So, first try a straightforward compilation with the default options to get the hang of things and then take it from there!

You can find more information on installations, with a general focus on web servers but also mentions of CLI usage, in the PHP Manual at `www.php.net/manual/en/install.php`.

Compiling and Installing (Extra) Core Extensions

As you saw in the previous section, the most common way to install core extensions is to enable the relevant flags at the configure stage during compilation of the main PHP installation (note, by default, many extensions are automatically enabled). However, it's not uncommon to come across the need to install an additional extension later, for instance, as the requirements for your program change from its initial design. There are two ways to approach this. The first, which you'll find recommended a lot online, is to redo the compilation/installation of PHP from scratch, adding the newly required modules at the configure stage (after issuing php -i to remember what configure options you used the first time). While this works perfectly well, compiling the full PHP binaries is a bit of a slog and can take older PCs in particular a long time to complete. There is a shortcut, however.

Each of the core extensions is actually a separate .so binary and can be compiled independently. To do this, follow the instructions in the previous section to download and unpack the PHP source code and step into the directory. If you haven't deleted it from when you compiled PHP, it should be ready to go. Within the source code is a directory called ext, inside of which are separate directories for each of the extensions.

```
~$ cd ext
~$ ls
```

This will show you all the core extensions available. For instance, if you want to add the pcntl extension, you can enter the pcntl directory and compile/install just that extension in a similar manner to how you compiled the whole PHP package in the previous section.

```
~$ cd pcntl
~$ phpize
~$ ./configure
~$ make clean
~$ make
~$ sudo make install
```

The additional command, phpize, is used to prepare the build environment for the extension. This is not necessary when building the full PHP binaries, but it is when building individual extensions. If you find that you don't have phpize on your system, it is often available through your system's package manager in the php-dev package. You can find more details about phpize and getting it at http://us.php.net/manual/en/install.pecl.phpize.php.

Once you have run the previous commands, you should find that a .so file (pcntl.so in this example) has been compiled and placed in PHP's extension directory. The final step is to tell PHP about it by adding the following line somewhere in your php.ini file:

```
extension=pcntl.so
```

If you're not sure where your php.ini file is, you can run php -i | grep "Loaded Configuration File" on the command line to find out or php --ini on the command line if you want full details of all INI files loaded. You can also use php -i to check that your extension is now correctly installed and available for use.

Installing Multiple Versions of PHP

Sometimes (particularly on development machines) you may want to install multiple versions of PHP at the same time, for instance, if you are deploying to end users with PHP already installed but who may have different versions. One straightforward way to achieve this is to create a set of virtual machines (I use VirtualBox for this) with a different version of PHP installed in each. In this scenario, you can always be sure which version you are running and that the installation and configuration of one version isn't interfering with that of another. The downside is that it can be slow to start up and shut down different VMs (or a hit on resources to run them all at once), and if you are using proprietary OSs like Windows, you can incur additional licensing costs. It is possible to have multiple versions installed and running directly on the same machine; however, if you are not careful, it can become a nightmare trying to keep the versions and their dependencies separate and making sure you know which version you are using at all times. As such, I am not going to delve into it in this book. However, the two articles in the "Further Reading" section are from respected PHP community members who have done just that; they may give you some pointers on what to do and the pitfalls involved. I suggest that before you try this, you become intimately familiar with compiling and installing PHP, the file and directory structures and locations that PHP uses, and how to check which versions of PHP and extensions are running.

There are also a couple of relevant tools listed in the "Tools" section. The first is php-build, which automatically builds multiple versions of PHP from source, although you still need to exercise care installing and using them simultaneously. The second is 3v4l.org, a web service that allows you to test chunks of code in 200+ versions of PHP at the same time. This may help you avoid the need for installing multiple versions at all.

Further Reading

- Installing multiple versions, using SVN

  - `http://derickrethans.nl/multiple-php-version-setup.html`

- Installing multiple versions, using Git

  - `http://mark-story.com/posts/view/installing-multiple-versions-of-php-from-source`

Tools

- php-build automatically builds multiple PHP versions from source that can be used in parallel.

  - *Main web site*: `https://php-build.github.io/`

- 3v4l.org is a web service that allows you test chunks of code in 200+ versions of PHP with the click of one button.

  - *Main web site*: `http://3v4l.org`

PEAR and PECL

PHP Extension and Application Repository (PEAR) is a library of code and extensions written in PHP, with an easy-to-use packaging and distribution system. PHP Extension Community Library (PECL) is essentially the same but is for extensions written in C.

Both PECL and PEAR work in a similar way to package managers such as Debian's apt-get. For example, to install the Cairo graphics extension from PECL, simply use `sudo pecl install cairo` at the command line. This will download, compile, and install Cairo for you, and you can then start using it from within your PHP scripts. Similarly, to install the RDF extension from PEAR, use `pear install rdf`.

The pear and pecl commands are included as standard with PHP; however, some package managers put them in the optional `php-dev` or `php-pear` package. On Ubuntu, for instance, use `sudo apt-get install php-pear` to install the package containing both `pecl` and `pear`.

You can find more information on both tools, as well as the hundreds of extensions and libraries available, at `http://pear.php.net` and `http://pecl.php.net`, respectively.

Composer

Composer is a dependency manager. While it deals with packages, it is not a package manager like PEAR. Rather than installing packages centrally, it deals with them on a per-project basis, ensuring that the appropriate versions of the relevant packages, and their dependencies, are installed automatically for that project.

The basic Composer workflow happens as follows:

1. You install Composer.

2. In the base directory of your project, you create a JSON-formatted file called composer.json that specifies which packages (and versions) your project needs.

3. In that directory, you run Composer. It will fetch and install all of the specified packages and will automatically also install any of the other packages that those you have specified depend on (and so on until all dependencies are satisfied).

4. In your PHP code, simply add the function require 'vendor/ autoload.php'; and your libraries will be automatically available when you use them.

Fully comprehensive documentation, aimed at beginners as well as advanced users, is available on the Composer web site. Composer itself doesn't host any packages; that is the job of package repositories. Packagist is the main, and currently the only, comprehensive public repository, and it is the default used by Composer. You can browse the thousands of available packages on the Packagist web site. You can, of course, specify a different repository and indeed create and use your own packages privately if you need.

The following are resources for Composer, the easy way to keep libraries consistent and up-to-date on a per-project basis:

- *Main web site*: `http://getcomposer.org`

- *Package repository*: `https://packagist.org`

- *Tutorial*: `http://code.tutsplus.com/tutorials/easy-package-management-with-composer--net-25530`

Symfony2 Bundles

If you're using the Symfony2 framework, you can choose from and download more than 3,000 useful code bundles from Knp Bundles. These can be installed manually or often using the Composer dependency system (see the previous section). Visit `http://knpbundles.com/` for more information and to browse the available code.

Getting Help

Even with excellent books like this on the market, you will sometimes need a little additional help when you come across a tricky problem with PHP. The following are some potential sources of easy (and mostly free) help.

The PHP Manual

You can find the official PHP Manual online at `http://php.net/docs.php`. The manual mostly provides fairly comprehensive documentation on PHP installation, syntax, functions, and many extensions. Of particular note are the user comments at the bottom of each page. These are generally helpful and offer real-world advice related to the function or topic of the page. Occasionally some poor-quality advice is given in the comments; however, this is usually corrected or mentioned in a subsequent comment, so it's worth reading through all the comments on a given page.

A handy function of the online manual is that you can do a quick lookup of a function or topic by typing it as the first part of a URL. For instance, if you can't remember what the parameters of `strripos()` are, you can simply type `http://php.net/strripos` into your browser, and you will be sent straight to the relevant page. Likewise, if you want a quick refresher on how PHP handles arrays, visit `http://php.net/array` and you'll go straight to the array page in the language/types section of the manual.

If you don't always have an Internet connection, you can also download a copy of the manual from `www.php.net/download-docs.php`. It is available as HTML, as Unix-style man pages, and in Microsoft Compiled HTML Manual (CHM) format.

Official Mailing Lists

There are a number of official mailing lists at `http://php.net/mailing-lists.php` covering a wide variety of topics. Of note for getting help are the "General user list" for general queries and the "Windows PHP users list" for Windows-specific questions. Beware when subscribing that some of the lists are quite busy and you will get a large number of e-mails each day. The archives are available online if you just want to browse them or get a feel for the volume generated on each list.

Stack Overflow

If you're not familiar with it, Stack Overflow (`http://stackoverflow.com`) is a prolific "question and answer" site aimed at programmers. Unlike some Q&A sites, you don't need to join or pay to view the answers to questions, ads are limited, and there are millions of answered questions on the site. This includes a good chunk of PHP-related questions.

All questions and answers are "tagged" with their topics so that you can find the ones relevant to you. To browse questions tagged with PHP, visit `http://stackoverflow.com/questions/tagged/php`. You can also use the site's search facility; to narrow your search to only PHP-related answers, add `[tag]` to your search. For example, if you want to search for questions about the date function, which is a common word in English and a common function name in many programming languages, search for *[php] date* to get only PHP-specific information. At the time of writing, there were 1,068,469 questions tagged with `php`, and almost 100 tagged with `[php]` and `[functional-programming]`. The moderators are usually very quick at shutting down duplicate questions, so you can see from these numbers that a lot of relevant information is available.

Other Books

While you may think that this is the only book on PHP you will ever need, I have been told that there may be other PHP books available. While I can't recommend any specifically (other than those I have already noted in the relevant chapters), if you browse any big-name bookseller, you will find a plethora of PHP-related titles. And of course you can browse the 100+ PHP-related books by my esteemed publisher at `www.apress.com/gb/search?query=php`.

Newsgroups

PHP has a set of official newsgroups listed and archived at `http://news.php.net/` that cover a wide range of PHP topic areas. These may be worth a browse and sometimes can elicit a response to queries (although some of the internal lists are definitely not for the faint-hearted).

PHP Subredit

The PHP "subreddit" on Reddit.com at www.reddit.com/r/PHP/ is a mixture of PHP news, opinions, useful links, and requests for help. Although usually genuinely interesting with helpful responses to questions, an occasional assortment of trolls and unhelpful/rude people can be found here as well. A more tolerant subreddit for getting help is PHPhelp at https://www.reddit.com/r/phphelp, which was specifically set up to answer questions (even from beginners), although it's frequented somewhat less than the main PHP subreddit.

PHP on GitHub

Sometimes the best way to solve a problem is to look at similar code other people have written. GitHub, the popular source repository web site, has tons of the stuff to plow through. You can search all the code repositories at https://github.com/search, and you can use the modifier *language:php* in your search terms to narrow your results to projects using your favorite language. If you just want to keep an eye on what PHP projects are popular these days, you can check out the PHP trending list at https://github.com/trending?l=php.

File and Data Format Libraries for PHP

As you'll no doubt have gathered while reading through this book, functional programming is big on the reuse of code. When you've gotten the hang of writing IO monads and the like to handle your impure I/O needs, you may want to pause for a moment before writing functions to process Word documents (for instance) and see whether someone else has written one that you can use. This section lists extensions, libraries, and API bindings, broken down by category, that can be used to work with different file and data formats in PHP. Most of these won't be written in a functional style, but as I discussed earlier in the book, PHP *isn't* a functional programming language, and you would be foolish to ignore the other positive aspects of the language. One of those positive aspects is the wide ecosystem of libraries and extensions for dealing with different data formats and file types. When you've found a nonfunctional library that does what you need, it's often quicker and more reliable to wrap it up in some functions and monads than it is to write a pure functional replacement by hand.

Within each category covered next you will find the name of the library, followed by a list of file types (specified by their common file extension for brevity) that it supports, and the main web site for that library. Where there isn't a common file extension (for example, streaming data formats), the name of the format is used instead.

The following list is not exhaustive, and not all libraries allow you to both read and write the given formats or support all features of the format. Check the relevant documentation for the library and try it out before selecting it for your project. If you haven't found a library to help you with the file format you're looking for, try looking through the Packagist, PEAR, or PECL repositories using your favorite search engine to find one, or consider "shelling out" to non-PHP helper applications (using shell_exec, pcntl_exec(), or similar).

Office Documents

OpenDocument

- *Formats*: odt
- *Web site*: `http://pear.php.net/manual/en/package.fileformats.opendocument.php`

PHPExcel

- *Formats*: ods, gnm, gnumeric, xlsx, xls (biff), xls (SpreadsheetML), htm, html, sky, slk, sylk, csv, pdf
- *Web site*: `https://github.com/PHPOffice/PHPExcel`

php-excel-reader

- *Formats*: xls (biff)
- *Web site*: `http://code.google.com/p/php-excel-reader/`

Excel Writer (XML) for PHP

- *Formats*: xls (SpreadsheetML)
- *Web site*: `http://sourceforge.net/projects/excelwriterxml/`

php-export-data

- *Formats*: xls (SpreadsheetML), csv, tsv
- *Web site*: `https://github.com/elidickinson/php-export-data`

Spreadsheet_Excel_Writer

- *Formats*: xls (biff)
- *Web site*: `http://pear.php.net/manual/en/package.fileformats.spreadsheet-excel-writer.php`

SimpleExcel

- *Formats*: xlsx, htm, html, csv, tsv, json
- *Web site*: `http://faisalman.github.com/simple-excel-php/`

PHPPresentation

- *Formats*: pptx
- *Web site*: `https://github.com/PHPOffice/PHPPresentation`

PHPWord

- *Formats*: docx
- *Web site*: `http://phpword.codeplex.com/`

Cairo extension

- *Formats*: pdf, ps, svg
- *Web site*: `www.php.net/manual/en/book.cairo.php`

tcPDF

- *Formats*: pdf
- *Web site*: www.tcpdf.org/

DomPDF

- *Formats*: pdf
- *Web site*: https://github.com/dompdf/dompdf

Haru PDF extension

- *Formats*: pdf
- *Web site*: www.php.net/manual/en/book.haru.php

PDF extension (PDFlib)

- *Formats*: pdf
- *Web site*: www.php.net/manual/en/book.pdf.php

mPDF

- *Formats*: pdf
- *Web site*: www.mpdf1.com/mpdf/index.php

FDF extension

- *Formats*: fdf
- *Web site*: www.php.net/manual/en/book.fdf.php

DOM extension

- *Formats*: htm, html
- *Web site*: www.php.net/manual/en/book.dom.php

Contact_Vcard

- *Formats*: vcf, vcard
- *Web site*: http://pear.php.net/manual/en/package.fileformats.contact-vcard.php

File_MARC

- *Formats*: mrc, marc
- *Web site*: http://pear.php.net/manual/en/package.fileformats.file-marc.php

Compression, Archiving, and Encryption

File_Archive

- *Formats*: tar, gz, gzip, bz2, tgz, tar.gz, tbz, tar.bz2, zip, ar, deb
- *Web site*: http://pear.php.net/manual/en/package.fileformats.file-archive.php

Zlib extension

- *Formats*: gz, gzip
- *Web site*: www.php.net/manual/en/intro.zlib.php

BZip2 extension

- *Formats*: bz2
- *Web site*: www.php.net/manual/en/book.bzip2.php

RAR extension

- *Formats*: rar
- *Web site*: www.php.net/manual/en/book.rar.php

Zip extension

- *Formats*: zip
- *Web site*: www.php.net/manual/en/book.zip.php

RPM extension

- *Formats*: rpm
- *Web site*: www.php.net/manual/en/book.rpmreader.php

LZF compression

- *Formats*: lzf
- *Web site*: www.php.net/manual/en/book.lzf.php

File_cabinet

- *Formats*: cab
- *Web site*: http://pear.php.net/manual/en/package.fileformats.file-cabinet.php

Phar extension

- *Formats*: phar, tar, zip
- *Web site*: www.php.net/manual/en/book.phar.php

GNU Privacy Guard extension

- *Formats*: gpg, pgp
- *Web site*: www.php.net/manual/en/book.gnupg.php

Graphics

Gmagick extension

- *Formats*: art, avi, avs, bmp, cals, cin, cgm, cmyk, cur, cut, dcm, dcx, dib, dpx, emf, epdf, epi, eps, eps2, eps3, epsf, epsi, ept, fax, fig, fits, fpx, gif, gplt, gray, hpgl, html, ico, jbig, jng, jp2, jpc, jpeg, man, mat, miff, mono, mng, mpeg, m2v, mpc, msl, mtv, mvg, otb, p7, palm, pam, pbm, pcd, pcds, pcl, pcx, pdb, pdf, pfa, pfb, pgm, picon, pict, pix, png, pnm, ppm, ps, ps2, ps3, psd, ptif, pwp, ras, rad, rgb, rgba, rla, rle, sct, sfw, sgi, shtml, sun, svg, tga, tiff, tim, ttf, txt, uil, uyvy, vicar, viff, wbmp, wmf, wpg, xbm, xcf, xpm, xwd, yuv

- *Web site*: www.php.net/manual/en/book.gmagick.php

ImageMagick extension

- *Formats*: aai, art, arw, avi, avs, bmp,bmp2,bmp3, cals, cgm, cin, cmyk, cmyka, cr2, crw, cur, cut, dcm, dcr, dcx, dds, dib, djvu, dng, dot, dpx, emf, epdf, epi, eps, eps2, eps3, epsf, epsi, ept, exr, fax, fig, fits, fpx, gif, gplt, gray, hdr, hpgl, hrz, html, ico, info, inline, jbig, jng, jp2, jpc, jpeg, jxr, man, mat, miff, mono, mng, m2v, mpeg, mpc, mpr, mrw, msl, mtv, mvg, nef, orf, otb, p7, palm, pam, clipboard, pbm, pcd, pcds, pcl, pcx, pdb, pdf, pef, pfa, pfb, pfm, pgm, picon, pict, pix, png, png8, png00, png24, png32, png48, png64, pnm, ppm, ps, ps2, ps3, psb, psd, ptif, pwp, rad, raf, rgb, rgba, rfg, rla, rle, sct, sfw, sgi, shtml, sid,mrsid, sparse-color, sun, svg, tga, tiff, tim, ttf, txt, uil, uyvy, vicar, viff, wbmp, wdp, webp, wmf, wpg, x, xbm, xcf, xpm, xwd, x3f, ycbcr, ycbcra, yuv

- *Web site*: www.php.net/manual/en/book.imagick.php

File_DICOM

- *Formats*: dcm

- *Web site*: http://pear.php.net/manual/en/package.fileformats.file-dicom.php

Ming extension

- *Formats*: swf, flash

- *Web site*: www.php.net/manual/en/book.ming.php

Cairo extension

- *Formats*: pdf, svg, ps

- *Web site*: www.php.net/manual/en/book.cairo.php

EXIF extension

- *Formats*: exif

- *Web site*: www.php.net/manual/en/book.exif.php

Audio

MP3_id

- *Formats*: mp3
- *Web site*: http://pear.php.net/manual/en/package.fileformats.mp3-id.php

OGG/Vorbis extension

- *Formats*: ogg, oga, ogv, spx
- *Web site*: www.php.net/manual/en/book.oggvorbis.php

php-reader

- *Formats*: mp3, asf, wma, wmv flac, 3gp, 3gpp, avc, dcf, m21, m4a, m4b, m4p, m4v, maf, mj2, mjp, mov, mp4, odf, sdv,qt, abs, mp1, mp2, mpg, mpeg, vob, evo, ogg, oga, ogv, spx
- *Web site*: http://code.google.com/p/php-reader/

ID3 extension

- *Formats*: mp3
- *Web site*: www.php.net/manual/en/book.id3.php

ktaglib extension

- *Formats*: mp3
- *Web site*: www.php.net/manual/en/book.ktaglib.php

Multimedia and Video

PHP-FFmpeg

- *Formats*: 4xm, 8088flex tmv, act voice, adobe filmstrip, audio iff (aiff), american laser games mm, 3gpp amr, amazing studio packed animation file, apple http live streaming, artworx data format, adp, afc, asf, ast, avi, avisynth, avr, avs, beam software siff, bethesda softworks vid, binary text, bink, bitmap brothers jv, brute force & ignorance, brstm, bwf, cri adx, discworld ii bmv, interplay c93, delphine software international cin, cd+g, commodore cdxl, core audio format, crc testing format, creative voice, cryo apc, d-cinema audio, deluxe paint animation, dfa, dv video, dxa, electronic arts cdata, electronic arts multimedia, ensoniq paris audio file, ffm (ffserver live feed), flash (swf), flash 9 (avm2), fli/flc/flx animation, flash video (flv), framecrc testing format, funcom iss, g.723.1, g.729 bit, g.729 raw, gif animation, gxf, icedraw file, ico, id quake ii cin video, id roq, iec61937 encapsulation, iff, ilbc, interplay mve, iv8, ivf (on2), ircam, latm, lmlm4, loas, lvf, lxf, matroska, matroska audio, ffmpeg metadata, maxis xa, md studio, metal gear solid: the twin snakes, megalux frame, mobotix .mxg, monkeys audio, motion pixels mvi, mov/quicktime/ mp4, mp2, mp3, mpeg-1 system, mpeg-ps (program stream), mpeg-ts (transport stream), mpeg-4, mime multipart jpeg, msn tcp webcam, mtv, musepack, musepack sv8, material exchange format (mxf), material exchange format (mxf), d10 mapping, nc camera feed, nist speech header resources, ntt twinvq (vqf), nullsoft streaming video, nuppelvideo, nut, ogg, playstation portable pmp, portable voice format, technotrend pva, qcp, raw adts (aac), raw ac-3, raw chinese avs video, raw criadx, raw dirac, raw dnxhd, raw dts, raw dts-hd, raw e-ac-3, raw flac, raw gsm, raw h.261, raw h.263, raw h.264, raw ingenient mjpeg, raw mjpeg, raw mlp, raw mpeg, raw mpeg-1, raw mpeg-2, raw mpeg-4, raw null, raw video, raw id roq, raw shorten, raw tak, raw truehd, raw vc-1, raw pcm, rdt, redcode r3d, realmedia, redirector, redspark, renderware texture dictionary, rl2, rpl/armovie, lego mindstorms rso, rsd, rtmp, rtp, rtsp, sap, sbg, sdp, sega film/cpk, silicon graphics movie, sierra sol, sierra vmd, smacker, smjpeg, smush, sony openmg (oma), sony playstation str, sony wave64 (w64), sox native format, sun au format, text files, thp, tiertex limited seq, true audio, vc-1 test bitstream, vivo, wav, wavpack, webm, windows televison (wtv), wing commander iii movie, westwood studios audio, westwood studios vqa, xmv, xwma, extended binary text (xbin), yuv4mpeg pipe, psygnosis yop

- *Web site*: https://github.com/alchemy-fr/PHP-FFmpeg

Programming, Technical, and Data Interchange

File_Fstab

- *Formats*: fstab

- *Web site*: http://pear.php.net/manual/en/package.fileformats.file-fstab.php

File_Passwd

- *Formats*: passwd

- *Web site*: http://pear.php.net/manual/en/package.fileformats.file-passwd.php

YAML extension

- *Formats*: yaml

- *Web site*: www.php.net/manual/en/book.yaml.php

Assorted extensions

- *Formats*: xml

- *Web site*: www.php.net/manual/en/refs.xml.php

XSL extension

- *Formats*: xsl, xslt

- *Web site*: www.php.net/manual/en/intro.xsl.php

JSON extension

- *Formats*: json

- *Web site*: www.php.net/manual/en/book.json.php

Native file functions (fopen, etc.)

- *Formats*: txt

- *Web site*: www.php.net/manual/

Miscellaneous

File_Fortune

- *Formats*: fortune
- *Web site*: http://pear.php.net/manual/en/package.fileformats.file-fortune.php

APPENDIX B

■ ■ ■

Command-Line PHP

Virtually all the example code in this book is written to be run at the command-line interface (CLI). There are several reasons for this.

- It removes the need for boilerplate code to deal with HTML, HTTP interactions, and so forth, which muddy the waters when you're learning a new topic (and would extend the length of this book unnecessarily!).

- While it is perfectly at home on the Web, functional programming thrives in the CLI environment where scripts aren't limited by time or resource allocation. This makes it possible to create longer-running "software" rather than "scripts" that are executed and gone in the blink of an eye.

- As a programmer, you can take advantage of tools like REPLs (which you'll look at in this appendix) to develop your code interactively, which can be a great help when learning new coding techniques.

This appendix takes a look at the basic steps involved in breaking PHP free from the Web. I'll cover the technical steps involved and also the differences in programming practices and focus.

PHP Without a Web Server

Most PHP programmers have used PHP strictly in a web server environment. In such an environment, PHP is a CGI/Fast GGI or server module called and controlled by the HTTP server (usually Apache, IIS, Nginx, or similar). The HTTP server receives a request for a PHP-based web page and calls the PHP process to execute it, which usually returns output to the HTTP server to be sent on to the end user.

There have been a number of attempts to create local applications (scripting systems, desktop apps, and so forth) with PHP using a locally installed web server, with some success. However, the downsides of using this web-type model for local apps are numerous.

- For the value they provide in these scenarios, web servers such as Apache are often over-specified and resource-hungry.

- Unless properly locked down, a web server running locally introduces a point of access to your machine for malicious visitors from the outside world.

- HTTP is a verbose protocol and (arguably) ideally suited for the Web. However, it's often overkill for local interprocess communication and adds more resource and complexity overhead to your application.

- Your application interface typically runs in a web browser and therefore looks anything but local (and comes with additional support/upgrade headaches unless you install a browser specifically for your app).

© Rob Aley 2017
R. Aley, *Pro Functional PHP Programming*, DOI 10.1007/978-1-4842-2958-3

PHP, as of version 5.4, includes a built-in web server, which removes some of the problems described earlier. However, it was designed for local testing of PHP scripts destined to be deployed on a fully fledged HTTP server such as Apache in a live environment. It is a route that can be explored for some local apps, particularly where you want to run a private instance of a PHP web app that already exists. However, its stability, reliability, and suitability for production-ready local apps are yet to be proven; it doesn't support concurrent requests (which may or may not be a problem for local apps); and it still comes with the baggage of the HTTP protocol and web browsers.

Since version 4.3, PHP has had an ace up its sleeve that solves all of these problems. The PHP CLI Server Application Programming Interface (SAPI), to give it its formal name, is essentially a long way of saying "stand-alone PHP." It cuts out the need for a web server and provides a stand-alone PHP binary for you to interact with. For instance, typing the following at a shell prompt

```
~$ php /home/myfiles/myprogram.php
```

will simply execute your `myprogram.php` file (which you write mostly like any other PHP script) and return any output to the terminal (unless you tell it otherwise) instead of being sent to the web server (which doesn't exist!).

In general, PHP scripts called directly using the PHP CLI SAPI will behave in the same way as when called through a web server, although there are some differences. For instance, you won't find any `$_GET` or `$_POST` arrays containing user-supplied data, and PHP won't output any HTTP headers by default; these concepts don't mean much beyond the Web. Default settings such as `max_execution_time` are set to sensible values for local use (in this case to 0 so your scripts won't time out), output buffering is turned off, and error messages are displayed in plain text rather than HTML. You can of course change the settings back to match the web settings where appropriate by updating the `php.ini` settings file. There is usually a separate `php.ini` file for the CLI SAPI. To find it, run `php --ini` on the command line.

What's Different About the CLI SAPI?

The following are the main differences between the PHP CLI SAPI and the standard PHP web implementations:

- No HTTP headers are written to the output by default. This makes sense because they hold no meaning in the command line and so would be just extraneous text printed before your genuine output. If your output will later be funneled out to a web browser, you will need to manually add any necessary headers (for instance, by using the `header()` PHP function).

- PHP does not change the working directory to that of the PHP script being executed. To do this manually, use `getcwd()` and `chdir()` to get and set the current directory. Otherwise, the current working directory will be that from which you invoked the script. For instance, if you are currently in `/home/rob` and you type `php /home/peter/some_script.php`, the working directory used in PHP will be `/home/rob`, not `/home/peter`.

- Any error or warning messages are output in plain text, rather than HTML-formatted text. If you want HTMLified errors such as when, for instance, you are producing static HTML files, you can override this by setting the `html_errors` runtime configuration directive to true in your script using `ini_set('html_errors', 1);`.

- PHP implicitly "flushes" all output immediately and doesn't buffer by default. Online performance can often be harmed by sending output straight to a browser, so instead output is buffered and sent in optimal-sized chunks when the chunk is full. Offline this is not likely to be an issue, so blocks of HTML and other output from constructs such as print and echo are sent to the shell straightaway. There is no need to use flush() to clear a buffer when you are waiting for further output. You can still use PHP's output buffering functions to capture and control output if you want; see the "Output Control Functions" section in the PHP Manual for more information.

- There is no execution time limit set. Your script will run continuously until it exits of its own volition; PHP will not terminate it even if it hangs. If you want to set a time limit to rein in misbehaving scripts, you can do so from within the script using the set_time_limit() function.

- The variables $argc and $argv, which describe any command-line arguments passed to your script, are automatically set. These are discussed fully later in this chapter.

- PHP defines the constants STDIN, STDOUT, and STDERR, relating to the standard streams of the same name, and automatically opens input/output streams for them. These give your application instant access to "standard input" (STDIN), "standard output" (STDOUT), and "standard error" (STDERR) streams.

Further Reading

- "Output Control Functions" section in the PHP Manual

  - www.php.net/manual/en/ref.outcontrol.php

- Standard streams (STDIN, STDOUT, STDERR) on Wikipedia

  - http://en.wikipedia.org/wiki/Standard_streams

CLI SAPI Installation

To use the PHP CLI SAPI, you may need to install it first. Appendix A gives details on installing (and compiling, where necessary) PHP in all its forms. However, you may find that the CLI SAPI is already installed if you have PHP installed (often in a folder called sapi/cli in the PHP program folders), and if not, it is usually available in modern OS software repositories. (For example, in Ubuntu a package called php-cli exists and can be installed from any package manager or via the command line with sudo apt-get install php-cli.) If it is installed in the command-line search path, typing php -v on the command line will print the version details, confirming it is indeed installed. On other Debian-based distributions you can type apt search php at the command line to search for the package if it is named differently. On Windows, it comes automatically in the zip file with the precompiled version of PHP, and on OS X/macOS it is available through Homebrew and MacPorts (see Appendix A for details) as well as (a sometimes out-of-date version) being installed by default.

PHP Command-Line Options

The PHP binary will accept a number of command-line options/switches/arguments that affect its operation. You can see a full list in your installed version by typing php -h at the command line. Although some apply only to the CGI SAPI (used by web servers when there is not a "module" such as the PHP Apache module), the following are some of the more interesting and common ones used when interacting with the CLI SAPI:

- -f or --file: This allows you to specify the file name of the script to be run and is optional. The -f option exists to allow compatibility with software and scripts such as automation software, which can programmatically call command-line programs but require file name arguments to be formed in this way. It also allows default file-type handlers to be easily set on Windows for PHP scripts. In most cases, the two following lines are mostly equivalent:

```
~$ php -f myscript.php
~$ php myscript.php
```

The only real difference in usage between the two versions of command come when interpreting command-line arguments passed to the script, which you will look at in the "Command-Line Arguments for Your Script" section.

- -a or --interactive: This runs PHP interactively, which allows you to type in PHP code, line by line, rather than executing a saved PHP script. This mode of operation is often called a *read-eval-print loop* (REPL). As well as providing an interactive interface for testing and developing code, it can act as an enhanced PHP-enabled shell or command line. I covered this more closely in Chapter 4.

- -c or --php-ini: This specifies the php.ini file that PHP will use for this application. This is particularly useful if you are also running web services using PHP on the same machine; if it is not specified, PHP will look in various default locations for php.ini and may end up using the same one as your web service. By providing one specifically for your CLI applications, you can "open up" various restrictions that make more sense for offline applications. Note that by using the CLI SAPI, PHP will automatically override several php.ini settings regardless of whether you specify a custom .ini file using this option. These overridden settings are those that affect the behavior outlined in the "What's Different About the CLI SAPI?" section, and while the php.ini file is ignored in these cases, you can revert or change these settings directly in your code using the ini_set() function or similar. You can also use the -d or --define option to set options (for example, php -d max_execution_time=2000 myscript.php). If you are deploying software onto machines that you do not control (for example, if you are selling software for users to install on their own machines), it makes sense to use one of these mechanisms to ensure that PHP will be running with the settings you expect, not the settings the user may happen to have. See -n next as well.

- -n or --no-php-ini: This tells PHP not to load a php.ini file at all. This can be useful if you do not want to ship one with your application and instead set all the settings directly within your code using ini_set() or similar. PHP will use its default settings if no .ini file is provided, and it is worth remembering that these default settings may change from version to version of PHP (and indeed have done so in the past). You shouldn't rely on the current defaults being suitable for your application. You can use php --ini to show the default path that PHP will look for .ini files when the -n option isn't used and -c isn't used to specify a file.

- `-e` or `--profile-info`: This puts PHP into Extended Information Mode (EIM). EIM generates extra information for use by profilers and debuggers. If you're not using a profiler or debugger that requires this mode, you should not enable it because it can degrade performance. You can find more information on profilers and debuggers in Chapter 4.

- `-i` or `--info`: This calls the `phpinfo()` function and prints the output. This outputs a large range of information about the PHP installation, in plain-text format rather than the usual HTML (it detects you are calling it from the CLI SAPI). This can be useful in tracking down issues with the installation, as well as giving you version information, lists of extensions installed, relevant file paths, and so on. As with any other shell command, the output can be piped to other commands, such as grep. So, if you wanted to check whether IPv6 was enabled in your PHP binary for instance, on Linux or OS X you could try the following:

```
~$ php -i | grep -i "ipv6"
```

On Windows you could try the following:

```
> php -i | findstr /I ipv6
```

- `-l` or `--syntax-check`: This option parses the file, checking for syntax errors. This is a basic "lint" type checker; more advanced static code analysis tools are discussed in Chapter 4. Be aware that this option checks only for basic syntax errors—the sort that cause the PHP engine to fail. More subtle bugs, problems in your program logic, and errors that are created at runtime will not be detected. Your code is not executed, so it can help pick up basic errors before running code that may alter data and cause problems if it fails. Even when you run such code in a testing environment, resetting data and setting up for another test can take time, so a quick check for basic syntax errors first can be a time-saver. Some integrated development environments (IDEs) and text editors run php `-l` in the background to highlight syntax errors as you type. For instance, the linter-php package in GitHub's Atom editor uses this method for live linting of PHP code.

- `-m` or `--modules`: This lists all the loaded PHP and Zend modules/extensions. These are modules that PHP has been compiled with and may include things such as core, mysql, PDO, json, and more. This is useful for checking the PHP installation has the functionality that your application requires. You can also check from within your scripts using the `extension_loaded()` function or by calling the `phpinfo()` function. `-m` provides a subset of the information given with the `-i` flag described earlier, and `-i` (or the `phpinfo()` function) will return more information about the configuration, version, and so on, of the modules.

- `-r` or `--run`: This runs a line of PHP code supplied as the argument, rather than executing it from a file. The line of code should be enclosed by single quotes when using shells like bash as they will try to interpolate PHP variables as if they were shell variables if you use double quotes. However, on Windows you should use double quotes to avoid errors because of single quotes on the command line. The `-r` option performs a similar role to the `-a` interactive mode, except that PHP's "state" is cleared after each line is executed. This means that the line of code supplied is treated as the whole script to be executed, and execution is terminated once it has been run. Here's an example that will print out "4" followed by a newline character:

```
~$ php -r "echo (2+2).\"\n\";"
```

251

Note that the line must be well-formed, syntactically correct PHP, so don't miss the semicolon at the end! I will return to -r later in this chapter in the section "Different Ways to Call PHP Scripts."

- -B or --process-begin, -R or --process-code, -F or --process-file, -E or --process-end: These four arguments allow you to specify PHP code to be executed before, during, and after input from STDIN is processed by PHP. -B specifies a line of code to execute before the input is processed, -R specifies a line of code to execute for every line of input, and -F specifies a PHP file to execute for each line. Finally, -E executes a line of code at the end of the input process. In -R and -F, two special variables are available; $argn contains the text of the line being processed, and $argi contains the number of the line being processed. This is mainly useful when using PHP directly in shell scripts. For instance, to print a text file with line numbers, you can do something like this:

```
~$ more my_text_file.txt | php -B "echo \"Lets add line
numbers...\n\";" -R "echo \"$argi: $argn\n\";" -E "echo \"That's the
end folks\n\";"
```

This code will output something like this:

```
Lets add line numbers...
1: Lorem ipsum dolor sit amet, consectetur adipisicing elit, sed do
2: eiusmod tempor incididunt ut labore et dolore magna aliqua. Ut enim ad
3: minim veniam, quis nostrud exercitation ullamco laboris nisi ut aliquip
4: ex ea commodo consequat. Duis aute irure dolor in reprehenderit in That's the end folks
```

- -s or --syntax-highlight: This outputs an HTML version of the PHP script, with colored syntax highlighting. The PHP script is not executed or validated; it's simply made "pretty." The pretty HTML is printed to STDOUT and can be useful when pouring over code looking for errors, issues, and optimizations. This works only with PHP in files, not with code provided by the -r option. Most modern IDEs and code editors provide syntax highlighting by default; however, this can be useful if your only access to a machine is on the command line and the editor you are using doesn't do syntax highlighting. In this case, use -s to create a colored version of your script and either download it or view it through your web browser if the machine has a web server installed.

- -v or --version: This outputs the PHP version information. This can also be found in the output of the -i option described earlier. Be careful when assuming a particular format; some package repositories (Ubuntu, for instance) include their name and their own build numbers in the version string, so don't just filter it for any numerics.

- -w or --strip: This outputs the contents of the source code with any unnecessary white space and any comments removed. This can be used only with code files (not with lines of code supplied by -r) and does not work with the syntax highlighting option shown earlier. This is used to "minify" a file, in other words, reduce the file size. Contrary to popular opinion, this will not speed up most scripts; the overhead of parsing comments and white space is extremely negligible. You should also be wary of support and debugging issues, even if a copy of the "full" code is kept, as line numbers in error reports will no longer match between the original and stripped versions. It also does not minify identifiers such as variable names and so cannot be used to obfuscate your code. There are few reasons to use this option these days. To make a file smaller for distribution, using proper compression (for example, adding it to a zip file) is usually a better method.

- -z or --zend-extension: This specifies the file name/path for a Zend extension to be loaded before your script is run. This allows dynamic loading of extensions, which can alternatively be specified in the php.ini file if they are always to be loaded.

- --rf or --rfunction, --rc or --rclass, --re or --rextension, --rz or --rzendextension, --ri or --rextinfo: These options allow you to explore PHP structures using reflection. Reflection is the process by which PHP can perform runtime introspection, which is a way to allow you to look into elements and structures of your code at runtime. The first three options print reflection information about a named function, class, or extension. The last two print basic information about a Zend extension or a standard extension, as returned by the phpinfo() function. This reflection information, which is very detailed, is available only if PHP is compiled with reflection support. These options can be used as a quick but precise reference guide to the entities listed earlier and are particularly useful in interrogating unknown code written by others.

Further Reading

- Reflection information in the PHP Manual

  - www.php.net/manual/en/book.reflection.php

- "Introspection and Reflection in PHP" by Octavia Anghel

  - www.sitepoint.com/introspection-and-reflection-in-php/

Command-Line Arguments for Your Script

As you've seen, passing arguments to PHP is straightforward and done in the normal way. However, passing arguments for use by your PHP script is a little more complicated, as PHP needs to know where its own arguments stop and where your script's arguments starts. The best way to examine how PHP deals with this is through some examples. Consider the following PHP script:

```php
<?php

echo "Number of arguments given : ".$argc."\n";

echo "List of arguments given :\n";

print_r($argv);
```

There are two special variables in this script:

- $argc: This records the number of command-line arguments passed to the script.

- $argv: This is an array of the actual arguments passed.

Let's save the script as `arguments.php`. Now let's call it as follows:

```
~$ php -e arguments.php -i -b=big -l red white "and blue"
```

You will get the following output:

```
Number of arguments given : 7
List of arguments given :
Array
(
[0] => arguments.php
[1] => -i
[2] => -b=big
[3] => -l
[4] => red
[5] => white
[6] => and blue
)
```

As you can see, all the arguments given from the file name onward in the command are passed to the script. The first, -e, which is used by PHP itself, is not passed through. So, as a general rule, everything after the file name is treated as an argument to the script; anything before the file name is treated as an argument for PHP itself, and the file name is shared between the two.

There is, of course, an exception. As you learned earlier, in addition to specifying the file name of your script on its own, you can also pass it as part of the -f flag. So, if you execute the following command

```
~$ php -e -f arguments.php -i -b=big -l red white "and blue"
```

you get the following unexpected output:

```
phpinfo()
PHP Version => 7.0.15-0ubuntu0.16.10.4

System => Linux desktop 4.8.0-49-generic #52-Ubuntu SMP Thu Apr 20 09:38:39 UTC
2017 x86_64
Server API => Command Line Interface
Virtual Directory Support => disabled
Configuration File (php.ini) Path => /etc/php/7.0/cli
Loaded Configuration File => /etc/php/7.0/cli/php.ini
Scan this dir for additional .ini files => /etc/php/7.0/cli/conf.d
Additional .ini files parsed => /etc/php/7.0/cli/conf.d/10-mysqlnd.ini,
/etc/php/7.0/cli/conf.d/10-opcache.ini,
<rest of output removed for brevity>
```

You may recognize this as the output of calling `php -i`. Rather than treating arguments after the file name as belonging to the script, PHP has treated the -i argument (and those afterward) as one of its own. As -i is a valid PHP argument, it decides that it was what you wanted and invokes its "information" mode. If you need to pass the file name as part of the -f flag rather than as an argument on its own, you will need to separate your scripts arguments using two dashes (--). So, for the previous command to work as expected, you need to alter it to read as follows:

```
~$ php -e -f arguments.php -- -i -b=big -l red white "and blue"
```

Everything after the --, plus the script file name, is passed as arguments to the script, and you get the expected output.

This can make your scripts a little messy, particularly if you are passing lots of arguments, so you may want to look at the following sections on self-executing scripts, which show you how to embed PHP arguments within the script, allowing the script to claim any and all arguments passed as its own.

Different Ways to Call PHP Scripts

As you can probably tell from the command-line options in the previous section, there are several ways to execute PHP code when using the CLI SAPI. Although I've covered a couple of these already, I will discuss them here again for completeness.

From a File

You can tell PHP to execute a particular PHP source code file. Here's an example:

```
~$ php myscript.php
~$ php -f myscript.php
```

Note that -f is optional; the previous two lines are functionally equivalent. The PHP command-line options detailed earlier, where appropriate, work in this method. This example:

```
~$ php -e myscript.php
```

will execute the file myscript.php in Extended Information Mode.

As with the web version of PHP, source files can be interpolated (mixed) with HTML (or, more usefully on the command line, plain text). So, you will still need your opening <? or <?php tag; otherwise, your source code will just be printed straight out without being executed.

From a String

You can execute a single line of code with the -r flag, as shown here:

```
~$ php -r "echo(\"Hello World!\n\");"
```

Many of the other command-line options are not available with the -r method, such as syntax highlighting. Watch out for shell variable substitution (use single quotes rather than double quotes around your code in Bash shells) and other mangling of your code by the shell. Unless it really is a quick one-off, it is likely safer and easier to pop the relevant line into a file and execute that instead. One common use of the -r option is for executing PHP generated by other (possibly non-PHP) shell commands where the whole shell script needs to execute in memory without touching the disk (for instance, where permissions prohibit disk write access).

From STDIN

If you do not specify a file or use the -r option, PHP will treat the contents of STDIN as the PHP code to be executed, as shown here (note echo works like this only on Linux or macOS):

```
~$ echo '<?php echo "hello\n";?>' | php
```

You can also use this method with -B, -R, -F, and -E to make PHP a first-class citizen in shell scripting, giving you the ability to pipe data in and out of PHP. For instance, to reverse every line of a file (or any data source that you pipe into it), on Linux or macOS, use the following:

```
~$ cat file.txt | php -R 'echo strrev($argn)."\n";' | grep olleh
```

On Windows, use the following:

```
> more file.txt | php -R "echo strrev($argn).\"\n\";" | findstr olleh
```

In this line of code, you pipe the contents of a text file into PHP. The -R option tells PHP to execute the following PHP code on each line of input, where the line is stored in the special variable $argn. In this case, you reverse $argn using the string-reversing function strrev() and then echo the reversed string out again. Any echo'd output goes to STDOUT, which either is printed to the shell or, as in this case, can be piped to another shell command. In this case, you then use grep to display only the lines containing the string olleh, which is *hello* backward. You can find more details on -R and its siblings in the previous section. If you want to use options like -R but have too much PHP code to fit comfortably on the command line, you can put the code in a normal PHP source code file and include it with include(). Here's an example:

```
~$ cat something.txt > php -R 'include("complicated.php");'
```

If it is a nontrivial PHP script, it may be more efficient to package it up into functions and include it once with -B (-B means it's executed before the main code) and then execute the function each time with -R. The following example loads the content of my_functions.php once at the start, and then the function complicated() from that file is called on each line (each $argn) from the data file (data.txt).

```
~$ php -B 'include("my_functions.php");' -R 'complicated($argn);' -f 'data.txt'
```

Although these commands look relatively simple, there is of course no arbitrary limit to the PHP code you can put behind them. You can use classes and objects, multiple files, and most of the code and techniques explored in this book, exposing only functions or methods at the shell level as an interface for the user. You can also open the standard streams as PHP streams within PHP and access their file pointers to read data in from, negating the need to use -R, as discussed in the next chapter.

As a Self-Executing Script: Unix/Linux

On Unix/Linux systems you can turn a PHP script file into a directly executable shell command. Simply make the first line of the script file a #! line (usually pronounced "shebang line" or "hashbang line") with a path to the PHP binary, as in this example:

```
#!/usr/bin/php

<?php

echo('Hello World!');
```

Then set the executable bit using chmod or similar. Here's an example:

```
~$ chmod a+x myscript.php
```

Simply typing `./myscript.php` at the command line will execute it. You can also rename the file to remove the `.php` extension (assuming you had one in the first place), so you would just type the following at the shell prompt to run it:

```
~$ ./myscript
```

You can further simplify it to remove the initial `./` by moving it to a directory somewhere in your shell's search path. Note that when running a script in this manner, any command-line options are passed directly to the script and not to PHP. In fact, you cannot pass extra command-line parameters to PHP at runtime using this method; you must include them in the shebang line when constructing your script. For instance, in the previous example, if you wanted to use Extended Information Mode, you would alter the first line of the script to read as follows:

```
#!/usr/bin/php -e
```

If you were to instead call the script as follows:

```
~$ myscript -e
```

then the `-e` flag would be passed as an argument to your main script, not to PHP directly, and so PHP would not enter EIM. This is useful for scripts that have lots of user-supplied arguments but also makes options like `-B` and `-R` discussed in the previous method cumbersome to use for processing `STDIN` data because you have to include all the PHP on the shebang line where it is harder to change. However, you can simply use `include()` to include the necessary files and use standard file streams to process the `STDIN` stream (created and opened by the CLI SAPI automatically for you) line by line instead.

If your script may be used on other systems, please bear in mind that the PHP binary will quite often be located in a different directory than the one on your system. In this scenario, you will need to change the shebang line for each system if you hard-code the location in it. Fortunately, if installed correctly, PHP sets an environment variable (called php) with its location, available via the `/usr/bin/env` shell command. So, if you change the shebang line as follows, your script should be executable wherever PHP is located:

```
#!/usr/bin/env php
```

On Windows, the shebang line can be left in because PHP will recognize it as a comment and ignore it. However, it will not execute the file as it does on *nix.

Further Reading

- Standard I/O streams information in the PHP Manual
  - `http://php.net/manual/en/features.commandline.io-streams.php`

As a Self-Executing Script: Windows

In a similar manner, scripts can be executed by calling them directly under Windows. However, the process for setting up Windows to do this is slightly more involved. First, you need to add your PHP directory (the directory containing php.exe, phpwin.exe, or php-cli.exe) to the Windows search path (specified in the environment variable PATH) so that you can call PHP without having to specify the full directory path. To do this, follow these steps:

1. (pre-Windows 10) From the Start menu, go to the Control Panel and select the System icon from the System and Security group.

2. (Windows 10) From the Start menu, click Settings and search for "Environment" then select "Edit the System Environment Variables" from the drop-down.

3. On the Advanced tab, click the Environment Variables button.

4. In the System Variables pane, find the Path entry (you may need to scroll to find it).

5. Double-click the Path entry to edit it and add your PHP directory at the end, including a semicolon (;) before it (for example, ;C:\php). Make sure that you do not overwrite or remove any of the text already in the path box. In Windows 10, simply add a new line in the editor.

You also need to amend (or add) the PATHEXT environment variable in the same way, so find the PATHEXT entry in the same window and add .PHP, again using a semicolon to separate it from the rest of the entries while taking care not to alter them.

Next you need to associate the .php file extension with a file type and then tell Windows which program to run for files of that type. To do this, run the following two commands in the Windows command prompt, which you should run as administrator. Make sure to change the path/file name in the second command to match your installation.

```
assoc .php=phpfile
ftype phpfile="C:\PHP5\php.exe" -f "%1" -- %~2
```

These changes will allow you to run myscript rather than C:\php\php.exe myscript.php. Note that under Windows 10 you will not be able to run scripts in this way in an elevated (administrator) command prompt because the PHP executable is not run as administrator by default. To fix this, right-click the php.exe executable, select Properties and Compatibility, and select "Run this program as an administrator" in Settings. Apply the change to all users. Scripts should now execute as expected in all command prompts.

Windows php-win.exe

PHP for Windows also ships with php-win.exe, which is similar to the CLI build of PHP, except that it does not open a command-line window. This is useful for running system software in the background or running scripts that create their own graphical interface.

"Click to Run" Your PHP

In the previous section you looked at the different ways PHP commands can be formatted and saw them in the context of the command line, i.e., typing them in. But let's make things easier and give them clickable icons so that you can run them directly from the desktop. How you achieve this depends on the operating system.

Clickable Icons: Linux

On most Linux systems, specifically those that support the freedesktop.org Desktop Entry Specification standard, you can create a clickable "launcher" icon by simply creating a text file. Most mainstream Linux distributions and their window managers follow at least the basics of this standard. To create a launcher for your app, create a text file in the folder where you want it to appear (e.g., in /home/rob/Desktop) called, for instance, myscript.desktop. It is important that it has the .desktop extension. In the file, add the following lines:

```
[Desktop Entry]
Type=Application
Name=My Funky App
Terminal=true
Exec=/usr/bin/php /home/rob/scripts/myscript.php
Icon=/usr/share/icons/Humanity/emblems/32/emblem-OK.png
```

The first two lines tell the system what you are creating here. The Name= line gives your launcher a name that will be shown below the icon. The Terminal= line determines whether a terminal window is opened for this program. You will want to set this to true if you are creating a shell script that takes input from, or sends output to, the terminal. If your script interacts with the user via GUI elements, you will likely want to set it to false. Exec= specifies the command to execute when the user clicks the icon. This is the command to call your PHP script, as discussed in the previous sections. Finally, the Icon= line points to the location of a pretty icon for your app. You can supply your own icon file or use one of the system-provided ones. Here you have use the Ubuntu smiley-face "OK" emblem icon to show the look on your face when you get your first PHP desktop app working. You will usually need to also give the .desktop file execute permission, using chmod u+x myscript.desktop or similar.

There are many other options you can set in this file; see the following standards site for more information. Support for some options varies from distribution to distribution.

Further Reading

- Freedesktop.org Desktop Entry Specification standard

  - http://standards.freedesktop.org/desktop-entry-spec/latest/

Clickable Icons: Windows

As mentioned previously, there are two executables for Windows, the standard php.exe and the newer php-win. exe, which allows the windowless running of scripts. There are likewise two ways to make "clickable" scripts.

First is the simple Windows batch file. This is a text file with a list of commands to execute. Batch files have the .bat extension in their name and are executable by default. So, if you have a PHP script called display_stats.php that displays a list of numbers and then exits and you want to run it in Extended Information Mode, you can make it a clickable script by creating a file called, say, our_stats.bat with the contents.

```
"C:\Program Files (x86)\PHP\php.exe" -e "C:\users\Rob\PHP
Scripts\display_stats.php"

Pause
```

If you click our_stats.bat, it will open a command prompt window, execute your PHP script, display your statistics, and finally wait for the user to press a key before closing the command prompt window. The last step, achieved here with the pause command, is important because the command prompt window will close again as soon as the batch file finishes executing, and if you have output for the user to view, you will want to keep it open. This can, of course, be achieved directly in your PHP script by pausing execution or waiting for user input, but the previous script shows how you can mix PHP and other commands/programs in the same batch file. Don't forget to change the paths to php.exe and your script as appropriate. You can use relative file names or rely on default search paths, but it is often best to use the full path name to ensure that the correct instance of php.exe is used and avoid problems if moving your PHP script relative to the batch file.

The second way of making a clickable PHP script is by calling it from within a Windows VBScript. The previous example using a batch file will always open a command prompt window, even if you use php-win. exe rather than php.exe, as it does it by default to execute the commands in the file. A VBScript, on the other hand, needs no command prompt or other visual form by default. So, if you want to use php-win.exe to run a script that either provides its own GUI interface or runs hidden in the background, you should create a script with a .vbs extension. Let's say you have a PHP-GTK script (more on that in Chapter 5) called text_ editor.php that provides a visual text editor like Notepad. You can make it clickable by creating a file called, say, our_text_ed.vbs with the following contents:

```
Set WinScriptHost = CreateObject("WScript.Shell")

WinScriptHost.Run Chr(34) & "c:\Program Files (x86)\PHP\php-win.exe" &
Chr(34) & " -e c:\Users\me\text_editor.php", 0

Set WinScriptHost = Nothing
```

Click the .vbs file and your PHP script should spring into life, sans the command-line prompt. The WinScriptHost.Run line does the heavy lifting of running a command that you provide. You format that command in the same way you would if you were typing it in by hand at the command prompt, and you pass it as a string. Note that in VBScript & is the string concatenation operator (the same as . in PHP) and that Chr(34) is the double quote (") character (needed as the directory path to php-win.exe has a space). Don't forget to change the paths to php-win.exe and your script as appropriate.

The final piece of the puzzle, whichever of the two methods you use, is to give your clickable file a better icon. The files will have the default icon for batch files or VBScripts, and it is not possible to change this directly without changing it for all files of the same type. There are, however, two workarounds. Windows allows you to change the icon of a shortcut (by right-clicking and choosing Properties), so the first workaround is to hide your script file somewhere out of sight and create a shortcut icon where you want to be able to click it. Then change the icon of the shortcut. The other workaround is to change the file extension to one that Windows does not recognize (e.g., .phpsc) and create a new file extension with the same actions as .vbs or .bat but with a different icon.

Clickable Icons: Ubuntu Unity

To add an icon to the Unity Launcher in Ubuntu, you create a .desktop file in a similar manner to the Linux launcher you created before, but with a few more entries in the file. So, let's create a new myscript.desktop.

```
[Desktop Entry]
Name=My Super Script
Exec=/usr/bin/php /home/rob/scripts/myscript.php
Icon=/usr/share/icons/Humanity/emblems/32/emblem-important.svg
```

```
Terminal=true
Type=Application
StartupNotify=true
Actions=Window;

[Desktop Action Window]
Name=Open me a new window please
Exec=/usr/bin/php /home/me/scripts/myscript.php -n
OnlyShowIn=Unity;
```

Don't forget to make it executable with chmod. This should work in its current location as with the previous Linux example. However, if you drag it to the Unity Launcher (or "pin" it while the script is running), it will remain there and add a new feature, the "action" menu. Notice the Actions=Window line and the [Desktop Action Window] section in the code. These define a new action (in this case opening a new window, if your script had that capability via the -n flag), which is accessible by right-clicking the icon. Through this you can add any actions you want, by for example calling your script with different parameters or even calling a completely different script (or other program) in the Exec line. If you want to automatically add Unity entries or make them available to all users, I suggest the following articles.

Further Reading

- "Unity: adding items to the dock" by Daan van Berkel
  - http://themagicofscience.blogspot.co.uk/2011/05/unity-adding-items-to-dock.html
- Unity Launcher documentation and guide at Ubuntu.com
  - https://help.ubuntu.com/community/UnityLaunchersAndDesktopFiles

All the methods for starting scripts I've described can be executed in any number of scenarios. You can use them directly from a command line, as part of a shell script, as a cron job, as a system call from other PHP (and non-PHP) scripts, as default file type handlers, and so on. With appropriate precautions and permissions, you can even use these methods to call scripts from web-based PHP pages (there is usually a better and safer way to invoke them than via a web page, so I'll leave the details of how to implement and secure it as an exercise for you if you really must do so).

Quitting Your Script from Within

You've looked at starting your scripts, but what happens when it comes time to finish running them? Like web-based PHP scripts, CLI scripts will terminate happily when you hit the end of the script file and will tidy up all the resources used in the same way, closing resources such as database connections and releasing used memory. And again like web scripts, if you want to end early, you can call the exit (or equivalent die) language construct as normal.

However, in the world of CLI scripts, this isn't considered polite. Because CLI command are designed to work together, often in chains of commands, most shell programs and scripts will provide an "exit code" when they terminate to let the other programs around them know *why* they finished. Were they done? Did they encounter an error? Were they called incorrectly? Inquiring minds want to know.

It is particularly important to supply an exit code when your script may be the last item in a shell script because the exit code of the shell script itself is taken to be the last exit code returned within it. You can make your PHP script provide an exit code simply by including it as a parameter to exit or die. An exit code is an integer, and there are a number of common exit codes to choose from.

- *0*: Success. You've exited normally.

- *1*: General error. This is usually used for application/language-specific errors and syntax errors.

- *2*: Incorrect usage.

- *126*: Command is not executable. This is usually permissions-related.

- *127*: Command not found.

- *128+N (up to 165)*: Command terminated by POSIX signal number N. For example, in the case of kill -9 myscript.php, it should return code 137 (which is 128+9).

- *130*: Command terminated by Ctrl-C (Ctrl-C is POSIX code 2, so, as earlier, 128 + 2 = 130).

- Any other positive integer is generally construed as exiting because of an unspecified error.

So, for instance, if you decide the command-line arguments provided by your user are not in the correct format, you should terminate your script using exit(2). If instead all goes well and your script continues to the end of its script file, you can actually let it exit by itself (or by calling exit without a parameter) because it returns status code 0 by default.

Further Reading

- POSIX signals on Wikipedia

  - http://en.wikipedia.org/wiki/Unix_signal#POSIX_signals

As with web scripts, you can register functions to be executed when your PHP script exits using the register_shutdown_function() function. One use for this may be to check that all is well and evaluate which exit code should be returned. The exit code used as the parameter to exit or die within a registered shutdown function overrides the code used in the initial exit call that initiated shutdown. This means you can happily exit with exit(0) everywhere and then exit with exit(76) from your shutdown function if you detect that the foo conflaganation isn't aligned with the bar initispations in your metaspacialatific object. Or similar. 76 is one of the general "unspecified" errors, so you should ensure that your program documentation details the actual meaning and ideally output some informative text (ideally to STDERR) from your shutdown function to make sure the user knows what happened.

Thinking About Security

Every good programmer is at least aware of the security implications of building web sites and online apps. You deliberately expose your code to the public, to the world, and to anyone and everyone who will come (good people and bad). One of the early failings of PHP was to prioritize ease of use over security of code (the horror stories from relics like register_globals are only a quick Google search away). With newer, more secure defaults and functions like register_globals being depreciated, PHP is safer than ever online. And although most security problems are caused by the programmer rather than the language, even the newest web coders seem to have an appreciation of security issues from day one these days.

Step into the world of offline software, however, and things are markedly different. Typically, you see software for trusted users only, deployed locally on trusted machines and under the full control of the benevolent user. The user isn't going to deliberately attack the software or machine; they're working with their own data. Functionality absolutely can't be compromised. Security is rarely considered at all when developing command-line programs and desktop apps, let alone being features specified at design time, because it's not "necessary."

Except the world doesn't work like that. Take a look at the list of software with the most "CVE-ID" vulnerabilities, and you'll find a plethora of offline apps such as Adobe Reader, Microsoft Office, and even open source stalwarts like Mysql. The fact is, security is important even in local apps, for two main reasons. The first is the perennial problem of "typical user" behavior. This is not a problem for an intelligent tech-literate user who never makes mistakes (like you, dear reader), but for any software used by the rest of us, disaster is only an accidental-click-on-a-dodgy-link away. The second reason security is important is that for most machines, many nonweb applications aren't really "offline." Even when a desktop app or a system daemon doesn't interact with the Web, local network, or other external services itself, the machine it is connected to will invariably have an Ethernet cable plugged into it or a WiFi/3G/4G connection active. Your software will not run in its own cosy little realm, insulated from the world outside (perfectly sandboxed virtual machines notwithstanding, of course, if such a thing exists…).

Software security is the topic of a whole other book (of which others have written plenty; see the "Further Reading" section), and many of the same principles apply to CLI software as to web software, so you will be able to use your existing knowledge of web-based PHP security practices to guide you. The following list of typical vulnerability types and attack vectors in both user-facing and systems software should be considered when planning your script security measures and monitoring:

- *Compromised files from external sources (loaded deliberately or accidentally by users)*: These are usually data files, and particularly at risk is software registered as a default viewer for a particular file type because accidental and malicious file activation is much easier.

- *Malware looking for innocent software to exploit to gain privilege escalation*: Scripted software like PHP code can be easier for malware to rewrite or alter, and the availability of the source code in an uncompiled form can be of help to the malware authors.

- *Legitimate users misbehaving*: John Smith is looking for a way to view the files or surfing history of his boss, Jane Doe, on their shared business system, for instance.

- *Privilege escalation*: Similar to legitimate users misbehaving, this is legitimate software misbehaving, either accidentally or deliberately trying to gain and use access permissions it does not have.

- *PHP vulnerabilities and vulnerabilities in other dependencies and related software*: Your software will be completely free of security issues, of course, but it invariably depends on other libraries, software, and PHP extensions, and of course let's not forget the PHP interpreter. Any of these can contain security bugs and attack vectors.

These are common sources of security issues in all types of software, not just in PHP. Minimize your risks by planning for these in the design stage and testing for them before deployment. Then cross your fingers.

Further Reading

- *Securing PHP: Core Concepts and Securing PHP: The Usual Suspects* by Chris Cornutt

  - https://leanpub.com/securingphp-coreconcepts

  - https://leanpub.com/securingphp-usualsuspects

- *Survive The Deep End: PHP Security* by Padraic Brady

  - http://phpsecurity.readthedocs.org/en/latest/index.html

- *Building Secure PHP Apps* by Ben Edmunds

  - https://leanpub.com/buildingsecurephpapps

CLI-Specific Code Frameworks

There are many coding frameworks for PHP, and many of them can be used with CLI applications, although only one is specifically created for nonweb programming. Code in general-purpose or web-based frameworks may assume that it will be called in an HTTP-related context, so you may need to do extra work to code around this when using it offline.

When deciding whether to use a framework and choosing which one to use, you should bear in mind their applicability (in terms of their focus on the Web) and whether your application's performance will suffer from the overhead they may bring. You will usually also need to look at their license because they will normally have components that need to be distributed alongside your scripts, and you'll look at deployment and distribution issues in Chapter 10. That's not to say they can't be useful in general-purpose programming; however, there are none that I can at this time recommend specifically for nonweb projects. If you're currently comfortable using a particular framework on your web projects, it may be worth seeing whether it has a "CLI" or "console" module or recommended code path for CLI-type scripts.

Further Reading

- The CLImax CLI-oriented PHP framework

  - https://github.com/apinstein/climax/

- The PHP Framework Interop Group, standardizing interoperability between frameworks

  - www.php-fig.org

- The Symfony Console Component (also used to build the Laravel Artisan Console software)

  - http://symfony.com/doc/current/components/console/introduction.html

  - https://laravel.com/docs/5.1/artisan

- Zend/Console, which are console routes and routing in Zend Framework 2

  - http://framework.zend.com/manual/current/en/modules/zend.console.routes.html

- Example of using Zend Framework with a CLI script

  - http://stackoverflow.com/questions/2325338/runninga-zend-framework-action-from-command-line

- Framework comparison matrix

  - http://matrix.include-once.org/framework/

PHP REPLs

When you want to test a few lines of PHP, your default instinct may be to create a new PHP file, save it, and then execute it with PHP or call it through your web browser. There is a faster and more interactive way, however, available on the command line. The PHP "interactive shell," also known as the PHP REPL, is a quick and easy way to type in code and have it execute immediately. Unlike executing single lines of code using php -r, the REPL (started by calling php -a) keeps the script's state (for example, contents of variables and objects) in between each line that you type until you exit. You can use all of PHP's functions (although no libraries are loaded by default), and you can use include() or require() to include existing files of PHP code.

This latter capability is useful for debugging the final output of a problematic script; simply use include() to include your script, which will execute the script, and as long the script doesn't terminate prematurely, then you can use echo() or print_r() (or similar) to explore the state of the variables and other resources at the end of the run. Other brands of REPL are available and are listed later in this section.

Note that the REPL doesn't function in standard versions of Windows because of the lack of readline library support, but it will work in WSL (Windows Subsystem for Linux; see https://msdn.microsoft.com/en-gb/commandline/wsl/about).

By its nature, the PHP REPL can also be used as a CLI/shell in its own right, calling other PHP and non-PHP programs as you would in, for instance, a bash shell. The following example is a capture of an actual interactive REPL session using the standard PHP REPL:

```
~$ php -a
Interactive mode enabled

php > # As we can type any valid PHP, I have added (valid PHP) comments
php > # directly to the REPL, rather than afterwards in editing!
php >
php > # Lets start with some simple variable assignments:
php >
php > $a = 5;
php > $b = 6;
php >
php > # The REPL will throw Notices, Warnings and Errors as appropriate,
php > # in real-time:
php >
php > $c = nothingdefined;
PHP Notice: Use of undefined constant nothingdefined - assumed
'nothingdefined' in php shell code on line 1
php >
php > # Just as with normal PHP source files, we can split commands across
php > # lines. The interpreter only kicks in when it hits the terminating
php > # semicolon :
php >
php > $d
php > =
php > 7
php > ;
php >
php > # The following shows that the state in the variables above has been
php > # kept :
php >
```

```
php > echo $a + $b + $c + $d ."\n";
18
php >
php > # Next, a more interesting example. Use the REPL instead of the
php > # shell to get the first line from a file :
php >
php > echo file('/proc/version')[0];
Linux version 4.4.0-38-generic (buildd@lgw01-58) (gcc version 5.4.0 20160609
(Ubuntu 5.4.0-6ubuntu1~16.04.2) ) #57-Ubuntu SMP Tue Sep 6 15:42:33 UTC 2016
php >
php > # Of course all of the usual protocol wrappers are available, so we
php > # can see what is happening in the world...
php >
php > $page = file('http://news.bbc.co.uk');
php >
php > echo $page[1];
<html lang="en-GB" id="responsive-news">
php >
php > # and maybe get a hash of that...
php >
php > echo md5 ( implode ( $page, "\n" ) ) . "\n";
c3e2fb06927099590aebb1ffcb3f0b5d
php >
php > # when we are done ...
php >
php > exit;
php >
php > # doesn't work, as its just evaluated as PHP (and the REPL ignores
php > # exit/die calls). To exit the REPL, enter the word 'exit' on its own
php > # on a new line
php >
php > exit
~$
```

Sometimes you'll want to execute your commands within the "environment" of other scripts. For instance, you may have a script that declares constants, sets up database connections, and does other routine tasks that you normally include with include() at the start of your main PHP scripts. As noted earlier, you can include these files in the REPL too using include(), but you may forget to do so and then wonder why things didn't work as they should. One facility PHP offers you, which applies not only to the REPL but to all forms of PHP execution, is the auto_prepend_file configuration directive. This tells PHP to execute a given file each time PHP is run before it starts to do anything else (such as executing the script you have asked it to execute). This can be set either in php.ini or via the -d flag on the command line. The following is an example of presetting some constants/variables. First, you create a script called initialise. php with the following content:

```
<?php

const FOUR = 4; # Declare a constant value

$five = 5; # Instantiate a variable with another value
```

Then, at the command line, start and run the REPL session as follows, using -d to execute the initialise.php script first:

```
~$ php -d auto_prepend_file=initialise.php -a
Interactive mode enabled

php > echo (FOUR + $five)."\n";
9
php > exit
~$
```

As you can see, the constant and variable you set up in the initialise.php file were available for use from the REPL without having to manually declare them. The -d flag is used here, but the option could be set in php.ini as well if you want to always use the same file. If you regularly use a few different initialization files like this, you can create shell aliases to commands using the -d flag. For instance, you could add lines similar to the following to your ~/.bash_profile:

```
alias php-clients="php -d auto_prepend_file=clientSetup.php -a"
alias php-inhouse="php -d auto_prepend_file=ourSiteSetup.php -a"
```

As well as the built-in PHP REPL explored earlier, there are a number of third-party REPLs available, some of which include features such as a history of commands typed, tab completion of commands, protection from fatal errors, and even abbreviated function documentation. The most common are listed here.

PsySH

This is a runtime developer console, interactive debugger, and REPL for PHP.

- *Main web site*: http://psysh.org/

Boris

This is a small but robust REPL for PHP.

- *Main documentation and installation information*: https://github.com/d11wtq/boris

- *Extension for Symfony and Drupal*: http://vvv.tobiassjosten.net/php/php-repl-for-symfony-and-drupal/

phpa

This is a simple replacement for php -a, written in PHP.

- *Main web site, installation information, and documentation*: http://david.acz.org/phpa/

PHP Interactive

This is a web-based REPL that allows better support of displaying HTML output. The project is an alpha release.

- *Main web site*: www.hping.org/phpinteractive/

Sublime-worksheet

This is an inline REPL for the Sublime Text editor.

- *Main web site*: https://github.com/jcartledge/sublime-worksheet

phpsh

Developed at Facebook, phpsh is an interactive shell for PHP that features readline history, tab completion, and quick access to documentation. It is no longer actively developed but still works fine.

- *Main web site and documentation*: http://phpsh.org
- *Installation information*: https://github.com/facebook/phpsh/blob/master/README.md

iPHP

This is an extensible PHP shell.

- *Main web site*: https://github.com/apinstein/iphp

APPENDIX C

■ ■ ■

Functional Programming Resources

The term *functional programming* represents a whole field of endeavor, and a single book like this cannot hope to possibly detail anything more than a small fraction of the knowledge available on the topic. Even within the small subset that represents PHP, you would need more than a few hundred pages to cover it all. So, this final appendix aims to highlight other useful resources available online, including learning and reference material, libraries and other code, and videos for those who prefer that medium for learning. Some of the resources have already been mentioned in relevant parts of the book, but they're included again here to keep everything in the same place. I've included academic and other advanced texts to give a flavor of the theory behind various topics; if that's a little heavy going for you, do skip to the more practical resources. All links were available at the time of writing, but if you find any that have since disappeared, you can always try the Internet Archive (`https://web.achive.org`) as most of the material here is archived there.

Other Programming Languages

As mentioned numerous times in the book, PHP is not a purely functional language, and formal functional programming is still in its infancy in the PHP community. Thus, to give you the full picture, some of the resources that follow are from other programming languages (Haskell, Scala, JavaScript) because nothing comparable exists yet for PHP. Where possible, if it doesn't exist in the PHP world, I've aimed for JavaScript-based materials, for three reasons. First, most PHP developers are web developers and will have some familiarity with JavaScript. This means the syntax used won't be completely unfamiliar to you. Second, the similarities in syntax (as compared to, for example, Haskell) mean that code should be easier to translate and implement in PHP. Finally, once you understand functional programming, you'll be yearning to use it not just in your PHP back ends but also in your JavaScript front-end code as well!

Functional Programming and Other Paradigms

The following are resources for general information about functional programming, and other programming paradigms, in PHP and other languages.

Articles

A Comparison of Programming Paradigms on Wikipedia

- https://en.wikipedia.org/wiki/Comparison_of_programming_paradigms

© Rob Aley 2017
R. Aley, *Pro Functional PHP Programming*, DOI 10.1007/978-1-4842-2958-3

The History of PHP in the PHP Manual

- http://php.net/manual/en/history.php.php

Limitations of Procedural-Oriented Programming

- www.extropia.com/tutorials/java/procedural_programming_limits.html

"All Evidence Points to OOP Being Bullshit"

- https://content.pivotal.io/blog/all-evidence-points-to-oop-being-bullshit

"What Are Some Limitations/Disadvantages of Functional Programming?"

- https://www.quora.com/What-are-some-limitations-disadvantages-of-functional-programming/answer/Tikhon-Jelvis

Online Books

Professor Frisby's Mostly Adequate Guide to Functional Programming

- https://drboolean.gitbooks.io/mostly-adequate-guide/

Functional PHP

- https://leanpub.com/functional-php/read

Learn You a Haskell for Great Good!

- http://learnyouahaskell.com/chapters

Real-World Haskell

- http://book.realworldhaskell.org/

Functional Programming in Python

- www.oreilly.com/programming/free/functional-programming-python.csp

Real-World Functional Programming

- https://msdn.microsoft.com/en-us/library/hh273069(v=vs.100).aspx

Videos

Functional Programming (PHP Round Table)

- https://www.youtube.com/watch?v=E1LsFtDtGRk

Functional PHP (DrupalCon Austin 2014)

- https://www.youtube.com/watch?v=M3_xnTK6-pA

Bringing Functional PHP into the Fold (PHPSW 2016)

- https://www.youtube.com/watch?v=Sn8uTpySGWA

What Is Functional Programming?

- https://www.youtube.com/watch?v=UxR1CUz1a3E

Reasoning About Your Code

- https://www.youtube.com/watch?v=l8YFeA8lY6c

Why Functional Programming Doesn't Matter

- https://www.youtube.com/watch?v=kZ1P8cHN3pY

Functional Killed the OOP Star

- https://www.youtube.com/watch?v=__DXfGH0In4

Functional Programming Is Terrible

- https://www.youtube.com/watch?v=hzf3hTUKk8U

Functional Programming Basics in ES6 (Scenic City Summit 2016)

- https://www.youtube.com/watch?v=HvMemAgOw6I

Online Courses

There are a number of good free or cheap online courses (MOOCs) and video learning series that cover functional programming from scratch. Most courses are rerun regularly, so if a particular course listed here is not currently open, keep it bookmarked and check back every couple of months.

Future Learn
Functional Programming in Haskell: Supercharge Your Coding

- https://www.futurelearn.com/courses/functional-programming-haskell

edX/TUDelft
Introduction to Functional Programming (language-agnostic, with a focus on Haskell)

- https://www.edx.org/course/introduction-functional-programming-delftx-fp101x-0

Coursera
Program on a Higher Level (Scala)

- https://www.coursera.org/learn/progfun1

Université Paris Diderot
Introduction to Functional Programming in OCaml

- https://www.fun-mooc.fr/courses/parisdiderot/56002S02/session02/about

Udemy
Learning Path: Functional Programming for PHP 7 Developers (note that only the second video set is about functional programming specifically)

- https://www.udemy.com/learning-path-functional-programming-for-php-7-developers/

Deep Dive into Functional JavaScript

- https://www.udemy.com/deep-dive-into-functional-javascript/

Functional Programming with F#

- https://www.udemy.com/fsharp-programming/

Functional Programming Using C++

- https://www.udemy.com/functional-programming-using-cpp/

Functional Programming Design Patterns

You'll find that many functional programmers deny that design patterns exist in functional programming. Give them the name of a pattern, and they'll retort, "Ah, that's just a function!" Others disagree. I'm on the fence.

Are Design Patterns Missing Language Features?

- http://wiki.c2.com/?AreDesignPatternsMissingLanguageFeatures

Functional Programming Design Patterns

- https://www.youtube.com/watch?v=E8I19uA-wGY

Functional Programming Patterns for the Non-mathematician

- https://www.youtube.com/watch?v=AvgwKjTPMmM

PHP Functional Basics

This section highlights reference material in the PHP Manual that covers the basic PHP syntax used for functional programming.

User-Defined Functions

- http://php.net/manual/en/functions.user-defined.php

Anonymous Functions

- http://php.net/manual/en/functions.anonymous.php

Closure Class (Used to Implement Anonymous Functions)

- http://php.net/manual/en/class.closure.php

Variable Functions

- http://php.net/manual/en/functions.variable-functions.php

Variable Scope

- http://php.net/manual/en/language.variables.scope.php

Variadic Functions (The Splat Operator)

- http://php.net/manual/en/functions.arguments.php#functions.variable-arg-list

Data Structures

When the venerable PHP array doesn't offer you everything you need, other data structures are available.

Data Structures in the Standard PHP Library (SPL)

- http://php.net/manual/en/spl.datastructures.php

Laravel Collections

A class that wraps arrays in a fluent interface, resulting in a classically functional data structure

- https://laravel.com/docs/5.4/collections

A library that splits collections out for use outside of Laravel

- https://github.com/tightenco/collect

Hack Collections

Hack has seven types of collections, including vectors, maps, and pairs, which are specialized array-based objects.

- https://docs.hhvm.com/hack/collections/introduction#hack-collections

Purely Functional Data Structures

- www.cs.cmu.edu/~rwh/theses/okasaki.pdf

Mutability in PHP

PHP mostly leaves immutability to the programmer. The following resources are for when you want more structure help with mutability issues in your code.

Constants in the PHP Manual

- http://php.net/manual/en/language.constants.php

A Comprehensive Synopsis of the Differences Between define() and const

- http://stackoverflow.com/a/3193704

Immutable PHP (PHP Round Table)

- https://www.youtube.com/watch?v=TNqy3gZdWXQ

Map, Filter, Reduce and Other Array Functions

You've seen how map, filter, and reduce are backbones of functional programming in PHP. While you can implement many dozens of array manipulation algorithms using them, PHP provides many prewritten functions to manipulate arrays, saving you the trouble of implementing them yourself.

List of All Array Manipulation Functions and Links to Documentation

- http://php.net/manual/en/ref.array.php

PHP Arrays

A comprehensive guide to arrays in PHP

- www.apress.com/us/book/9781484225554

Recursion and Trampolines

These are resources for understanding and implementing recursive functions in PHP and optimizing them with.

Recursive Functions

- https://www.youtube.com/watch?v=m_mqmJm45Nc

PHP Recursion #101

- https://www.youtube.com/watch?v=HLSFxXPYDNI

Trampoline
Trampoline implementation for PHP

- https://github.com/functional-php/trampoline

Partial Functions and Currying

These are resources that will help you to make better use of your multi-arity functions.

php-curry
A PHP library for manual currying of functions

- https://github.com/matteosister/php-curry

JavaScript Tutorial: Curried Functions

- https://www.youtube.com/watch?v=3gEIAmtOh-U

Functional Composition

These resources will help you put your functions together to make something great.

The Composer of Functions

- https://www.youtube.com/watch?v=zNc5bHADOoA

Transducers-php
Composable algorithmic transformations in PHP

- https://github.com/mtdowling/transducers.php

Monads

Learn more about these functional devices, which are both a blessing and a curse.

MonadPHP
A simple monad implementation, useful for exploring the basics of monads in PHP

- https://github.com/ircmaxell/monad-php

Go Mad for Monads (PHPSW 2015)

- https://www.youtube.com/watch?v=F5fUgXFSHOQ

Monads and Gonads (Google Tech Talk)

Douglas Crockford explaining monads in JavaScript

- https://www.youtube.com/watch?v=bOEFOVTs9Dc

Don't Fear the Monad (MSDN)

Brian Beckman explaining monads with more math

- https://www.youtube.com/watch?v=ZhuHCtR3xq8

Haskell Manual

Haskell was responsible for popularizing monads in programming, and this is a fairly succinct treatment.

- https://wiki.haskell.org/Monad

An explanation of the three monad axioms/laws

- https://wiki.haskell.org/Monad_laws

A physical analogy for monads (via The Wayback Machine)

- https://web.archive.org/web/20100910074354/www.haskell.org/all_about_
monads/html/analogy.html

A fairly comprehensive time line of monad tutorials and related articles (not Haskell specific)

- https://wiki.haskell.org/Monad_tutorials_timeline

Monads, Monoids, and Make-Believe (JS.everywhere 2012)

https://www.youtube.com/watch?v=awEGF8giTcE

Fantasy Land Specification

JavaScript specification for interoperability of common algebraic structures like monads and monoids

https://github.com/fantasyland/fantasy-land

Types

Explore these options if you don't want to stick with PHP's native dynamic type system.

Type Declarations (Formerly Type Hints) in the PHP Manual

- http://php.net/manual/en/functions.arguments.php#functions.arguments.
type-declaration

Return Type Declarations in the PHP Manual

- http://php.net/manual/en/functions.returning-values.php#functions.
returning-values.type-declaration

Heresy! Combining Type Systems with PHP

- https://www.youtube.com/watch?v=aN22-V-b8RM

Zephir

A language for creating PHP extensions; one of its focuses is on type/memory safety

- https://zephir-lang.com/

Duck Typing vs. Type Hinting

- https://www.youtube.com/watch?v=Grli9Ssx-AY

Typed PHP

- www.apress.com/us/book/9781484221136

Type Systems for Programming Languages

- https://people.mpi-sws.org/~dreyer/ats/papers/harper-tspl.pdf

Type Theory and Functional Programming

- https://www.cs.kent.ac.uk/people/staff/sjt/TTFP/ttfp.html

Hack's Type System

- https://docs.hhvm.com/hack/types/type-system

Hack's Typechecker Tool

- https://docs.hhvm.com/hack/typechecker/introduction

Profiling

You can use functional programming to speed up your code. But you can only be sure you're actually doing that if you know how to profile your code performance.

The Need for Speed: Profiling PHP with XHProf and XHGui

- https://www.sitepoint.com/the-need-for-speed-profiling-with-xhprof-and-xhgui/

XHProf PHP Profiling

- www.geekyboy.com/archives/718

Profiling PHP Applications with XHGui

- https://inviqa.com/blog/profiling-xhgui

Profiling PHP Applications (PHP UK Conference 2014)

- https://www.youtube.com/watch?v=4TbxHDSDkiw

Profiling PHP Applications (PHP UK Conference 2012)

- https://www.youtube.com/watch?v=nFBQNQ1_5vI

Profiling PHP Apps with XHProf

- https://www.youtube.com/watch?v=J89GJ1luZJ8

XHProf

Function-level hierarchical PHP profiler

- https://github.com/phacility/xhprof

Tool for visual XHProf function graphs

- http://graphviz.org/

XHProf UI
Expanded profiler based on XHProf

- https://github.com/preinheimer/xhprof

XHGUI
A graphical interface for XHProf data built on MongoDB

- https://github.com/perftools/xhgui

Xdebug
Comprehensive debugger with built-in profiler

- https://xdebug.org/

Tool for use with Xdebug for visual profile information

- https://kcachegrind.github.io/html/Home.html

An alternative web-based profiling front end for Xdebug

- https://github.com/jokkedk/webgrind

"What Is PHP Doing?"
An article on low-level profiling

- http://derickrethans.nl/what-is-php-doing.html

Memoization

This is a resource if you want to cache the results of your functions.

Function-Level Caching in JavaScript Using Memoization

- https://www.youtube.com/watch?v=lsp82xOXdsY

Lazy Evaluation

This resource is for when you want your code to take the easy path.

Lazy vs. Eager Evaluation

- https://www.youtube.com/watch?v=qOHRCEKAcas

Relevant PHP Manual Sections

Logical Operators and "Short-Circuiting"

- http://php.net/manual/en/language.operators.logical.php

Operator Precedence and Order of Evaluation

- http://php.net/manual/en/language.operators.precedence.php

Generators (Simple Iterators)

- http://php.net/manual/en/language.generators.overview.php

The Iterator Class

- http://php.net/manual/en/class.iterator.php

Parallel Programming

Speed up your scripts by running things in parallel. Use functional programming to keep everything under control.

Pthreads
> An extension for writing multithreaded CLI scripts in PHP

- http://pthreads.org/

Pthreads section in the PHP Manual

- http://php.net/manual/en/book.pthreads.php

AMP
> A concurrency framework for PHP with abstractions for Pthreads and process control extensions

- http://amphp.org/

Testing

Functional programming helps you to write code that's easy to test. If you're not familiar with unit testing, these resources will get you going.

Unit Testing by Example (PHP UK Conference 2017)

- https://www.youtube.com/watch?v=ESl-ncXA4G0

Testing Complex Applications for PHP7 (PHP UK Conference 2017)

- https://www.youtube.com/watch?v=qKE3Pwkbhrc

Writing Unit Tests Using (PHP UK Conference 2013)

> https://www.youtube.com/watch?v=Jr8jAK86Uf0

Event-Based Programming

Event-based programming is a typical use case where functional programming's lack of side effects helps keep code manageable.

The Event (libevent) Extension

- http://php.net/manual/en/intro.event.php

Main Libevent Web Site

- http://libevent.org/

Asynchronous PHP

Often used for event-based programming, async code is gaining ground in PHP.

ReactPHP
> The main event-driven Async library for PHP, modeled after Node.js

- http://reactphp.org

Hack Async

Facebook's PHP-compatible language, providing an async interface for certain types of I/O

- https://docs.hhvm.com/hack/async/introduction

Amp

An asynchronous concurrency framework for PHP

- http://amphp.org/

A list of resources, code, libraries, and other material related to asynchronous processing in PHP

- https://github.com/elazar/asynchronous-php

Big Data/Hadoop

The Hadoop framework allows you to process Big Data across multiple machines, using humble PHP. Functional principles help keep that data straight across the massively parallel runs.

Large-Scale Data Processing with Hadoop and PHP (PHP UK Conference 2011)

- https://www.youtube.com/watch?v=elOaZdQCWEY

Implementing MySQL and Hadoop for Big Data

This is not PHP specific, but given MySQL's proliferation in the community, this is likely to be useful.

- https://www.youtube.com/watch?v=QhBPOb7hV6Y

REST API for HDFS

How to access HDFS using its REST API (from PHP or any other language)

- https://www.youtube.com/watch?v=EKr9ipjQQQo

Hadoop

- http://hadoop.apache.org/

Documentation

- https://wiki.apache.org/hadoop/

Hadoop streaming app for working with PHP scripts

- https://hadoop.apache.org/docs/r1.2.1/streaming.html#How+Streaming+Works

Bitnami Hadoop VM

The easiest way to try Hadoop

- https://bitnami.com/stack/hadoop

Bitnami Hadoop VM documentation

- https://docs.bitnami.com/virtual-machine/apps/hadoop/

MapReduce Is Not Functional Programming

Why MapReduce is not functional programming (though MapReduce can be implemented in functional programming)

- https://medium.com/@jkff/mapreduce-is-not-functional-programming-39109a4ba7b2

PHDFS

A library to help you access HDFS directly from PHP

- https://github.com/yuduanchen/phdfs

General-Purpose Libraries

The following libraries are general-purpose functional programming libraries for PHP. Many are available in the Packagist repository for installation via Composer; check the relevant web site for installation and usage information. For each library, I've provided a list of the functions available at the time of writing; this can help you to quickly identify candidate libraries for your particular needs. A number of the extensions don't provide comprehensive lists, and for some, these lists (which are mostly taken from the source code) are more up-to-date than the official documentation, which is why I've taken a few pages to list them here.

As you go through the literature listed in this appendix and come across new functions or features, look through the following lists to see whether there is a PHP implementation to help you learn the topic with. You'll also find functional implementations of common procedural PHP syntax, like ifElse, so if you're tempted to use an imperative structure, take a look to see whether there is a functional equivalent already written.

Be aware, though, that many of the libraries provide more than just the utility functions listed here, such as custom data types and data structures. Also be aware that similarly named functions in different libraries may be implemented differently or may indeed perform different functions. New functions or renamed functions may also cause issues, so always check the documentation and/or source code for the relevant library in conjunction with these lists.

Pramda

- https://github.com/kapolos/pramda

add	inc	props
all	join	reduce
allPass	last	reverse
add	lt	set
append	lte	size
appendTo	map	slice
apply	mathMod	sort
chain	max	split
compose	maxBy	subtract
concat	merge	sum
converge	mergeAll	tail
countBy	min	take
curry2	minBy	takeLast
curry3	modulo	takeWhile
curryN	multiply	toArray
dec	nd	trampoline
divide	negate	unapply
each	nth	unary
eq	of	uniq
eqBy	partition	values
file	pipe	zip
filter	pluck	zipAssoc
flatten	prepend	zipWith
flip	prependTo	
gt	product	
gte	prop	
head	propOf	
identity	propOr	

Phamda

- https://github.com/mpajunen/phamda

add	first	pathEq
all	flatMap	pick
allPass	flatten	pickAll
always	flattenLevel	pipe
any	flip	pluck
anyPass	fromPairs	prepend
append	groupBy	product
apply	gt	prop
assoc	gte	propEq
assocPath	identity	reduce
binary	ifElse	reduceRight
both	implode	reject
cast	indexOf	reverse
clone	invoker	slice
comparator	isEmpty	sort
compose	isInstance	sortBy
concat	last	stringIndexOf
construct	lt	stringLastIndexOf
constructN	lte	substring
contains	map	substringFrom
curry	max	substringTo
curryN	maxBy	subtract
defaultTo	merge	sum
divide	min	tail
each	minBy	tap
either	modulo	times
eq	multiply	toPairs
evolve	nAry	true
explode	negate	twist
false	none	twistN
filter	not	unary
find	partial	unapply
findIndex	partialN	where
findLast	partition	zip
findLastIndex	path	zipWith

Underscore.php

- https://github.com/brianhaveri/Underscore.php

after	initial	Objects
all	intersection	once
any	invoke	pluck
bind	isArguments	range
bindAll	isArray	reduce
chain	isBoolean	reduceRight
clon	isDate	reject
compact	isElement	rest
compose	isEmpty	shuffle
debounce	isEqual	size
defaults	isFunction	sortBy
defer	isNaN	sortedIndex
delay	isNull	tap
difference	isNumber	template
each	isObject	throttle
escape	isRegExp	times
extend	isString	toArray
filter	isUndefined	union
find	keys	uniq
first	last	uniqueId
flatten	lastIndexOf	value
functions	map	values
groupBy	max	without
has	memoize	wrap
identity	min	zip
includ	mixin	
indexOf	noConflict	

Underscore

- https://github.com/ImOrtality/Underscore

from	map	all
range	pluck	any
times	merge	contains
clone	intersection	find
compact	reject	indexOf
defaults	shuffle	lastIndexOf
difference	sortBy	value
extend	tail	toArray
filter	tap	size
flatten	thru	min
groupBy	uniq	max
head	values	has
initial	where	reduce
invoke	without	reduceRight
keys	zip	
last	collection	

Underscore.php

- https://github.com/Anahkiasen/underscore-php

accord	last	replaceValue
after	length	rest
append	limit	set
append	lower	set
at	matches	singular
average	matchesAny	size
cache	max	slice
clean	merge	sliceFrom
contains	methods	sliceTo
diff	min	sort
each	once	sort
endsWith	only	sortKeys
explode	padding	startsWith
filter	paddingLeft	sum
find	paddingRight	throttle
find	pluck	title
first	pluck	toArray
flatten	plural	toBoolean
fromCSV	prepend	toCamelCase
fromJSON	prepend	toCSV
fromXML	random	toggle
get	random	toInteger
group	range	toJSON
group	reject	toObject
has	remove	toPascalCase
implode	remove	toSnakeCase
initial	remove	toString
invoke	removeFirst	unpack
isEmail	removeLast	upper
isIp	repeat	values
isUrl	repeat	without
keys	replaceKeys	words

Saber

- https://github.com/bluesnowman/fphp-saber

The functions in Saber aren't documented and depend on the Sabre data type that you are using, so you'll need to dive into the appropriate classes to determine which functions you can use. The types supported by Saber are as follows:

Control	None	IFloat
Choice	ISeq	IReal
Data	IArrayList	IIntegral
IBool	ILinkedList	IReal
IChar	IString	IInt32
ICollection	ISet	IInteger
IEither	IHashSet	ITrit
Left	ITuple	IRatio
Right	INumber	IFractional
IMap	IFloating	IObject
IHashMap	IFractional	IRegex
IOption	IDouble	IUnit
Some	IReal	

Functional PHP

- https://github.com/lstrojny/functional-php

average	if_else	pluck
capture	indexes_of	poll
compare_object_hash_on	intersperse	product
compare_on	invoke	ratio
compose	invoke	reduce_left
const_function	invoke_first	reduce_right
contains	invoke_if	reindex
curry	invoke_last	reject
curry_n	invoker	retry
difference	last	select
drop_first	last_index_of	select_keys
drop_last	map	some
each	match	sort
every	maximum	sum
false	memoize	tail
falsy	minimum	tail_recursion
first	none	true
first_index_of	partial_any	truthy
flat_map	partial_left	unique
flatten	partial_method	with
flip	partial_right	zip
group	partition	zip_all
id	pick	

php-fp

- https://github.com/php-fp

php-fp is actually a collection of libraries/utilities. I've listed all of the functions collectively here, but see the documentation for each to work out which one you need to use for a given function.

ap	exec	nothing
ask	flip	of
bimap	fork	on
chain	get	put
compose	id	reduce
concat	ifElse	right
construct	just	run
either	K	tell
empty	left	tryCatch
equals	map	unsafePerform
evalState	modify	

PHPz

- https://github.com/divarvel/phpz

Rather than a set of functions, PHPz provides a set of functional structures, listed here:

ArrayMonoid	ArrayFunctor	ArrayMonad
BaseMonoid	BaseFunctor	BaseMonad
MaybeMonoid	MaybeFunctor	MaybeMonad
StringMonoid		

fyrfyrfyr

- https://github.com/ikr/fyrfyrfyr

add	curryN	mergeAll
always	flip	minBy
append	fromPairs	pathOr
assoc	identity	pick
assocPath	inc	pickAll
compose	indexBy	prop
converge	map	propOr
curry	merge	reduce

Functional Framework

There is only one general-purpose framework built in a functional style that I am aware of. The Laravel framework does have some functional elements like its collection class, which is linked to elsewhere in this appendix.

Bullet
General-purpose micro-framework with functional style

- http://bulletphp.com/

Bullet: The Functional PHP Micro Framework

- https://www.youtube.com/watch?v=F9EMPLORS60

Lisp in PHP

When you want to start emulating a pure functional language in PHP, these libraries are worth a look.

Pharen
A Lisp dialect that compiles to PHP

- www.pharen.org

pEigthP
A basic LISP implementation that can be embedded in a PHP app

- https://github.com/cninja/pEigthP

Other Miscellaneous Topics

These are other materials of interest that don't fit cleanly into the previous sections.

A Functional Pattern System for Object-Oriented Design

- http://homepages.ecs.vuw.ac.nz/~tk/fps/fps-sans-escher.pdf

Implementing Functional Languages: A Tutorial

- https://www.microsoft.com/en-us/research/publication/implementing-functional-languages-a-tutorial

PHP RFCs: The Future

Requests for comments (RFCs) are the way that the PHP project decides what features make it into the next version. At the time of writing, there are a number of RFCs relating to functional programming, and I've listed those next. Some have been accepted and will be making an appearance soon (possibly by the time you read this book), some are still under discussion, and some have been closed and are unlikely to see the light of day. This should give you a flavor of the development process; even closed RFCs are useful to read as they hint at the future direction of PHP, and the related discussions can give you an idea of the mind-set of the PHP developers (and the surrounding community). They may even temp you to weigh in with your own ideas for improving the state of functional programming in PHP by submitting your own RFCs. To see the current list of RFCs and details of the process to submit your own, see https://wiki.php.net/rfc/.

PHP RFC: Arrow Functions
A short form of closures similar to ES6's arrow functions

- `https://wiki.php.net/rfc/arrow_functions`

Related to PHP RFC: Short Closures

- `https://wiki.php.net/rfc/short-closures`

PHP RFC: Additional Usage for the Splat Operator
How to allow the splat operator to be used in array literals

- `https://wiki.php.net/rfc/additional-splat-usage`

PHP RFC: Pipe Operator
Pipe/compose type composition operator

- `https://wiki.php.net/rfc/pipe-operator`

Related to the Hack pipe operator

- `https://docs.hhvm.com/hack/operators/pipe-operator`

PHP RFC: Chaining Comparison
Implement arbitrary chaining of comparator operations

- `https://wiki.php.net/rfc/chaining_comparison`

PHP RFC: Immutable classes and properties
Proposes introduction of immutable classes and properties

- `https://wiki.php.net/rfc/immutability`

PHP RFC: Nullsafe Calls
A "Maybe monad" type of operator to allow safe chaining of method calls

- `https://wiki.php.net/rfc/nullsafe_calls`

The Wikipedia Glossary

Wikipedia has a surprisingly well-curated selection of pages on various functional programming topics, giving relatively easy-to-understand (and mostly technically correct) basic overviews of particular terms and subject areas. You've already heard my take on most of these terms elsewhere in the book, so rather than provide a glossary of terms here, I'll let the many editors of Wikipedia provide their well-honed explanations of these terms instead.

- *Anonymous functions*: `https://en.wikipedia.org/wiki/Anonymous_function`

- *Asynchronous programming*: `https://en.wikipedia.org/wiki/Asynchrony_(computer_programming)`

- *Big Data*: `https://en.wikipedia.org/wiki/Big_data`

- *Closures*: `https://en.wikipedia.org/wiki/Closure_(computer_programming)`

- *Collections*: `https://en.wikipedia.org/wiki/Collection_(abstract_data_type)`

- *Composition*: `https://en.wikipedia.org/wiki/Function_composition_(computer_science)`

- *Currying*: https://en.wikipedia.org/wiki/Currying
- *First-class functions*: https://en.wikipedia.org/wiki/First-class_function
- *Function objects*: https://en.wikipedia.org/wiki/Function_object
- *Generators*: https://en.wikipedia.org/wiki/Generator_ (computer_programming)
- *Higher-order functions*: https://en.wikipedia.org/wiki/Higher-order_function
- *Iterators*: https://en.wikipedia.org/wiki/Iterator
- *Lambda calculus*: https://en.wikipedia.org/wiki/Lambda_calculus
- *Lazy evaluation*: https://en.wikipedia.org/wiki/Lazy_evaluation
- *Memoization*: https://en.wikipedia.org/wiki/Memoization
- *Monads*: https://en.wikipedia.org/wiki/Monad_(functional_programming)
- *Monoids*: https://en.wikipedia.org/wiki/Monoid
- *Mutability*: https://en.wikipedia.org/wiki/Immutable_object
- *Parallel computing*: https://en.wikipedia.org/wiki/Parallel_computing
- *Partial function application*: https://en.wikipedia.org/wiki/Partial_application
- *Recursion*: https://en.wikipedia.org/wiki/Recursion#In_computer_science
- *Referential transparency*: https://en.wikipedia.org/wiki/Referential_transparency
- *Unit testing*: https://en.wikipedia.org/wiki/Unit_testing
- *Variadic functions*: https://en.wikipedia.org/wiki/Variadic_function

Index

Get the eBook for only $5!

Why limit yourself?

With most of our titles available in both PDF and ePUB format, you can access your content wherever and however you wish—on your PC, phone, tablet, or reader.

Since you've purchased this print book, we are happy to offer you the eBook for just $5.

To learn more, go to http://www.apress.com/companion or contact support@apress.com.

Apress®

All Apress eBooks are subject to copyright. All rights are reserved by the Publisher, whether the whole or part of the material is concerned, specifically the rights of translation, reprinting, reuse of illustrations, recitation, broadcasting, reproduction on microfilms or in any other physical way, and transmission or information storage and retrieval, electronic adaptation, computer software, or by similar or dissimilar methodology now known or hereafter developed. Exempted from this legal reservation are brief excerpts in connection with reviews or scholarly analysis or material supplied specifically for the purpose of being entered and executed on a computer system, for exclusive use by the purchaser of the work. Duplication of this publication or parts thereof is permitted only under the provisions of the Copyright Law of the Publisher's location, in its current version, and permission for use must always be obtained from Springer. Permissions for use may be obtained through RightsLink at the Copyright Clearance Center. Violations are liable to prosecution under the respective Copyright Law.